T0207940

THE TRANSPACIFIC EXPERIMENT

THE
TRANSPACIFIC
EXPERIMENT

*How China and California Collaborate
and Compete for Our Future*

MATT SHEEHAN

COUNTERPOINT
Berkeley, California

The Transpacific Experiment

Copyright © 2019 by Matthew Sheehan
First hardcover edition: 2019

To explore photos, videos, and interactive graphics related to this book, visit transpacificexperiment.com.

ISBN: 978-1-64009-420-8

The Library of Congress Cataloging-in-Publication Data is available.

Cover design by Sarah Brody
Book design by Jordan Koluch

COUNTERPOINT
2560 Ninth Street, Suite 318
Berkeley, CA 94710
www.counterpointpress.com

Printed in the United States of America

TO ALL OF MY TRANSPACIFIC FAMILY—
YOU KNOW WHO YOU ARE

塞翁失马，焉知非福

The old frontiersman lost his horse—
how to know it's not a blessing?

—CHINESE PROVERB

Contents

Introduction: Welcome to the Transpacific Experiment. 3

1 | Freshman Orientation 20
2 | Silicon Valley's China Paradox 59
3 | Toward the New Tech Landscape 100
4 | Is Mickey Mouse an American? 140
5 | The Mayor Who Loved China 183
6 | A Phoenix Rising from the Toxins. 220
7 | "Chinese Americans for Trump" 256

Conclusion: Backlash or New Beginning?. 288

Acknowledgments 297
Notes 301

THE TRANSPACIFIC EXPERIMENT

WELCOME TO THE TRANSPACIFIC EXPERIMENT

Nestled against the western shores of the San Francisco Bay, Angel Island is both a monument to the past and a window into the future of the world's two most powerful countries. On the northeast corner of the island lies the Immigration Station, a relic of the Chinese Exclusion Act of 1882. That act of Congress was the capstone to the first era of major face-to-face engagement between Chinese and American people. California was the stage on which these two groups made their first introductions and impressions. They didn't exactly hit it off.

After the discovery of gold in 1849, tens of thousands of Chinese men made landfall in San Francisco—a city they called "Gold Mountain." Fleeing famine at home and dreaming of rivers running with precious metals, these men left their villages in southern China and clambered onto wooden ships that would carry them across the Pacific. In California they dug for nuggets, cooked for cash, and earned a reputation as cheap but extremely valuable laborers. When Leland Stanford and his fellow robber barons set out to build the western segment of the transcontinental railroad, they enlisted Chinese workers for the most crucial and the most dangerous tasks.

But these men entered an America rife with economic anxiety and racial resentment. To Irish laborers in San Francisco—men like my great-great-grandfather—these Chinese arrivals were seen as a threat to their jobs and an affront to their identity. Newspapers and dime novels spread fears of a "yellow peril" descending on American shores. Demagogues thrived, blaming the new Chinese arrivals when banking crises dragged down the American economy. Thugs carried out lynchings at Chinese labor camps, and California's own governor demanded that Congress "check this tide of Asiatic immigration."

Those clamoring for a law excluding Chinese laborers sparred with men like Wong Chin Foo, a naturalized American citizen who became one of the most outspoken defenders of Chinese rights.

"As residents of the United States, we claim a common manhood with all other nationalities," Wong wrote in 1893, "and believe we should have that manhood recognized according to the principles of common humanity and American freedom."

But those principled appeals largely fell on deaf ears among white immigrants resentful of the new competition. My own great-great-grandfather arrived in San Francisco in the 1870s, working at the Pacific Rolling Mill and living in a tough part of town known as Irish Hill. Our family doesn't have any record of him participating in anti-Chinese activity, but he certainly fit the demographic profile: a working-class Irish Catholic immigrant laborer, scratching to carve out his space in a new city and country.

His son and my great-grandfather, Tommy Sheehan, was born in San Francisco in 1879, three years before the Chinese Exclusion Act became law. Orphaned at a young age, Tommy grew up in Saint Vincent's Home for Boys and went on to become a San Francisco longshoreman and union organizer. In that role, he befriended Peter C. Yorke, a priest and vocal advocate for Irish laborers. Tommy used to drive Yorke around the city on weekends, smoking cigarettes and talking shop. In our family, Yorke is remembered as a righteous defender of the working man. But he did not extend that empathy to Chinese laborers. Keynoting the 1901 California Chinese Exclusion Convention, Yorke railed against Chinese people who remained in the country during the exclusion era.

"We are face-to-face with an immigration which is emphatically not Christian," Yorke told the crowd. "Their thoughts are not our thoughts; their blood is not our blood; their outlook is not our outlook."[1]

Four years after that speech, construction began on the Angel Island Immigration Station, where thousands of Chinese people looking to make a home in California would be held. One of the few exceptions in the Chinese Exclusion Act allowed for children and spouses of Chinese people in America to follow their relatives over. The Immigration Station hosted interrogations designed to separate out true blood relatives from "paper sons"—people who would claim a false familial relation in order to enter the country.

Immigration officials would have new arrivals draw their family trees and maps of their home villages. Virtually all Chinese laborers in the U.S. were recruited from just a handful of counties in the south of China near Hong Kong, allowing immigration officials to cross-reference these diagrams with those drawn by earlier immigrants, attempting to weed out the "paper sons" in the process. Detentions could go on for weeks or even months. Some were finally granted entry to the country; others were sent back across the Pacific.

Thousands of miles from home but barred from San Francisco's shores, the Chinese prisoners carved poems into the wooden walls of the Immigration Station, engravings that you can still see there today.

America has power, but not justice.
In prison, we were victimized as if we were guilty.
Given no opportunity to explain, it was really brutal.
I bow my head in reflection but there is
nothing I can do.[2]

THE TRANSPACIFIC PANORAMA

Today, Angel Island offers a panoramic view of a new transpacific reality, one being forged by the new era of large-scale face-to-face engagement between Chinese and American people. The surrounding landscape is where the world's two superpowers are getting reacquainted with one another at ground level in the twenty-first century. For a window into that process at work, we just need to take a short walk south from the Immigration Station.

Exiting through the front door of the building, hang a right, and head south along the island's paths for about a mile. Reaching the shore, scramble out to Point Blunt, at the southeast corner of the island. These boulders offer up a sweeping view of the Bay Area: Berkeley and Oakland to the east, Treasure Island in the middle of the Bay, and San Francisco to the west. If the fog hasn't rolled in, you can just barely catch glimpses of Silicon Valley in the distance to the south.

Starting in the east, you see the Campanile, a gothic clock tower at the center of University of California, Berkeley. Over the last decade, the number of Chinese undergrads at UC Berkeley has multiplied by a factor of ten, a microcosm of a nationwide boom in Chinese enrollment on U.S. campuses.[3] In the aftermath of the financial crisis, public universities that saw their funding slashed at home turned to China, hoping that an influx of international undergrads paying higher tuition could fill the gaping holes in university budgets. Many Americans saw an additional benefit to the new arrivals: a chance to "show the light" to China's next generation, exposing them to free speech and planting the seeds of China's own democratic reforms.

But things haven't exactly gone as planned. When confronted by the political evangelism of their American peers, many Chinese students feel increasingly confident in—or defensive about—their home country. It's a group that isn't necessarily buying into American political values. And the sheer number of new arrivals has stirred anxiety among some California students and parents, who fear that admission to America's top public universities is being auctioned to the highest bidder. That backlash is now going national, with members of the Trump administration accusing these undergrads of spying for their home country and proposing a total ban on Chinese students.

Panning east to west across the Bay Bridge, you catch sight of the two largest housing developments in the region, both of which needed funding from Chinese investors to get off the ground. Past the cranes of the Oakland shipyards lies Brooklyn Basin, a 2,300-unit development going up just past Jack London Square. And across the water in San Francisco's Bayview–Hunter's Point neighborhood, Chinese immigrant investors have poured hundreds of millions of dollars into the San Francisco Shipyard, the city's largest housing and retail development in decades.[4] That development rubs up against San Francisco's only remaining predominantly black neighborhood—the last island of affordability in a city that has seen a massive exodus of African Americans amid tech-fueled gentrification. As Chinese money comes in and the buildings go up, longtime residents look on with hope for new jobs and fear of displacement.

Gazing south toward Silicon Valley, you can see the home of America's most influential industry, a thriving technology ecosystem that some fear will be "disrupted" by competition from across the Pacific. Chinese billionaires, coders, and internet juggernauts have arrived in Silicon Valley seeking out "unicorn" start-ups, top U.S. researchers, and the next big idea. Local start-ups have learned to pitch to Chinese investors, while in my hometown of Palo Alto, Mark Zuckerberg has devoted himself to studying Chinese.

But when the giants of Silicon Valley return the visit in Beijing, they receive a much cooler reception. Google, Facebook, Twitter, Snapchat, Instagram, and many more pillars of the global internet are outright blocked by China's "Great Firewall." Still, entranced by the potential of a billion new customers, these companies are bending over backward to curry favor with the Chinese Communist Party leadership and its censors. Facebook has worked on software tools that would seal off Chinese users from political content abroad, and Google has offered to build a fully censored search app for China to regain access to its market. A decade ago, techno-utopians gleefully predicted that a free internet would be the midwife to democracy in China. Today the question isn't how Silicon Valley will change China. It's how China is changing Silicon Valley, and the very structure of the global internet.

Four hundred and fifty miles farther south, the same dynamics are playing out in the other great bastion of American cultural dominance:

Hollywood. For years, Hollywood films dominated Chinese screens and the people's popular imagination. But today a booming Chinese box office, strict government controls, and the rise of Chinese-made blockbusters are eating away at Hollywood's hegemony. Like their peers in Silicon Valley, Hollywood studios are now rewriting plotlines to please government censors, all in a bid for greater market access. And as China's film industry comes into its own, American films are increasingly forced to compete with Chinese movies that marry Hollywood techniques to local sensibilities, creating China's own equivalents of nationalistic blockbusters like *Rambo II* and *Captain America*.

Finally, complete the panorama from Angel Island by scanning the horizon on all sides—from the brightly painted hilltops of San Francisco to the mansions of Silicon Valley and the Spanish-style homes lining the East Bay. These housing markets have already seen dizzying price hikes from an influx of Silicon Valley tech money, and in the last five years, wealthy Chinese home buyers have pushed prices up even higher. Political and economic turbulence in China has led many of the country's wealthiest citizens to seek financial security in international real estate, turning multimillion-dollar U.S. homes into "the new Swiss bank account." The phenomenon of wealthy Chinese home buyers touches not just on real estate prices, but also on social values. California today prides itself on embracing immigrants from all over the world, but that embrace has become more complicated when the new arrivals are wealthier than the longtime residents. It's challenging many Californians to ask themselves, Do we welcome all immigrants, or just those of the "poor, tired, huddled masses" variety?

As this new generation of Chinese immigrants sets down roots, they're now shaking up long-standing political coalitions. Earlier generations of working-class Chinese immigrants had become staunch Democrats, often building pan-ethnic coalitions and struggling alongside black and Latino activists in campaigns for civil rights and racial justice. But the new immigrants are leaving China and entering America under far different circumstances. Instead of earning minimum wage at jobs in Chinatown, they often have high-paying tech and investing jobs in wealthy suburbs. For this cohort, affirmative action has become a lightning-rod issue, catalyzing a new generation of Chinese American activists that coalesced around an unlikely champion: Donald Trump. Now they are fanning out across city councils and serving as foot soldiers in a new wave of conservative Chinese American politics.

The phenomena glimpsed in this panorama are playing out to different degrees in cities and towns all across America. They are bringing the U.S.–China relationship down from the realm of geopolitics and directly into the lives of ordinary Americans. In doing so, they're shifting key dimensions of the relationship from the White House to the state house, and from the politburo to the PTA meeting. To see where the world's two most powerful countries are meeting, cooperating, and competing today, we need to get outside of Washington, D.C., and Beijing.

Welcome to the Transpacific Experiment.

WHAT IS THE TRANSPACIFIC EXPERIMENT?

The Transpacific Experiment is the living laboratory for a new breed of grass-roots superpower diplomacy. It is the fluid ecosystem of students, entrepreneurs, investors, immigrants, and ideas bouncing back and forth between the Golden State and the Middle Kingdom. It's the Chinese undergrads expanding their horizons on California campuses, and the Silicon Valley start-ups scratching for a toehold in China; the California mayors courting Chinese factory investment, and the Chinese governors studying California carbon markets.

As the top destination for Chinese investors, students, tourists, technologists, filmmakers, and home buyers, California is ground zero for this experiment in deep and multifaceted engagement between China and the United States. The results of this experiment—the personal ties, economic frictions, and technological innovations—are already reshaping China and the United States and filtering out into the international system that orbits around them.

All of these interactions bring new opportunities—for investment, jobs, tuition dollars, and fascinating cultural fusion—but also new anxieties.

When international diplomacy enters our everyday lives, it is transformed. Greater contact can humanize the other side, turning a faceless "other" into a neighbor, classmate, or even friend. But that close-up contact can also drag things in the other direction, sharpening awareness of our differences and making geopolitical problems feel personal. In the Transpacific Experiment, we see both of these forces at work: a magnetic pull toward greater integration and synergy, as well as an intense backlash when one side feels manipulated or taken advantage of.

Here we catch a glimpse of the tension that animates this experiment in grassroots diplomacy. This new breed of deep U.S.–China engagement has the potential to bring tremendous benefit to people in both countries, but in that process, it creates entirely new problems that hit closer to home.

Heightening the drama is the grand geopolitical backdrop to these interactions. In the century and a half since Chinese and American people first came face-to-face in California, the relative positions of the two countries have changed dramatically. During that first wave of engagement in the 1800s, China was a once-great dynastic empire slowly being torn apart by colonial aggression and internal strife. The United States was instead an up-and-coming nation of immigrants, an unproven democratic experiment mixing lofty ideals, messy realities, and mounting military strength.

Today, the people of these countries are getting reacquainted on different footing: as citizens of the world's two superpowers. Now, the United States plays the role of the incumbent juggernaut. It is home to powerful global industries and proud national traditions but also an increasingly fraught economic, social, and political order. And China is now the up-and-comer, a nation that has emerged from decades of domestic turmoil to challenge the United States for global leadership. To complicate matters further, China has not risen to this position by walking the path prescribed for it by Western theorists: free markets, free speech, and democratic politics. Instead, it has relied on its own unique alchemy of Leninist politics, state-guided development, and strict controls on speech and culture.

That geopolitical role reversal infuses every aspect of the Transpacific Experiment. New ties may be forged at the grassroots, but they are often colored by our sense of relative standing on the world stage. How Americans feel about their new Chinese neighbors is intimately wrapped up in our feelings about China as a rising power, as well as insecurities about the trajectory of our own national experiment in democracy. Chinese people's perceptions of these interactions are similarly bound up in questions of national pride and insecurity. On a good day, the United States and its top companies might be looked at with admiration, as a source of inspiration for artists, entrepreneurs, and educators. On a bad day, that same country is seen as mired in steep and unsalvageable decline, an aging nation that will expend its last ounce of energy attempting to hold China down.

As Chinese investors, immigrants, and ideas make their presence felt on U.S. soil, they pose a question that challenges something deep within the American psyche: Are Americans ready for a world in which they engage with Chinese people, companies, and ideas on equal footing? Or a world in which the Chinese side has the upper hand?

Today, California is the space in which these tensions, frictions, and possible futures are taking shape. In many ways, China and California make for an odd couple. America's most liberal state, and one of the world's most sophisticated authoritarian regimes. A bastion of environmental protectionism, and an industrial behemoth that leads the world in carbon emissions. The free-spirited home of everything from the hippies to the Kardashians, and an ancient Confucian culture built on ritual and personal restraint.

And yet, those apparent contradictions are often what have drawn these two states into their dialectical dance. Chinese leaders see a vision for their own country's future in California: blue skies, top universities, innovative technology, and global blockbusters. They know that if China is going to make the leap from a middle- to a high-income country, it needs to move up the global value chain, fostering technological and cultural industries. In that light, California offers both inspiration and a tremendous wealth of resources to be accessed or acquired.

For Chinese families, the stakes are less grandiose but no less important:

they want clean air for their lungs, a good education for their kids, and a place to stash their life savings that is safe from the vagaries of the Chinese political system. They often don't think of themselves as volunteer diplomats in the most pivotal international relationship of the twenty-first century, and yet circumstance and happenstance have made it so.

On the U.S. side of the equation, these same phenomena have a tendency to challenge dearly held values and pose uncomfortable questions about our own nation.

At the neighborhood level, the new Chinese arrivals are turning many American ideas about immigration on their head, confronting Californians with complicated questions about acceptance, assimilation, and citizenship. Residents of suburbs like my hometown often feel comfortable—even self-righteous—in their open-armed embrace of immigrants and refugees targeted by President Trump. They abhor "build the wall" chants and proudly decorate their lawns with signs declaring NO HUMAN IS ILLEGAL. Looking back on the Chinese Exclusion era, they condemn the racist white workers who resented Chinese laborers for "stealing" their jobs.

But tweak a few of the variables and bring these issues to their own doorstep, and you might get far different reactions from these same people. What if the immigrant isn't a poor laborer, but a rich family escaping the Beijing smog? What if the resource being competed for isn't a working-class job, but a house in your hometown? What if, like many of the early immigrant laborers, the new arrivals have no intention to remain in the country long-term? Suddenly that comfortable moral clarity is harder to come by, forcing a closer examination of exactly what principles to hold on to and which to amend.

For California's trademark industries—technology and culture—the rise of competitive Chinese ecosystems also challenges long-standing orthodoxy about the sources of innovation and creativity. For over half a century, California has been a global haven for personal freedoms and alternative lifestyles. During that same period, it has also dominated the world of technology and culture. That correlation—between personal freedoms, technological innovation, and cultural production—led many to believe these phenomena were inextricably woven together. A country without political freedoms could not truly innovate, and people without freedom of expression couldn't create a thriving cultural industry. It's a mantra woven deep into our American psyche, and one that seemed to be confirmed by the country's successive triumphs over rivals such as the Soviet Union.

But the rise of China's technology and movie industries is steadily peeling apart that once-solid correlation. In the process, it is challenging certain core beliefs about what makes innovation and creativity possible. Instead of putting stock in abstract personal freedoms, China is instead betting that you can build these industries up brick by brick. Throw together a critical mass of computer programmers, free-flowing capital, film sets, movie screens, and disposable income, and hope that innovation and commercial culture emerge from it. The game is far from over in these industries, but China has consistently outperformed expectations, and that surprising run of success is changing the conversation about technology and culture on both sides of the Pacific.

Looked at from a 40,000-foot perspective, these issues can appear abstract or distant from everyday life. But all of these open questions and thorny problems are playing out in real time. They are affecting lives and livelihoods today, driven forward by real people with big ambitions, fears, and hopes for what the Transpacific Experiment will mean to them.

Over the past six years, I've used my own work as a journalist, analyst, consultant, and general hanger-on in California and China to follow these people's stories and fit together the pieces of this puzzle as best I can. The book you're now reading is the result of that piecing together. It's an imperfect, incomplete, and subjective snapshot of these phenomena. In the process of writing, the people, places, and questions dissected here became a part of my life. Much of the writing here reflects that closeness, with both the insight and the bias that closeness brings.

Bridging two distinct countries and cultures is a delicate and often fraught process. If done right, it can open entirely new vistas for the people and the places involved. If done wrong, it can turn minor frictions into a major backlash, fueling mutual suspicion and outright resentment along national, cultural, and personal lines. This book tells the stories of people who have tried, and sometimes failed, to build those bridges between China and California.

But before telling you their stories, I'll briefly share my own. Over the last five years, the Transpacific Experiment has exerted a similar pull on me: part personal, part professional, and whole lot of dumb luck. That run of luck began with a broken ankle and a visa problem.

ANKLES AND OPPORTUNITIES

I grew up in the Bay Area, but before 2008 had virtually no interest in China. My high school didn't offer Mandarin courses, and even if it had, I would have stuck with Spanish. In our survey courses on "world history," we blew through a dozen Chinese dynasties in a couple of weeks. By the time I got to college, I could sum up my knowledge of modern China in three phrases: Mao Zedong, Tiananmen Square, and Factory of the World.

But in the summer after my sophomore year in college, I stumbled into a job as a counselor at an academic summer camp in Beijing. It was June 2008, and the city was ramping up to host the summer Olympics, furiously repaving roads and launching campaigns to discourage spitting in public. Despite those efforts, Beijing was still a city with an untamed heart. I found myself fascinated by the high-functioning chaos that reigned all around me: the lawless fluidity on the roads, the bruising bartering in the markets, and the no-holds-barred competition for every seat on the subway.

Underneath that gruff exterior, there was also real warmth and openness toward Americans. Many working-class Chinese people had never interacted with an American before, and a big smile combined with some creative sign language went a long way in the cause of grassroots diplomacy. I made friends with the security guards at our dormitories, gifting them my Frisbee on my last day there, and receiving one of their Beijing Public Security uniforms in return. Sitting in the airport lounge waiting for my flight to San Francisco, I knew I had to come back to China.

So, after graduating college in 2010, I found a job teaching English in the central Chinese city of Xi'an. As I slowly gained Chinese language skills, that city and the whole country became even more captivating than on my first trip. After a year in Xi'an, I headed back to Beijing to study language full-time at a university. Graduating from that program, I began a job at a local TV station that broadcast English-language pseudopropaganda about China in countries like Iran.

By the spring of 2013, I knew that I wanted to work as a proper journalist. Reading American media coverage of the country, I felt that it wasn't capturing what I saw in the daily life of my Chinese friends. I wanted to fill that gap with their stories. I gave myself six months and $5,000 in savings to try to string freelance writing gigs into a job as a China correspondent.

I hitchhiked across central China looking for stories, writing about a fight I witnessed at an airport and about the personal evolution of Chinese students who returned from studying in the U.S. When I eventually ran out of time and money, I had collected a handful of publications but no job offers. Resigned to reality, I began interviewing for more mundane careers: selling real estate in central China or working for the U.S. Chamber of Commerce in the country's northeast.

And then, a miracle happened: I badly mangled my ankle during a game of Ultimate Frisbee in Beijing. By the time I dragged myself into the lobby of a local hospital, my ankle was the size of a cantaloupe, but the doctor who glanced at my X-rays declared it to be "no problem"—if I stayed off it for a week or two, all would be back to normal. A few days later, I flew home to California for a long-scheduled visit of a couple weeks. There, my family doctor saw things differently: the ankle was severely broken in two places, and with an injury like that I absolutely should not fly for at least two months.

I was stranded back in the Bay Area with one working foot and no job. The prospect of two months sitting at home left me worried that I would lose the pulse of what was happening in China. I'd spent the last six months obsessively following—and trying to contribute to—news coverage of the country. Right before coming home, I had completed an intensive Mandarin program in which I vowed to speak no English for three months, a pledge that I broke at the exact same moment as my ankle. Now I was trapped in the leafy suburbs of the Bay Area, 6,000 miles from the action in Beijing.

But then, the action started coming to me. At the time, prospective Chinese home buyers were arriving in my hometown of Palo Alto in droves. They were boarding luxury buses for mobile real estate tours of the city, purchasing million-dollar homes the way my parents might snap up a nice piece of furniture. I called up the real estate agency hosting the tours and talked my way into joining one of them, eventually writing an article about it for the website of *The Atlantic*.

The home-buying tours were a truly transpacific phenomenon: the rush to move money out of China reflected jitters about that country's economy, and the sudden influx of rich Chinese buyers was ruffling feathers in California suburbs. It was one of the first signs I saw that the economic, social, and human narratives that I'd been tracing within China were now making their way onto American soil.

When my ankle healed up, I headed back to China and resumed my job search. Soon after arriving back in Beijing, a well-timed introduction and a lucky break landed me my dream job: as the first China correspondent for *The WorldPost*, a new media collaboration between *The Huffington Post* and the Berggruen Institute, a think tank. Before I could begin that work, I had to apply for a journalist visa.

That application process is never easy, but my timing was particularly bad. A year earlier, *The New York Times* and *Bloomberg* had dropped bombshell investigations into the family wealth of China's top leadership, reports that led to a freeze on visas for those publications. Chinese leadership had no beef with *The WorldPost*, but we faced a different hurdle: China had never before granted full journalist credentials to an all-online media platform. The print–online distinction was functionally meaningless but bureaucratically momentous. Tensions with *The New York Times* hung heavy over the Chinese Ministry of Foreign Affairs, and no one there was eager to hand out credentials to a new American outlet. I flew back to San Francisco in

December of 2013, unsure if the powers that be would see fit to grant me the visa.

But this time around, I was ready to track down some more transpacific narratives. When state labor inspectors raided the Southern California factory of a Chinese electric car company, I interviewed the eccentric mayor who had courted the company and covered the fallout from the investigation. I began visiting and interviewing people in the Hunters Point neighborhood being transformed by a Chinese-funded mega-development. I hung out with Chinese entrepreneurs in Silicon Valley and met the Airbnb team planning the company's China strategy. I even helped organize a delegation of small-town Bay Area mayors making a trip to China to pitch their cities as ideal destinations for investment.

All these stories provided small windows into massive changes within China itself. When I first set foot in Beijing just six years earlier, China was still squarely a developing country. Awe-inspiring Olympic ceremony aside, it was a majority-rural country whose economy ran on low-wage labor. China was considered a technological backwater and an afterthought for the U.S. entertainment industry. Cheap Chinese goods stocked the shelves of our nation's Walmarts, but that was about as close as Chinese people got to the everyday lives of most Americans.

Now, as I followed these stories up and down the state of California, I saw early glimpses of a country transformed. Chinese technology companies had become some of the largest in the world, and they were making their presence felt in Silicon Valley. The Chinese movie industry was growing at breakneck speed and casting a spell over executives in Hollywood. Chinese students, tourists, investors, and home buyers abroad were carving out a new reputation for their countrymen: rich, sometimes cultured, sometimes crass, and very ready to spend.

Watching as Chinese tourists lugging enormous cameras poured into Stanford's Quad, I couldn't help but ask myself: Is this how Italians in 1950s Rome felt when all the Americans began crowding into the Colosseum?

This new wave of arrivals didn't quite reflect the life of the average Chinese person back home: the country was still middle-income, with large swaths of the population scraping out a living in factories or on farms. And many Chinese immigrants arriving on U.S. soil did so in a low-key, thoughtful, and genuinely curious way: more in the tradition of James Baldwin in Paris than obnoxious Americans in Thailand. But China's growing footprint in California does offer clues into the country's future: the industries it wants to promote, the lifestyles it hopes to adopt, and the kind of wealth it hopes to cultivate.

THE BAY AREA, BEIJING, AND BACK AGAIN

After seven months in visa limbo, I was abruptly informed by the Ministry of Foreign Affairs that I would indeed receive a journalist visa. I tied up some loose ends with my reporting, packed my things, and in the late summer of 2014 headed back to Beijing.

But sitting in the airport departures lounge, I once again knew that I would be coming back—this time to California. China still felt like the center of the action, but the Transpacific Experiment felt like the next frontier.

Back in China with my newly minted journalist credentials, I pinballed around the country, covering everything from democracy protests in Hong Kong to down-and-out coal towns in Shaanxi Province. I also traced the transpacific stories back to their source, meeting the Chinese students who were heading to California and those who had returned, the artificial intelligence (AI) researchers who left Google to found their start-up back in China, and the wealthy "birth tourists" who gave birth to American citizens on U.S. soil before heading home to Beijing.

In 2016 I moved to Oakland, California, and since then I've continued weaving in more layers and more characters as these stories evolved. Tracing these trends from source to destination and back again continues to drive home the interconnectedness of these two places. In this world of deep China–U.S. entanglement, an anticorruption crackdown in Guangzhou can drive up housing prices in Pasadena, and an ideological campaign in Beijing can reshape the movie slate of Hollywood studios. We don't know what long-term consequences these ties will yield, but it's clear that they are already molding the industries, technologies, universities, and communities that affect the entire world.

Each of the following chapters charts these trends in one of six key arenas: education, technology, film, green investment, real estate, and American politics. Each chapter seeks to explore that arena through the eyes of the people who are living out these phenomena in real time: students, film producers, mayors, entrepreneurs, and community activists. Woven into those stories are my own intersections with them, the chances I've had to both observe and sometimes affect the Transpacific Experiment in action. I've learned a tremendous amount about both countries from watching this strange new world take shape, and I hope you will as well.

Let's dive in.

1

FRESHMAN ORIENTATION

Tim Lin has crystal-clear memories of the first time he woke up in an American dorm room. Tim was at Miami University in Ohio, nearly 7,000 miles east of his hometown in northwest China, and he was eager to get a jump on student life halfway around the world. But waking up early that morning, he got a different kind of education. Slumped across the bed of his roommate was a woman, fast asleep and completely naked.

"I was seventeen years old. I had never seen a real naked girl. I'd seen something like that, but on the computer or on the TV," Tim recounted to me.

He remembered thinking to himself, "Oh, so this is what it really is. . . ." From there, Tim was quickly inducted into the rites and rituals of collegiate America: Saturday football games, campus controversies, and tequila shots.

Fast-forward three years from Tim's 2012 graduation, and I'm watching blood rush to his head as he hangs upside down from a spine-stretching device at his start-up's headquarters in Beijing. A couple of his employees look over with a mix of curiosity and concern as Tim's face turns a deep red. But he is at ease, calmly explaining to me the origins of his start-up: College Daily.

After graduating from Miami University in 2012, Tim spent a couple years bouncing between continents: working in Silicon Valley, volunteering in East Africa, and eventually landing back in China. That's when Tim created College Daily, a media company devoted entirely to the needs of Chinese students on foreign campuses. He began by writing articles explaining the things about American collegiate life that he wished he'd known during his undergrad years: What does it mean to get "sexiled" by your roommate? How can Chinese students enter the H-1B lottery for American work visas? And what is this "Super Bowl" that everyone is talking about?

Tim began by posting the articles in a Chinese smartphone app called WeChat, and they quickly connected with a rapidly growing population of Chinese students in the United States. In the decade between when Tim enrolled at Miami University in 2008 and 2018, the number of Chinese students at American colleges had more than tripled from 98,000 to just over 360,000.[1] California led all other states with over 60,000 Chinese students, nearly 50 percent more than second-place New York.[2] Along with College Daily's audience abroad, the start-up also targets the millions of parents in China who have international ambitions for their child's education. That reach earned Tim venture-capital funding, which he used to rent an office in a chic Beijing complex and hire a team of writers and editors.

College Daily's readers are an advertiser's dream: united by a clear shared interest and predominantly wealthy. Chinese students of generations past often showed up on American soil with almost no money, just a dream of turning a technical PhD into a decent salary and an American green card. But today's Chinese students are a different breed. They are wealthier, younger, and far less invested in putting down roots in the United States. These traits often rub their classmates the wrong way, but it's the first of those qualifications that helped spur the boom in the first place.

Following the financial crisis of 2008, American public colleges and universities saw their funding gutted. University administrators scoured the horizon for a way to replace the vanishing taxpayer support, and many of them settled on a quick fix: international students. While in-state students at public universities receive steep discounts, out-of-state or international students pay full tuition, often triple the amount of their local classmates. So schools threw open their gates to international students.

The timing turned out to be impeccable. China's middle class was booming, and parents who had scratched their way up through an insanely competitive Chinese education system were hoping to spare their kids that same struggle. They hired English tutors, signed their kids up for SAT-prep classes, and paid "education consulting" firms huge sums to guarantee entrance at American colleges. Once that acceptance letter came, the parents were happy to fork over the $35,000 a year for the privilege of an American university degree. China quickly came to dominate international student demographics, and by 2017 China accounted for one in three international students in the U.S.[3]

From the outside, it looked like a perfect match: American universities could patch holes in their budgets, and Chinese students could gain exposure to a topflight international education. Beyond that financial exchange, there was also hope that these on-campus interactions could promote cultural understanding and even pull the world's two superpowers closer together. What better way is there to promote world peace than to have the future leaders of China and the United States chugging Bud Lights with one another?

But on the ground, things weren't exactly playing out as imagined. University administrators may have seen Chinese students as a financial life jacket, but some California students observing changing campus demographics began to ask a new question: are these foreign students subsidizing us or just replacing us? The collegiate cultural melting pot also wasn't functioning as imagined. As the number of Chinese students grew, so too did the insularity of that group. Some Chinese students could get through four years at a UC school without truly mastering English or making more than a couple American friends.

And in many cases the politics of international campuses turned out to be more fraught than friendly. The Chinese government sometimes looked upon returning students with a wary eye, fearful that they brought with them the infectious disease of a desire for electoral democracy. American politicians turned out to share a mirror image of those suspicions. Media reports showing that the Chinese government helped fund some Chinese student groups led to fears that America was being infiltrated via its campuses. When those Chinese student groups organized campus protests against speakers they deemed "offensive," such as the Dalai Lama, the question became whether the Chinese government was using these students to export its domestic restrictions on speech.

By 2018, the backlash against Chinese students had gone from campus politics to national politics. Prominent senators and the FBI director were all piling on, accusing the students of acting as pawns and spies in a massive Chinese government scheme to steal technology and squash dissent. In private, President Trump remarked that "almost every student that comes over to this country is a spy," and he entertained a proposal for placing an outright ban on student visas for Chinese citizens.

This wasn't how the story of Chinese students in America was supposed to go.

MISSIONARIES AND MILITARY TECHNOLOGY

It's a story that has its origins as far back as the 1800s, when a smattering of Chinese students sailed across the Pacific to take up studies in the upstart nation known as *meiguo*, "beautiful country." But even these early international scholars were burdened by expectations both political and religious. Many early arrivals were sponsored by American Christian missionaries, who hoped that they would absorb that faith and return to China to spread it among their own people. The Chinese government had other ideas. In 1872, it sponsored what became known as the Chinese Educational Mission, a group of 120 boys who were sent to America to learn the art and science of American technology, particularly military technology.[4]

At the time, imperial China was approaching an all-time low. Long confident that it possessed the most advanced civilization on earth, China had been shaken from its slumber during the two Opium Wars of the mid-1800s, when European militaries armed with modern weaponry repeatedly steam-rolled the Chinese forces. The devastating Taiping Rebellion and skirmishes with Western troops drove home the message: if China wanted to hold its own as an empire, it needed to learn these technologies from the West. Officials in the Qing Dynasty approved the first batch of young Chinese men to be sent to the United States.

But as those boys settled into life in New England, they began picking up more than just Western engineering concepts. Some converted to Christianity. Others earned thoroughly American nicknames like Ajax, Fighting Chinee, and By-jinks Johnnie. The conservative Chinese official tasked with supervising the mission became alarmed that these boys were abandoning their Confucian culture and losing their loyalty to the Chinese emperor. Rubbing salt in that wound, the State Department refused to allow the Chinese students to enroll in West Point or other military academies, claiming there was no room available.

After the students completed nine of the planned fifteen years, Chinese officials canceled the mission and ordered the boys back to China, where they were detained and thoroughly interrogated on arrival. Several boys from that group would go on to take up leadership positions in the Chinese military and bureaucracy, but they couldn't reverse the rot of the Qing Dynasty, which continued to wrestle with a love-hate relationship with the technology and culture of the West.

A year after the boys' 1881 departure from the "beautiful country," the United States passed the Chinese Exclusion Act. It would be nearly a hundred years before the Chinese government would send another large batch of students to learn from America.

SECOND-WAVE SCHOLARS

That next group of students made the journey at another low point for China. The year was 1978, and the country was still in a daze from the madness of Mao Zedong's Great Proletarian Cultural Revolution (1966–76). During that decade, China's education systems were largely crippled by fanatical student Red Guards who tormented their teachers for teaching anything "feudal" (traditional, Confucian) or "foreign" (most modern academic and scientific knowledge that didn't adhere to "Mao Zedong Thought"). The government sent scholars of math and science to work in coal mines and eventually dispersed the Red Guards to the Chinese countryside to "learn from the peasant farmers." By the time the dust settled on the Cultural Revolution, China was decades behind the West in most fields of modern science and technology.

Eager to make up lost ground, China's new leader, Deng Xiaoping, struck a deal with U.S. president Jimmy Carter to send a cohort of fifty-two Chinese scholars to study at a handful of American universities.[5] They were to spend a few years immersed in fields such as computer science and return to China to plant the seeds of the country's technological rebirth.

When the first batch of twelve scholars arrived at Princeton University, Professor Stanley Kwong was there to greet them. An assistant dean at Princeton, Professor Kwong had grown up between Hong Kong and the United States and had visited China in 1973 as part of an early delegation of Chinese American students and scholars. On that trip, Chinese premier Zhou Enlai had personally asked him to help take care of Chinese students in the United States.

They needed the help. The students may have had the backing of the central government, but at the time China's per capita GDP was on par with Rwanda's.[6] The scholars were kept on a tight financial leash.

"They ended up having white bread for breakfast and white bread for lunch," Professor Kwong recalled.

To boost those nutrients, he and some other Chinese American professors would get together once a month to cook a big chicken dinner for the students. After a few years of work and study in the U.S., those scholars returned to China and took up leading posts in Chinese academia, heading up university departments and laying the foundations in new fields of study.

They were soon followed by a new kind of Chinese student: those who came to America on their own. By the mid-1980s, a steady trickle of these young Chinese began arriving in the United States. Many relied on relatives in the United States to sponsor their visas by pledging to financially support the students. But those relatives were often barely scraping out a living in Chinatown restaurants or garment factories, and the new students had to fend for themselves financially.

That meant pairing full-time studies with hard work, often as waiters in restaurants or manual laborers in factories or warehouses. Work restrictions on student visas meant much of that labor had to be done in Chinatown's under-the-table cash economy. Earlier waves of immigrants who now ran these businesses used the students' precarious legal position as bargaining leverage, often paying them as little as half of minimum wage.

"Whatever they could squeeze, they squeezed," one student-turned-immigrant in San Francisco told me.

For these students, the payoff—a shot at a United States green card—was worth the struggle. China was steadily turning itself into a manufacturing powerhouse, but the economic gap between it and the United States remained enormous. In terms of quality of life, it was still better to be relatively "poor" in America than "middle-class" in China. Once these students got a hold of life in America, they didn't want to let go.

BUDGET CUTS AND INTERNATIONAL BOOMS

What a difference a generation makes. By 2008, three decades of breakneck economic growth had produced a large cohort of very wealthy Chinese parents: factory owners, real estate developers, technology entrepreneurs, and government officials who could skim off all these industries. Having a child studying abroad became a status symbol in these circles, and Chinese applications to American colleges skyrocketed.

They found a very receptive audience in the admissions offices of American public universities. Public funding for higher education has been shrinking for several decades, but during the financial crisis of 2008 that steady decline turned into a sudden plunge.

California was a prime example of the trend. Between 2007 and 2012, California state support for public higher education (including the UC system and the parallel California State University system) dropped by $2 billion, a cut of over 30 percent.[7] School administrators scrambled to make up the difference, but lawmakers proved indifferent to their pleas, and any attempt to raise tuition was met with protests. Henry Brady, dean of UC Berkeley's Goldman School of Public Policy, described the dilemma facing these schools.

"You've got a budget constraint, costs are going up, state funding is going down or staying steady, and you're not allowed to increase tuition," Brady told the *San Francisco Chronicle*. "We're producing a Cadillac education for the cost of a Chevy, and the state's saying you should do it at a motorcycle price. At some point you have to ask, 'What's realistic?'"

With their backs up against the financial wall, public universities quickly began ramping up out-of-state and international student enrollment. The logic is straightforward: these students often pay around triple the tuition of local students and generally receive no financial aid. During the 2014–15 school year, local undergraduate students at UC Berkeley paid roughly $13,328 in tuition, with 55 percent of those local students qualifying as low-income and thus paying no tuition at all. Their out-of-state and international classmates put down $36,833 for the same education and were generally excluded from public financial aid.[8] Theoretically, every Chinese student who enrolled could effectively subsidize the tuition of two of her California classmates.

The stage was set for the great Chinese student boom.

Between 2008 and 2012 Chinese enrollment in U.S. colleges and universities grew by over 20 percent every year, according to the Institute for International Education. By 2013, total Chinese enrollment was more than triple the levels before the 2008 financial crisis, and during the 2017–18 school year, China set a record with over 360,000 undergraduate and graduate students. The country had vaulted past India as the top source of international students in the United States, and by 2017 accounted for more students in the U.S. than the next five countries combined.[9]

Big state schools, many of them in the Midwest, absorbed the largest number of Chinese students. The University of Illinois Urbana–Champaign emerged as the unlikely leader in total Chinese enrollment—the school went from hosting just 37 Chinese undergraduates in the year 2000 to enrolling nearly 3,000 by 2014.[10] Flagship public campuses in Wisconsin, Indiana, and Ohio all followed the same pattern, throwing open their doors to students from across the Pacific.

But at a statewide level, California led the nation with more than 60,000 students from the People's Republic. Between 2007 and 2017, Chinese enrollment at the ten campuses of the University of California system (UC Berkeley, UCLA, etc.) multiplied by a factor of nearly ten.[11] At the start of the 2017–18 school year, 22,325 Chinese students were enrolled across the UC campuses, more than double the number of African American students in the system.

FERRARIS AND CHINESE TAKEOUT

And when these students arrived, many of them did so in style. Professor Stanley Kwong had a front-row seat to the changing demographics of Chinese students. After greeting those first Chinese students at Princeton in 1978, Professor Kwong had spent the intervening thirty years as a global marketing executive for IBM. Following his retirement from IBM in 2009, he returned to academia as a professor at the University of San Francisco (USF), a private Jesuit school near the center of the city. Professor Kwong was beginning to see more and more Chinese students in his marketing classes, but it was their after-hours activities that attracted the most attention.

At the time, Professor Kwong frequently appeared as a guest on local Cantonese radio stations, discussing Chinese economics and politics. Many of his listeners lived in the Richmond neighborhood abutting USF, a quiet part of town home to many elderly immigrants from Hong Kong and Taiwan. Beginning around 2013, Professor Kwong started to get more callers in his radio programs complaining about one thing: the sound of Ferrari engines at night.

As students from mainland China increased at USF, Chinese restaurants in Richmond began adapting to the new patrons, swapping out Cantonese seafood dishes for the spice of Sichuan cuisine. They also expanded their hours, with some staying open until three a.m. to catch the students returning from a night of karaoke. The bustle of normal business was one thing for elderly neighbors, but these late-night crews often announced their presence by gunning their engines.

"If a Ferrari is driving in your neighborhood," Professor Kwong told me, "you notice that because of the roar, right?"

Chinese students were by no means universally rich. Many middle-class Chinese parents had worked hard and saved up for decades to give their kids a chance to study in America. Some of those students spent two years at American community colleges, often working side jobs on nights and weekends, for the chance to transfer to a place like UCLA.[12] Even among students from wealthy backgrounds, most opted to keep a low profile and blend in on campus. For many of their families, a diploma from a top U.S. college stood right at the intersection of an up-by-your-bootstraps American dream and deeply held Confucian values about the paramount importance of education.

But the Ferrari-driving cohort were the most noticeable to outsiders, in part because of how different they appeared from the humble PhDs of generations past. Tim Lin had arrived in America just as the transition got under way, and College Daily documented the shifting profile of Chinese students on American campuses.

"Ten years ago nobody bought Mercedes, BMW, or luxury brands," Tim Lin told me on my first visit to his office headquarters. "They bought second-, third-, or even fourth-hand 1995 Toyota Corollas. But right now, it's 2015. We see a lot of students fly first-class to the U.S. When they arrive in the U.S. they've already bought the [luxury] car. They ask the students who are already there to buy the car first and just give them the car at the airport."

SHOULD I STAY OR SHOULD I GO?

It wasn't just money that separated these Chinese students from their predecessors. They were also younger, less academically elite, and far less likely to
stay in the U.S. long-term.

From the 1980s through the early 2000s, very few Chinese students
enrolled in U.S. undergraduate programs. Instead, the vast majority of Chinese students at American universities were pursuing graduate studies, often PhDs in technical fields. These scholars represented the cream of the
academic crop in China: products of prestigious institutions like Tsinghua
or Peking University, with a track record of excellence that gained them
entrance to top American research programs.

And when this group earned their degrees, they almost always stayed to
work in the country. One study by the National Science Foundation showed
that of Chinese students who had earned PhDs in the United States from 2002
to 2004, 86 percent of them were still in America a decade after graduating.
That retention rate was tied with India for the highest of any country, and
nearly triple the 32 percent stay rate of South Korean doctoral recipients.

But after 2008, all of these markers began to shift. More Chinese high
school students began applying directly to U.S. colleges. They were not necessarily the highest-performing students at their schools, but rather students
who could afford to enroll in international high school programs. In 2011,
the number of Chinese undergrads in the UC system surpassed the number
of graduate students for the first time, with that milestone replicated at the
national level a couple years later.[13] Within a few years of earning a bachelor's degree, many of these students returned to China.

Chinese people who study abroad and then return to China are
known as *haigui*, a pun on the Chinese word for "sea turtle" that means to
return from overseas. During earlier waves of overseas study in the 1980s
and 1990s, "sea turtles" were a rare breed, and when they returned home
they were often rewarded with coveted positions in universities or mul-
tinational corporations. But as the number of students going abroad
multiplied, so too did the number of sea turtles.

There isn't comprehensive data on return rates among more recent arrivals, but a mix of statistical indicators and anecdotal evidence points to a sea change in decisions about whether to stay. In 2017, a record-setting 480,000 students returned to China after studying abroad. China's Ministry of Education estimated in 2016 that return rates had risen to 70 to 80 percent beginning around 2013.[14] Those numbers were approximately in line with the results of a survey on the postgraduation plans of Chinese students at Purdue University in Indiana: 57 percent planned to return to China after a few years in the U.S., while 9 percent wanted to return to China immediately and 13 percent hoped to stay in the U.S. indefinitely (21 percent said they didn't know).[15]

Those shifting return rates reflect both a push (away from the U.S.) and a pull (back to China). A main factor pushing students to return is the increasing difficulty in obtaining H-1B visas, the most common visa for high-skill foreign citizens who have found a job in the United States. The United States caps the number of new H-1B visas each year, entering all applicants into a lottery that picks the lucky winners. Recent years have seen a steady rise in applications, while the 85,000-visa cap has remained unchanged. That means Chinese graduates who found jobs in the U.S. have seen their odds of "winning the lottery" to obtain a visa steadily fall.

But that push to return to China isn't always as blunt as a visa rejection.

"When I graduated from college, I believed in American dreams: I can get a good living, a good future in America, we follow the rules, and blah blah blah," Tim Lin told me. "But when we start to work we realize there is a glass [ceiling] for Chinese students."

Tim bumped up against that glass in his first job out of college, at an accounting firm in San Jose, California. What initially looked like a promising gig quickly fizzled over cultural barriers. Tim felt lost during Sunday football parties with the firm's partners, and what he saw at management levels told him the deck was stacked against Chinese and other Asians when it came to promotions.

Earlier generations of Chinese graduates often had to swallow their pride and stick with these jobs; their H-1B visa, and chance of obtaining a

U.S. green card, depended on it. But China's economic transformation and the wealthier family background of many of these students have changed that calculus. An American degree is no longer the golden ticket out of an impoverished country. For many of these students, especially those who are heirs to a successful family business, their earning potential is higher in their home country.

That reversal of fortunes is changing the way these students approach their time at school. In many places, the undergrad lifestyles of Chinese students in the U.S. are starting to resemble that of many Americans: a time to cut loose, have fun, and explore.

"They are enjoying the time studying there," observed Tim. "They're not pursuing some better life. They can have a better life back in China."

"HIGHER EDUCATION HOLOCAUST" OR "UPWARD-MOBILITY MACHINE"?

Not everyone was so happy about these changes. In a 2014 editorial titled "UCSD Is Selling Our Seats to the Rich," the student newspaper of Southwestern College, a community college in San Diego County, railed against the rise in foreign enrollment at the University of California, San Diego. Between the freshmen classes of 2007 and 2013, UCSD had multiplied its Chinese admissions by a factor of eight, from 258 to 2,099.[16] The newspaper's staff accused UCSD of perpetrating a "higher education holocaust" by simultaneously accepting progressively fewer transfer students from the local community college.

"UCSD flat out does not want Southwestern College students," the editors wrote. "We do not bring in as much cash as foreign students. Guilty as charged."

The accompanying cartoon showed UCSD's chancellor sitting at a desk with overflowing boxes of applications labeled "out-of-state" and "foreign," casually dropping applications from Southwestern College students in a paper shredder.

"UCSD has all but sealed shut the doors for first-generation college scholars from working-class families, most of them under-represented minorities," the newspaper's staff wrote. "No one here is accusing UCSD of intentional racism, but discrimination does not always burn crosses and wear hoods."

Criticism of growing foreign enrollment also came in the more measured tone of a report from the California State Auditor. That report ran with the self-explanatory title "The University of California: Its Admissions and Financial Decisions Have Disadvantaged California Resident Students." It accused the UCs of padding budgets by lowering admissions standards for out-of-state and foreign students, all while making things harder on local students.

"Despite a 52 percent increase in resident applicants, resident enrollment increased by only 10 percent over the last 10 years while nonresident enrollment increased by 432 percent," the report stated.

The report took particular umbrage with a 2011 decision to change official admission standards for nonresidents: instead of requiring that they "generally be in the upper half of admitted students," the UCs now only asked that nonresidents "compare favorably to California residents admitted." As a result, between 2009 and 2014, additional tuition generated from nonresident enrollment (the amount over and above what local students pay) rose from $325 million to $728 million.[17] During that period, the percentage of UC students from California had fallen from 89 to 81 percent.[18]

The California State Auditor used much of the remainder of the report to criticize the financial management of the UCs, accusing them of insufficiently adhering to recommendations from previous audits and paying excessive salaries to UC administrators. It recommended the legislature amend state law to cap nonresident enrollment at the UCs, and to make continued public funding for the system contingent on not exceeding those caps.

Predictably, UC leadership was not happy. In a strongly worded letter to the auditor, UC president Janet Napolitano rejected the fundamental premises of the report, arguing that the UCs essentially had no choice but to massively increase nonresident enrollment. She pointed out that the UCs have three main sources of funding: state appropriations (which were cut by 33 percent); resident tuition (which causes student protests when raised); and nonresident tuition (which the UCs increased to make up the difference). Using the auditor's own estimate of $728 million in additional nonresident revenue, Napolitano argued that eliminating this sum would mean a 20 percent tuition hike for all local students.

Beyond pleading helplessness in the face of budget cuts, the UC response argued that it had actually expanded enrollment for disadvantaged students. From 2007 to 2016, the UC system increased its percentage of underrepresented minorities (17 to 25 percent), first-generation college students (36 to 42 percent), and Pell Grant recipients (a proxy for low- and middle-income families, 30 to 38 percent). At UCSD, the school charged with perpetrating the "higher education holocaust," those three categories of students all held steady or increased.[19]

Those stats earned the UC system national recognition in *The New York Times*'s annual College Access Index, a ranking of schools "doing the most for the American dream," based on tuition, enrollment, and graduation rates for low- and middle-income students. UC schools dominate the rankings, taking the top five spots in 2015 and 2017. The *Times* dubbed the UC system "California's Upward-Mobility Machine."

Yes, Chinese students were entering the UC system, but their tuition dollars were also a source of fuel that kept the machine running.

BLACK CATS ON SKYPE

It wasn't just the sheer number of Chinese students that was causing frictions on American campuses. It was also how they got there.

Troubles first surfaced at USF during freshmen orientation in 2012. The school had begun ramping up Chinese enrollment a few years earlier, but some members of the administration feared there was a language barrier when communicating with the new arrivals. So one enterprising dean decided to offer headsets with simultaneous English-to-Mandarin translation for the Chinese students during a welcome ceremony. It probably sounded like a decent idea in the abstract, a way to accommodate students from "diverse backgrounds."

But the optics—dozens of Chinese students putting on headphones to understand a welcome lecture at their school—were all off. It had their American classmates and teachers asking the same question: "If they can't understand English, why are they here?" The move felt like an insult to the American students who had worked hard to get accepted. Professors felt the language barrier was messing with classroom dynamics, reducing discussion, and forcing them to dumb down their language to be understood. One associate dean at USF's business school quit soon after the orientation.

There was some important context to the headset fiasco. Like many schools, USF admitted some Chinese students on a conditional basis, requiring them to take anything from a semester to multiple years of English classes before joining undergrad classes. Those ESL students usually pay full university tuition but attend classes taught by retired high school teachers, a lucrative side hustle for these schools.

But the incident still shone a spotlight on the uncomfortable truth that neither Chinese students nor school administrators wanted to acknowledge: Chinese applications to U.S. universities are rife with fraud.

Rapid expansion of U.S. admissions spawned a cottage industry of "education consulting" companies. Employing young Americans living in China, these companies often charge fees ranging from $5,000 to $50,000 to help Chinese kids apply to U.S. colleges. The services they offer are on a spectrum as well, from totally legitimate admissions guidance to the ghostwriting of essays and the fabrication of extracurricular activities. A friend of mine who worked for an education consulting company in Beijing described the business proposition in simple terms: "The more you pay, the more we promise."

For 250,000 RMB (roughly $40,000), the company would guarantee entrance to a top-twenty-five school in the *US News & World Report* rankings. For around half that amount, it would promise a certain level of involvement in selecting schools, crafting personal statements, and coaching the student for taking the SATs and English-proficiency TOEFL test.

Reporting a Chinese student's high school grades brought its own challenges and opportunities. Most schools there use number rather than letter grades, and they tend to grade dramatically harder than U.S. schools; the grade of the best Chinese student in a class of 300 might translate to B+ if converted directly to the American system. So many students, schools, and parents work together to create a better-looking transcript. My friend who worked as an educational consultant put it bluntly: "If a parent is actually influential and has money, then that high school Chinese transcript is like a chalkboard."

What emerged at the end of this application process was often a polished picture of a brilliant Chinese student who was full of potential and fluent in English. When many of those students arrived on campus with severely limited English skills, colleges quickly realized something was amiss.

Some schools began requiring Skype interviews for their Chinese applicants, hoping to at least ferret out students whose language skills couldn't cut it. But these schools discovered that even a live conversation with the real applicant could be faked. A report on admissions fraud by Vericant, a Beijing-based company that conducts certified video interviews for schools, recounted the story of one Skype interview gone wrong:

> As they began, the [admissions] officer noticed the ear of a black cat in the student's lap. Although the officer thought it was strange, he continued with the interview. At one point mid-way through the interview the "cat" moved, and the admissions officer was astonished to realize there was a woman lying in the student's lap! The woman, presumably the mother, had been there throughout the interview, whispering answers to her daughter.[20]

Stunts like the whispering cat-mom can be anything from comical to criminal. As the full scope of admissions fraud became apparent, some observers began to pin the blame on Chinese culture, invoking stereotypes about Chinese people as devious, corrupt, or unconcerned with morality.

But American universities—institutions with "truth" and "justice" carved into their ivy-framed plaques—were often just as complicit. My friend's company funneled a good portion of its highest-paying students through one admissions officer at a prestigious California university. A student's application would have to be polished, and their test scores above a certain threshold, but beyond that the officer could work to push the student through the admissions committee. At the end of the day, all parties had a sense of what was going on.

"On the admissions side, are they shocked that these things were forged, that the integrity of their academic program is jeopardized? Are they mad?" my friend asked. "Or did they say, 'Yo, we have a budget deficit. We need $450,000 from international students over the next year. Give me the best you can.'"

"THEY NEVER REALLY LEFT CHINA"

Education consultants helped the two sides navigate the admissions process. But once the Chinese students landed on U.S. soil, platforms like College Daily took on the duties of cross-cultural translation. Even if a student's English skills were up to snuff, getting a handle on the many facets of life in America—pop culture, politics, and dating apps—could still be daunting.

In that process, the sheer number of Chinese students could be a handicap. Earlier waves of Chinese students were immediately thrown into the deep end: they were largely cut off from their home country and surrounded by American peers. Students who didn't learn English and make friends with Americans would live a very lonely existence. But by 2012, many American universities had reached a critical mass of Chinese students such that they didn't *need* to venture outside their own circles: they only made Chinese friends, consumed Chinese-language media, and spoke Mandarin all day long.

Tim Lin had chosen Miami University specifically because it would force him to make friends with Americans, and he lamented the inward turn of more recent arrivals: "You could say they never really left China."

No app or news platform can force these students to engage with their American peers, but College Daily did its best to give them the tools they would need if they wanted to venture outside their comfort zone. The articles clearly resonated with an audience: by fall 2015, College Daily boasted over 400,000 subscribers to its daily publications, a number that far exceeded the 300,000 Chinese students in the United States.

When I visited Tim's Beijing headquarters that year, his team of editors and writers were busy mashing up the day's slate of news, gossip, and life hacks. The articles are largely written by Chinese students in the U.S., and they reflect their needs: how-to guides on applying for a green card, pointers for using Tinder ("Those interested in Chinese people are just in it for the novelty"), and think pieces on Donald Trump ("taking America charging hysterically into the unknown—a place with politics, dark humor and 100% naturally grown hair").

Reading those stories gives a window into an activity familiar to many Americans, whether they're immigrants to this country or students spending a semester in Spain: piecing together the puzzle of a country and a culture not your own.

A TALE OF TWO SYSTEMS

People like Tim were working overtime to bridge the gap for Chinese students, to interest and engage them with American culture. It was much rarer to find Americans engaged in the same project, trying to understand their new Chinese classmates and where they were coming from. Exploring that background—the education system, family expectations, and college application process—goes a long way toward understanding the sources of cultural frictions once Chinese students arrive in the states.

I dove into that background while profiling a pair of identical twin brothers who were high school seniors in Beijing: Ding Xuanyu and Ding Xuancheng. They had grown up going to the same schools, hanging out with the same friends, and playing the same sports. But when it came time to think about college, their paths diverged. Xuanyu preferred to stay in China, while Xuancheng (English name: Frank) decided he wanted to study in America.

Both of those choices seemed like natural fits for the guys. Xuanyu was a bit more serious and studious; Frank leaned more extroverted and expressive. Xuanyu had a close-cropped haircut; Frank sported a more stylish flop, with one side shaved close and the rest grown out. But what really separated them for that last year of high school were the different college application processes they faced.

For the vast majority of Chinese high school students, applying to university means one thing: passing the country's notorious college entrance exam, the *gaokao* (pronounced "gow-cow"). Their score on that two-day test will be the sole determinant of which—if any—college they gain admission to. High school grades get thrown out, extracurriculars don't exist, and no college wants to see your "personal statement." It all comes down to *gaokao*.

The test is sometimes compared to the SAT, but in reality there is no comparison. *Gaokao* is an all-consuming black hole at the end of high school, the culmination of over a decade of intellectual cramming that makes American high schools look like daycare centers. High school seniors often study more than twelve hours a day, six to seven days a week. Some extreme schools have even hooked students up to IV drips during cram sessions and installed suicide nets at student dorms.

Xuanyu's high school was progressive by Chinese standards, but hearing him recount his *gaokao* preparation regimen left me feeling pathetically weak of will. Monday through Friday he would be in class, taking practice tests or studying from 8 a.m. to 11:25 p.m., with an hour each for lunch and dinner. He would take Friday evening after dinner off, and then put in two more eight-hour days of studying on both Saturday and Sunday.

As draining as *gaokao* may be, it has the virtue of simplicity: a single test score and a single standard for admissions. It is also widely perceived as a fundamentally fair system in a nation where personal connections and casual corruption often erode public trust.

By choosing to study in America, Frank opted out of the *gaokao* pressure cooker. But what American college admissions lacked in intensity, they made up for in complexity: AP classes, extracurricular activities, TOEFL tests, the SAT test, SAT subject tests, letters of recommendation, and personal statements.

That last item can be particularly puzzling for Chinese students. Frank is an engaging and curious student with good English. He likes to dance and sketch and will reference eighth-century Chinese poetry while discussing current New York fashion trends. But when it came time to write a personal statement, his ideas about the essay reflected Chinese values that do not translate well to the American admissions context.

"I thought maybe in a good personal statement you'll just show off your strong will to the guy reading this," he told me. "Like you'll just say, 'I focused on studying math for four years.'"

Some time working with an education consultant set Frank straight. The company Frank's family hired for the process was on the more legitimate end of the spectrum, helping him brainstorm topics and proofreading the essays. He ended up writing about the inspiration he drew from Joyce Carol Oates and his nostalgia for fishing in his family's ancestral village. Those essays helped him gain entrance to the University of Illinois Urbana–Champaign, where he enrolled that fall.

Frank's decision to go abroad was a personal one: a chance to explore a new country and culture. But for his twin, Xuanyu, the choice of where to study was imbued with broader social dimensions.

"If everyone just goes to America, China will never truly develop," he told me. "If China wants to grow into its own country—not just a second America—Chinese people need to feel more responsibility for their nation."

For Xuanyu, that meant cultivating and reimagining the intellectual traditions that made China distinct.

"Lots of people in my generation love entertainment and international things. They're going toward a kind of uniformity, where everything is the same across countries," he said. "China has its own unique things, like Confucius and Taoist thinking. It's just that they haven't been fully expressed."

That fear of losing Chinese culture in the whitewashing of a Western education goes back as far the 1880s, when Confucian officials ordered By-jinks Johnnie and his classmates to return immediately to the Middle Kingdom. But as I spent more time on American campuses, I began to hear echoes of that age-old concern coming from the Chinese students themselves. To understand how they handled this cross-cultural tug-of-war, I signed up to be a judge at a Mandarin-language speech contest down the road from my apartment, at UC Berkeley.

"THAT'S WHY WE TRY TO FIT IN"

First up at today's qualifying round is a Chinese student who goes by the English name Ham. Dressed in a black jacket and a crisp Golden State Warriors baseball cap, Ham is holding forth in Mandarin on one of today's three speech prompts: When a fellow student says they're depressed, are they just trying to get attention? Ham doesn't think so. He cites statistics on mental health and draws out a metaphor around sneezing, colds, and cries for help. He's a great public speaker, and I recommend that he advance to the next round.

Today's contest is being put on by a Chinese coworking space in San Francisco. A dozen students, almost all of them Berkeley undergrads, are competing to be a contestant on the internet TV show that the company will film in a few weeks. Tryouts are being held in a small classroom on the third floor of a building on UC Berkeley's campus. Tomorrow we'll head down to Stanford and repeat the selection process with Chinese students and recent graduates in the area. My friend Tina is managing this event for the coworking space, and she invited me to act as a judge.

I've been on a decent number of Chinese internet and television shows, and I know what my role is: speak some Chinese for the cameras and add that "international" flavor. I agreed to do it as a favor for Tina, but also because I wanted to hear what these students thought about the third debate prompt: "Should Chinese students pretend to be different than they are to blend into American culture?"

It's a question close to my own heart. I spent over five years in China desperately working to pick up the language, inflections, and mannerisms of the people around me. I wanted so badly to be able to understand what made them tick and to express myself in a way that resonated. It mostly worked. By the end of my time there I felt totally comfortable navigating those worlds, using Mandarin to express my own thoughts. My favorite thing to do was put those skills to work sharing parts of California culture with Chinese people. I started an Ultimate Frisbee team with one of my best friends there and put up goofy online videos teaching the sport.

All of that feel-good cultural exchange was facilitated by a form of national and racial privilege: many Chinese people are excited to learn about American culture, and they're often very happy to meet an American (especially a white American) who is interested in their culture. Speaking even a little bit of Chinese wins undeserved accolades, and there's often a tacit understanding that when it comes to the best movies, TV, music, and sports, America is the place to be.

Linghong Zhang got a much different reception when she tried to share her own culture with Americans. She's a freshman at Berkeley, and the fifth speaker in today's contest. Linghong talks about growing up in a part of southern China where locals still valued sons over daughters, a tendency that put a chip on her shoulder from a young age. She came to Los Angeles during high school, living with a Mexican family while attending local schools.

But Linghong felt isolated. She spoke English with a heavy accent, didn't get her classmates' jokes, and felt that they looked down on her. So she went to work learning their culture. She watched six seasons of *The Vampire Diaries* and pretended that she liked the same shows as the other girls. But she still felt like they didn't really accept her, and she thought she knew why: people don't want to be friends with someone *pretending* to be interested in the same stuff as them. She decided to stop faking it and take pride in her own culture.

A couple years later, Linghong was volunteering at an international film event, staffing the desk for one of China's most famous animation companies. She was a big fan of cartoons and was proud to be representing the company as it promoted *The Monkey King*, an animated film inspired by the protagonist of China's most famous novel, *Journey to the West*. But when she tried to talk to an American director about the movie, he laughed it off. He told her no one in America was going to watch it. When she tried to argue with him, he offered her a bet: he would give her $200 if she could find ten Americans who had heard of the Monkey King. She scavenged the event for people who knew about this treasure of Chinese culture. She came up empty, unable to find a single American who had any idea what she was talking about.

It felt like a slap in the face. It reminded her that "mainstream" or "global" culture is basically defined by what American people like. But the more she thought about it, the more she put the blame on her own people.

"Chinese people aren't confident enough," she tells our panel of three judges. "With something like the Monkey King—the essence of our culture—we're embarrassed to bring it out and show it to our American classmates."

It's clear that this touches a nerve with Linghong. Her Mandarin keeps picking up speed as she talks, and I put down my pen to listen closely. For just a moment, I think that she's on the verge of bursting into tears. Linghong has lived in America for several years, learned a new language, and earned admission to one of the country's best universities. But despite all that—or maybe because of it—she feels ever more acutely that on a deep level, Chinese people lack confidence in their own country.

"That's why we always think foreign culture is better than our own. That's why we"—and here she switches to English—"try to fit in."

"WHAT A BIG TREE"

Tensions over assimilation spanned both the personal and the political. Chinese students in the United States have long served as a screen on which the two countries project their hopes and fears when it comes to technology, theology, and politics.

Many Americans have imagined that these students' time in the United States will give them an eye-opening introduction to the wonders of liberal democracy. Finally free to read, think, and say what they want, these students will learn the truth about political repression in their home country. Many will choose to stay in this land of the free, and those who return home could well turn into seeds for a movement that will finally bring democracy to the People's Republic of China. In the end, these students and their home country will become "more like us."

There's a historical basis for these kinds of hopes. Sun Yat-sen, the leader of the revolutionary movement that overthrew China's last dynasty in 1911, was deeply influenced by Western political ideas, having studied under British missionaries in Hawaii and converted to Christianity in Hong Kong. Sun was actually in Denver on a fund-raising trip when he learned the revolution he was plotting had broken out unexpectedly.

Many of the men who would go on to lead the Chinese Communist Party itself had their political awakenings while studying in the West. Deng Xiaoping—a longtime CCP leader who both spearheaded China's economic reforms and ordered the tanks toward Tiananmen Square—first encountered Marxism in France in the 1920s. There he met other young intellectuals like Zhou Enlai, who sought to study the political and social structures of Western countries and use that foreign knowledge to "save China." They ended up forming Chinese Communist cells, laying the groundwork for the eventual overthrow of Chiang Kai-shek's Nationalist Party and the creation of a "new China" led by the CCP.

During the 1989 student protests in Tiananmen Square, Chinese students in the U.S. engaged in vigorous public debates about democracy and the future of China. Professor Stanley Kwong used to drop in on these debates at UC Berkeley, with some conservative students arguing for the more incremental reforms and others calling for full-on transition to a democratic political system. Following the CCP's violent crackdown in Beijing, the U.S. government allowed any Chinese students who were in the U.S. at the time to obtain permanent residency here if they feared persecution in their home country.

Students in the most recent wave have shown far less interest in fomenting revolution. Most of them have known nothing but rising standards of living and a steady elevation of China's place in the world, changes that have opened up vast new life possibilities for them and their parents.

But the CCP has remained suspicious of what these students are learning overseas and what they're bringing home. The Ministry of Education and other organs of the Chinese state have regularly singled out overseas students as priority targets for "political education" that will imbue them with greater levels of "patriotic energy" while overseas and after returning home. That brand of paternalistic "guidance" has sometimes taken the form of censorship.

On June 4, 2016, Tim Lin's College Daily published what looked like a relatively innocuous post: a picture of a tree. Above it was written, "Today we're suspending publication for one day. Reply with the words 'What a Big Tree' to read yesterday's story."

Readers who replied to the post with the prescribed phrase were sent a small commemoration of Hu Yaobang, the relatively liberal general secretary of the CCP during the early 1980s. Hu had worked toward greater political reforms but had been forced to resign in 1987 after refusing to discipline the leaders of pro-democracy demonstrations on college campuses. When Hu died in 1989, commemorations of his life had been the spark that ignited the student protest movement in Tiananmen Square. During the movement, a poem memorializing Hu was set to music and sung in both mourning and hope. The title: "What a Big Tree." The College Daily post on June 4—the anniversary of the 1989 crackdown—was a not-so-subtle commemoration of that movement and those who lost their lives.

The response was swift. The post was quickly taken down and College Daily was blocked from publishing anything for one month. The punishment was something between a slap on the wrist and truly damaging retaliation. During that month, Tim's team opened other accounts that allowed them to continue publishing, though the work didn't reach nearly as many readers. When the month was up and College Daily went back to publishing, Tim put out a post boasting that their subscribers had actually increased during the publishing blackout.

Behind the scenes, Tim was more cautious. He told me he'd learned his lesson and wouldn't be putting something like that out again. What had begun as a passion project was now a business, one with a responsibility to its investors and the employees who counted on it for their salary every month.

But even that caution was no guarantee against interference. A couple months after getting publishing privileges back, Tim began planning College Daily's election-night coverage for the showdown between Hillary Clinton and Donald Trump. He planned and advertised a live stream from the publication's New York office, with College Daily writers and editors explaining the mechanics of the electoral college and breaking down returns in real time. And then, just a couple hours before the stream was set to begin, they got a call from the relevant authorities. There was to be no live stream. No explanation was given, and the decision was not up for debate.

#CHINESESTUDENTSMATTER

Censoring public discussion in China is one thing, but after the 2016 election, worries began to mount that China was exporting some of those restrictions to U.S. campuses—and Chinese students were acting as the conduit.

The issue made national headlines in the spring of 2017, when UC San Diego announced its pick to deliver that year's commencement address: His Holiness the Dalai Lama. UCSD's administration probably thought they'd scored a major coup by securing the long-exiled Tibetan leader. If they did, the feeling didn't last long.

Within hours of the announcement, Chinese student groups were issuing statements of protest, claiming that the invitation "contravened the spirit of respect, tolerance, equality, and earnestness" upon which the university was built. They demanded a meeting with the UC chancellor and vowed to protest the speech. The leader of those calls was the local chapter of the Chinese Students and Scholars Association, which declared that it had already contacted the Chinese consulate in Los Angeles regarding the matter.

What was all the fuss about? In the West, the Dalai Lama is viewed as an apolitical symbol of universal love, a mascot for world peace and Buddhist wisdom. But the Chinese government still views and portrays him as an enemy of the state and a "wolf in sheep's clothing." At issue is the status of Tibet, a region that for centuries has seesawed between independence and Chinese rule. The current Dalai Lama was just a child when the People's Republic of China regained control of Tibet in 1950. Ever since he fled the country for India during a 1959 uprising, China has blamed him for instigating unrest in the region. China's Ministry of Foreign Affairs regularly issues indignant statements of protest when heads of state invite the Dalai Lama to visit, and it does its best to keep his message from reaching the Chinese people.

But this time the outrage over a Dalai Lama speech was coming from a different source: the students themselves, the very people who were supposed to be basking in their newfound freedom to access information censored in their home country.

That reaction surprised many Americans who had taken for granted the idea that Chinese students becoming "more like us" meant falling into lockstep with mainstream American political values. Conversations with, and surveys of, Chinese students revealed a far more complex picture.

A 2016 Purdue University survey of over 800 Chinese students at a Big Ten school revealed that exposure to America was no guarantee of more positive opinions about U.S. political values. Students in the survey were asked whether their time in the U.S. left them with more positive or more negative impressions of both the United States and their home country. When it came to the United States, the students were evenly split: 26 percent gained a more positive view of America, while 29 percent had a more negative view (44 percent reported no change).

On views of China, the results skewed positive: 44 percent reported a more positive view of their home country, while only 17 percent felt more negatively toward their home country during their time abroad. When asked about their views on democracy as a form of government, the students were divided: 37 percent either agreed or strongly agreed that it is the best form of government, while 28.1 percent disagreed or strongly disagreed with that statement (35 percent felt "neutral").

Chinese students may not have wholeheartedly embraced America's take on liberal democracy, but they did tap into the protest zeitgeist on U.S. college campuses. The UCSD controversy played out during a period of major tumult on U.S. college campuses, with student protests often shutting down public lectures by people they deemed objectionable. Chinese students at UCSD were now latching onto the vocabulary of those protests: "diversity," "inclusive spaces," and "respect for all cultures." They deployed it in public statements and hundreds of Facebook comments criticizing the decision.

Some called the decision "insulting" to Chinese students' heritage; others compared it to inviting Osama bin Laden or white supremacist David Duke to deliver the commencement. One Chinese student captured the zeitgeist in a melodramatic hashtag: #ChineseStudentsMatter.

THE LONG ARM OF THE CHINESE GOVERNMENT

Not everyone saw the protest as a shining example of student activism. Many media accounts of the affair cited a claim by the Chinese Students and Scholars Association (CSSA) that it had been in touch with the Chinese consulate, pointing to that contact as evidence that the Chinese government was using student groups to censor political speech abroad. The incident put CSSAs in the national spotlight, and journalists began investigating how the "long arm" of the CCP was reaching onto American campuses.

Most universities with a large contingent of Chinese students play host to a CSSA chapter. Those chapters act as hubs for Chinese students on campus: organizing orientation events, hosting job fairs with Chinese companies, and putting on the school's annual Chinese New Year Gala. For many

Chinese students, the CSSA is the organization that gives them a sense of community and helps them find their footing on a foreign campus.

CSSAs also maintain relationships with the Chinese government, often via the nearest Chinese embassy or consulate. Chapter presidents often gather at the consulate once per semester for meetings or dinners, and the chapters provide the consulates with student volunteers for public events. In return, the embassy or consulate will appropriate a certain level of funds to each CSSA, often between a few hundred and a couple thousand dollars per semester. That money goes toward organizing events like the New Year Gala, a major undertaking with mountains of food and lots of live performances.

But money from the embassy also sometimes goes toward political activities. In early 2018, *Foreign Policy* reporter Bethany Allen-Ebrahimian began publishing a series of reports on the ways the Chinese government mobilizes CSSAs for its own purposes. When President Xi Jinping was visiting Washington, D.C., in 2015, the Chinese embassy reportedly asked local CSSAs to bring students out to line the streets for his motorcade, offering twenty dollars to each student who came out. During a major CCP political gathering in the fall of 2017, the consulates reportedly asked the CSSAs to organize "watch parties" on campus for Chinese students and to send back pictures and reports on the events. In other pieces, Allen-Ebrahimian described how a reference to Taiwan—the self-governing island locked in a multidecade dispute with the PRC—was removed from her personal biography at an event sponsored by the Confucius Institute.

American analysts began to refer to these activities as "influence operations"—an umbrella term for any attempts by the Chinese state to affect American institutions or alter the parameters of discussion on U.S. soil. Several CSSA student officials interviewed by Allen-Ebrahimian said that the consulates had increased the emphasis on political activities in recent years, beginning around 2016.

"I feel like the tendency is that the consulate tries to control CSSAs more and more," one chapter president told *Foreign Policy*. "I don't think this student group should be involved with government in any way."

Speaking with CSSA officials at several California universities, I got a mixed bag of responses about political pressures. Yin Yikai, the president of the Stanford CSSA, said that his group received little funding and no political marching orders from the nearby consulate. He described the events in San Diego as an "extreme" case and said that his organization focused on safety issues and social events.

But members of other CSSAs described a rising emphasis on "political education," particularly during major CCP events like the Nineteenth Party Congress in the fall of 2017. Along with organizing watch parties on their home campuses, CSSA presidents were reportedly required to write an essay on what the "spirit of the Nineteenth Party Congress" meant to them.

In one instance, a CSSA member told me about being asked to report on the activities of fellow Chinese classmates. The student attended a historically Christian university and said that the local consulate was worried these students would be targeted for conversion by Christian groups. They described being invited to the consulate multiple times and asked by the consul general which students were falling under the influence of Christian groups. When I asked if the consulate did anything based on the information, they said the consulate would only act if the students appeared to be forming religious groups "like Falun Gong," a persecuted spiritual group in China.

What was most striking—and troubling—about that conversation was that despite having lived in the United States for over six years, the students appeared to have no idea that reporting on the religious activities of other students would be seen as a deep affront to American values and freedoms. To them, low-level surveillance of your peers' religious beliefs just felt like business as usual.

HIS HOLINESS AT UCSD

But even during the Dalai Lama affair at UCSD, the picture was more complicated than it initially appeared. Yes, the CSSA was spearheading the Dalai Lama protests, and yes, they had contacted the consulate about the event. But conversations with the actual students involved revealed that it wasn't the Chinese government pulling the strings.

While delivering a lecture at UCSD in 2018, I arranged to meet Lisa Hou, a junior and an officer in the school's CSSA. Lisa is from a midsize city in southwest China, and before arriving at UCSD she had hoped to study philosophy. But upon arrival she discovered that her English wasn't up to the obtuse verbiage of philosophy. When it came to improving her language skills, it didn't help that her roommate and almost all the girls on her freshman dorm's hall were other Chinese students. Lisa decided to major in math and computer science, and she joined the CSSA.

She said news of the Dalai Lama's visit triggered an immediate reaction among Chinese students, including herself. That reaction didn't stem from a deep-seated hatred of the Dalai Lama himself, but rather from a sense that the university didn't understand or care about how Chinese students would feel.

"Normally, Chinese students are completely silent. We have no influence or voice," she told me. "When we speak, no one really listens. So we felt that we definitely want to stand up and say something."

Members of the CSSA leadership quickly fired off a public statement on the group's WeChat account, including the part about contacting the Chinese consulate in Los Angeles. For them, the reference to the consulate conveyed gravitas and the seriousness of the situation. For outsiders, it made the students look like stooges of a foreign government. Lisa felt it was a mistake, but they had to move on.

The CSSA planned to hold a small protest along the school's Library Walk, a stretch of sidewalk where student groups frequently hand out flyers and put up posters for different causes. Lisa was put in charge of preparing material for their informational posters. She didn't know much about the Dalai Lama growing up. She had heard a little about him during the 2008 riots in Tibet, but only really began to read about his work while preparing the posters.

In doing that research, Lisa decided to use Western sources because the Chinese ones were "really biased." As she read on, she found that she agreed with many of the Dalai Lama's current teachings about compassion and tolerance. But she also felt that his pristine public image in the West obscured his political past, such as the fact that he and his organization took millions of dollars of financing from the CIA during the 1960s.[21]

The posters Lisa ended up creating had titles such as "Why Is the Dalai Lama Controversial?" and "Monk or Politician?" They displayed copies of declassified U.S. intelligence documents on the CIA's payment to him and quotes from Western historians about institutional serfdom in Tibet during the Dalai Lama's rule there.

On the appointed day, members of the CSSA propped those posters up along the Library Walk and tried to engage passing students in conversation. The reception was not always friendly.

"Tons of people doubted or questioned us. Whatever we would say about the Dalai Lama, they'd bring up things from Chinese history. They'd say, 'Well, can you explain Tiananmen to me?'" she told me. "They don't actually care about this. The feeling I got from them was, 'No matter what you say, it's ridiculous, because you're from an authoritarian country and you don't have freedom of speech.'"

It was a frustrating line of argument for the Chinese students. Lisa wanted to tell them that China had changed a lot, that there was a kind of freedom of speech even if it had limits, and that she wasn't ignorant of the problems in her own country. But it was difficult to get that across in a back-and-forth with students who believed her to be fundamentally brainwashed. They weren't going to change too many minds here, and the UCSD administration had said early on that it would not consider canceling the appearance by His Holiness.

Still, looking back on the event, Lisa was proud of what they achieved.

"I felt like it was successful," she told me. "If there's debate, then that's a success, because at least we were able to show them another side of things."

"WHOLE-OF-SOCIETY THREAT"

If students like Lisa had a hard time convincing their fellow students they weren't brainwashed, they were going to have an even harder time convincing the FBI they weren't spies. On February 13, 2018, the heads of the six major intelligence agencies sat down opposite the Senate Intelligence Committee for a hearing on threats posed by Russian hackers, North Korean missiles, and other "worldwide threats." But when it came time for Senator Marco Rubio to pose a question to the panel, he zeroed in on a new topic.

"What, in your view," he asked FBI director Christopher Wray, "is the counterintelligence risk posed to U.S. national security from Chinese students, particularly those in advanced programs in the sciences and mathematics?"

Wray launched into a discussion of China's use of "nontraditional collectors"—students, professors, and scientists—to infiltrate U.S. academic institutions and gather things of value. He said that reports of these activities were coming in from nearly all the FBI field offices, covering all major disciplines.

"They're exploiting the very open research and development environment that we have—which we all revere—but they're taking advantage of it," Wray told the committee. "So one of the things we're trying to do is view the China threat as not just a whole-of-government threat, but a whole-of-society threat on their end. And I think it's going to take a whole-of-society response by us."

On the one hand, Wray was stating the obvious: all countries try to use the assets at their disposal to conduct espionage on each other. There happen to be a large number of Chinese students at U.S. universities, many of them working in cutting-edge fields, and China's spy agencies are certainly trying to turn some of those students into intelligence assets. The United States intelligence community would be derelict in its duties if it wasn't trying to do the same thing.

But Wray's choice of words—"whole-of-society threat"—set off alarm bells in some quarters. That phrase seemed to cast suspicion on all Chinese students, and perhaps even Chinese Americans. A coalition of prominent Asian American community organizations wrote an open letter to Wray expressing "feelings of both anger and sadness" at his remarks, warning that such generalizations will lead to racial profiling against Chinese people.

The groups had reason to be worried. In the years prior to Wray's re-marks, a string of prominent Chinese American researchers had been inves-tigated, arrested, and charged with espionage, only to have the cases against them prove unfounded. The public humiliation and damage to their reputa-tions led several scientists to simply relocate back to China afterward.

But the FBI chief's testimony crystallized a growing trend in Wash-ington, D.C.: the tendency to view Chinese students as pawns or puppets working on behalf of the CCP, suppressing free speech on American soil or stealing our advanced technology. It was a transition that reflected the sea change in the balance of power between the two countries. When China was poor and weak, these students were welcomed as aspiring immigrants or the seeds of China's democratic future. But as the People's Republic became a legitimate strategic counterweight to U.S. power, the students were looked upon with suspicion, as foreign agents or intellectual leeches, sapping the United States of its hard-earned edge in advanced technology.

Those sentiments came to a rolling boil during an Oval Office meeting in the spring of 2018. With backlash against the students mounting and a trade war looming, President Trump's influential policy adviser Stephen Miller pushed a draconian proposal: a full ban on student visas for all Chi-nese citizens. Miller had staked out a position as one of Trump's far-right advisers, and he was instrumental in shaping President Trump's hard-line immigration policies. According to a report in the *Financial Times*, he ar-gued that along with hurting China, a ban on the students would also be a blow to the elite Ivy League universities and their faculty, who comprised some of Trump's harshest critics.

With President Trump undecided on the proposal, he convened a meet-ing with both Miller and his ambassador to China, Terry Branstad, the for-mer governor of Iowa. Ambassador Branstad pushed back against the ban, arguing that it would do more damage to small colleges in places like Iowa, which had come to rely on the students. Chinese enrollment at the Univer-sity of Iowa has skyrocketed after the financial crisis, and by 2015 Chinese students were paying an estimated $70 million in tuition and adding over $100 million to the local economy. Over the course of the Oval Office meeting, President Trump came to side with Ambassador Branstad, who himself had graduated from the University of Iowa. Turning to his ambassador, the president reportedly joked, "Not everyone can go to Harvard or Princeton, right, Terry?"

Instead of the outright ban, he opted for a more targeted approach. In May of 2018, the Trump administration issued new restrictions on visas for Chinese graduate students in fields such as robotics, aerospace, and advanced manufacturing. Validity of their visas would be reduced from five years to one. In a tweet following the new restrictions, Senator Rubio hailed the decision as a "great move!" He described Chinese student visas as "weapons" that the government uses in a concerted campaign to "steal & cheat their way to world dominance." The prospect of much tighter restrictions continued to loom large. In August of 2018, President Trump told a group of American business executives at a private dinner that "almost every student that comes over to this country is a spy."

It was a bizarre twist in the story of Chinese students in the U.S. As far back as the 1800s, Americans have imagined that Chinese students arriving in the U.S. would suddenly see the light—whether that light be Christianity or liberal democracy. Many of the Middle Kingdom's best and brightest would choose to settle down in the land of the free, and those who returned to China would act as a Trojan horse for American ideals. Now Americans feared the exact reverse: that Chinese students had turned into vessels for Chinese values, tools for suppressing free speech, and conspirators in an international technology heist.

When ideology wasn't an issue, economics was. Wealthy students had subsidized American universities reeling from budget cuts, but they also sparked a backlash from American students and professors who worried college admissions were being bought and sold on the free market. In 2018, the University of California system finally began implementing a policy to assuage those concerns: enrollment by non-California residents would be capped at 18 percent, or at the percentage in the 2017–18 year for schools in which it already exceeded that percentage.[22] For now at least, California looks to have hit its peak for Chinese students.

Undergirding all these changes has been a tectonic shift in geopolitical balance: today's Chinese students are coming from a country that is far more prosperous, powerful, and stable than at any point in recent history. It's a change that affects their motivations to come, their decisions to leave, and their posture toward everything they encounter in America. This group doesn't always feel the pull of American culture, and when they encounter liberal democracy up close, they're not necessarily impressed.

International, national, and state politics are all at play here. But if you zoom in a little further, the experience of Chinese students in the U.S. is still intensely personal and can be, in its own way, liberating.

CONCLUSION: KAFKA IN SAN FRANCISCO

Groups of painfully shy Chinese students are milling around near the neon-lit red carpet. Tonight, the University of San Francisco is hosting the first-ever "Golden University Student Micro-Film Festival," and the award nominees look equal parts excited and anxious. The event is put on by the local CSSA chapter, and ten teams of aspiring filmmakers from seven different California colleges are out here. Earlier in the year, I had created an online video series titled *The California Spirit* introducing California culture in Chinese. The first episode has been nominated for awards in a couple of categories—basically, serving as a token American project to increase the "international" flavor of the event.

The red carpet has been laid out in an alleyway behind the USF theater, splitting the difference between a chain-link fence and the back of the building. Neon-blue lights illuminate the way, and toward the end of the thirtyish yards of carpet, a camera crew waits to interview each nominee. We all take turns walking the carpet and answering a few stiff questions before heading into the school auditorium. I plop down in the center of the auditorium alongside a friend I've brought to the event, and we're soon joined in the row by a handful of chatty Chinese guys dressed in ties and sweaters. They're clearly enjoying themselves, and we strike up a conversation.

One of them is currently enrolled at San Francisco City College, and two of them recently graduated from UC Berkeley. One of the Berkeley grads, Wu Qiyin, now works in Google's Cloud department and does creative writing on the side. He's the scriptwriter behind their film: *Kafka*. I ask what it's about.

"It's about me!" the middle of the three blurts out. "My name is Kafka."

We all have a laugh at how eager Kafka is to take center stage, and the author explains the film's background. It's not *specifically* about his friend, but it is about a gay Chinese student in America named Kafka, his struggle to make a genuine connection with those around him, and his difficulty in coming out to his family.

Kafka asks where I uploaded my own video: YouTube or on Chinese video sites? I tell them I put it on both and ask the same question to them.

"Just YouTube," scriptwriter Wu tells me. "If we put it on Chinese sites, I think people would just criticize it—criticize *us*. We'll just leave it up in the U.S. and that's enough."

Our hosts for the night step onto the stage, including the president of the USF CSSA, a skinny film lover who I had met earlier through Professor Stanley Kwong. He makes awkward banter with his cohost and invites a series of sponsors and esteemed guests to the stage, including a representative from the education department of the nearby Chinese consulate in San Francisco, who makes a few standard-issue remarks on the importance of educational and cultural exchanges.

Sitting there, it occurs to me that in a certain light, an event like tonight could be interpreted as another Chinese "influence operation." It was put on by the CSSA, an increasingly politicized group. In attendance were multiple members of the Chinese Communist Party and representatives from the Chinese consulate. I imagine that any films touching on sensitive issues like the Dalai Lama or Taiwan would have been barred from competing; for all I know, that kind of censorship may have happened at USF that night.

And yet, that narrative doesn't get to the heart of what's happening here. The restrictions described above are real, but so are the new possibilities being explored by students through their films. As the auditorium goes dark, the screen lights up with short clips from each of the projects, small snatches of the stories that these students wanted to tell. One depicts the relationship between an old man and his granddaughter in a poor corner of rural China. Another follows a Chinese PhD student at Stanford who is haunted by paranoid fantasies and eventually saved by faith in God.

Kafka follows its title character from high school in China through college at Berkeley. It shows him getting bullied as a teenager in public by the same boy who is intimate with him in private, and then Kafka echoing that same behavior as a closeted college student. It shows him meeting David at a club in San Francisco's Castro District, and the tentative first steps of their relationship. Woven throughout are surreal montages and a monologue reciting parts of astronomer Carl Sagan's book *Pale Blue Dot*.

As the show progresses, awards are doled out and shy acceptance speeches delivered from the stage. My film comes up empty at the end of the night. The same goes for *Kafka*, despite nominations for best actor, best original screenplay, and best picture. It's a disappointment for the *Kafka* crew, but not a major one. They made their movie and were happy to put it out there into the world. Back in the lobby, we all take a picture together and add each other on WeChat.

Kafka featured several shots of the Bay Bridge, and as I drive my car back over it toward Oakland, something Tim Lin said to me three years earlier keeps running through my head.

"When Chinese students go to American colleges, they immediately find out that life can go many different ways. Not a linear one, not a single way."

2

SILICON VALLEY'S CHINA PARADOX

I t's eleven a.m. on a smoggy Friday in Beijing, and this busload of Chinese geeks is buzzing about smartwatches. As the bus driver muscles through gnarly traffic, programmers fiddle with watchband prototypes and debate the merits of different wrist-flick functions. The Apple Watch will be released later today, and the most popular models will sell out within seconds.

But the debut of the next big thing from Apple is not what has this group excited. The bus is carrying employees of Beijing-based artificial intelligence start-up Mobvoi to a twenty-four-hour smartwatch hackathon in a scenic village outside the city. The goal for the day and night ahead: build the apps for Mobvoi's own smartwatch operating system, Ticwear. Mobvoi hopes Ticwear can rival Apple's and Google's efforts in defining what a smartwatch does here in China—and eventually around the world.

That's a daunting task for any start-up, but one made easier by the background of Mobvoi's founders and the geopolitics of tech today. Résumés for Mobvoi's top brass read like a cross-section of the best in U.S. education and innovation: Google, Harvard Business School, Microsoft, Stanford research labs. The waves of Chinese students filing into American universities have generated an equally important undertow: ambitious Chinese engineers who are returning home with a U.S. diploma, work experience in Silicon Valley, and the desire to make a mark in China's emerging start-up scene.

Giving another boost to Ticwear's prospects is the fact that the operating system's main competitor, Google's Android Wear, remains effectively blocked in China.

The Communist Party treats Chinese cyberspace like the country's physical turf—something to be policed, cultivated, and controlled. The Great Wall of China was constructed and maintained over millennia to repel invading "barbarians"—Mongols and a variety of steppe people who raided and invaded the Chinese heartland. To deal with twenty-first-century "barbarians," the country has created the digital "Great Firewall," a complex system of controls that blocks access to many U.S. tech juggernauts: Google, Facebook, Snapchat, Twitter, and many media outlets.

Like its brick-and-mortar predecessor, the Great Firewall is far from impenetrable. Internet users in China can circumvent most controls by using a VPN (virtual private network), a tool that routes their traffic through servers overseas and grants access to the global internet. Chinese people call this *fanqiang*—scaling the wall. But VPNs are slow, unreliable, and frankly an all-around pain in the ass. Slim minorities of Chinese people use them, and your average internet user here inhabits a distinctly Chinese version of cyberspace, one devoid of the companies and apps that Silicon Valley churns out.

The initial goal in building the Firewall was information control: maintaining a Leninist grip on the channels of information and communication, thus protecting the Communist Party's grasp on power. But one of the side effects of that desire for information control has been the nurturing of China's own thriving digital economy.

By keeping out global technology leaders, the government also created breathing room for homegrown Chinese tech brands to blossom and eventually dominate their country's markets. Google's 2010 exit from mainland China cleared the way for Baidu to own the Chinese search market. Twitter's absence (and inspiration) made possible Weibo, the Chinese microblogging platform that eventually overtook Twitter in number of global users.

The ban on Facebook opened up the social media space for WeChat, the omnipresent social app on the mainland. And, crucially for Mobvoi, the block on Android Wear means the market for Android operating systems on wearables is wide open. Mobvoi intends to fill that void.

Towering technological walls may insulate the Chinese internet, but you'd never know that from the chatter here on the bus. Conversations flow seamlessly between new Facebook features, Chinese smartphone brands, and one programmer's favorite food: stinky tofu. Coders wear Google hoodies while typing out WeChat messages. They've got opinions on the algorithms in Chinese shopping apps and the best Hunan food in the Bay Area. Whenever the topic turns to technology or business, Chinese sentences are suddenly peppered with English phrases: "actionable path," "back end," and "why not?"

These are the twenty- and thirtysomethings driving China's tech renaissance. Apps and algorithms conceived by these types of coders are fueling a rash of billion-dollar valuations and business-model innovations that have caught the world's attention. Many on this bus studied at top-notch American universities and worked for the same companies that the Firewall blocks. They move fluidly across borders, languages, and cultures, mixing Silicon Valley idealism with a dose of Chinese reality. Having honed their chops in the global epicenter of technological innovation, they're now putting those skills to use in the rough-and-tumble world of Chinese tech.

These returnees are the *haigui*—"sea turtles"—who make up a good chunk of the audience for Tim Lin's College Daily, and they've been a driving force in China's tech scene for over two decades. In the mid-1990s, a batch of returnees founded the first wave of Chinese internet companies to get listed on global stock markets. Today, sea turtles from places like Stanford, Berkeley, and Harvard are founding and funding the companies vaulting China's tech scene to the top of global rankings.

Up at the front of the bus, dressed in an Android-branded jacket, sits Mobvoi's founder and CEO Li Zhifei (surname Li, given name Zhifei; pronounced "Jur-fay"). Li embodies this game of transpacific technological ping-pong. Born and raised in central China, he did stints at Beijing start-ups in the late nineties, earned a PhD in computer science at Johns Hopkins University, and spent two years as a researcher for Google Translate at the company's Mountain View, California, headquarters. But when Li wanted to found his own company, he picked up stakes and headed back to China, splicing what he calls the "Google DNA" into his own start-up's culture.

Ensconced behind China's Firewall, Li's company now produces apps, operating systems, and smartwatches, many of them filling the vacuum created by China's decision to block Li's former employer, Google. You might think that Li's decision to ditch Google and found a competitor in a protected market would have engendered some bad blood between the parent company and the start-up, but the opposite is true. In 2015, Google decided to invest in Li's company, and in subsequent years Mobvoi has served as a trusted partner and potential back door for Google's long-anticipated return to Chinese markets.

TRANSPACIFIC FLOWS AND GREAT FIREWALLS

Li and Mobvoi's story takes us to the heart of the fundamental paradox that long bound together Silicon Valley and China: while the transpacific flows of people, money, and ideas reached new heights, technology companies and the internet itself have never been more divided by national boundaries.

Chinese companies have set up research labs in Silicon Valley. American executives have taken the helm at their Chinese competitors. Venture capitalists from both countries began splashing around cash on both sides of the Pacific. Product managers in Silicon Valley are studying WeChat, and Chinese AI scientists are looking to Google for inspiration. And ultimately, a dose of the cultural zeitgeist of Silicon Valley has seeped into China's tech scene. As entrepreneurs and engineers bounce between the two places, they cross-pollinate the philosophical underpinnings and the management practices of the two technology ecosystems.

But that's where the exchange stops. Apart from Apple, virtually every major consumer-facing Silicon Valley company that's entered China has either been outcompeted or outright blocked. Chinese companies attempting to pierce U.S. markets have faced fewer legal obstacles, but their business ventures on U.S. soil have largely fallen flat.

China may have begun blocking foreign websites as a practical quest for information control, but an increasingly robust Chinese technology sector and the revelations of Edward Snowden helped turn those efforts into an ideology: cyber sovereignty, the right of a nation to absolute control over its domestic "cyber sphere." The result is a global internet that increasingly mirrors traditional economic and political systems, with governments asserting control at home and vying for influence abroad.

THE ETHICS OF ENGAGEMENT AND THE NEW TECH TENSIONS

Stakes are high for all the key players in this environment. But for the Chinese Communist Party, they verge on existential. That's because the rise of the internet touches on two of the key pillars of the Party's legitimacy: information control and economic growth.

Since its founding in 1921, the CCP has seen "ideological work" as core to its ability to gain and maintain power. Controls on information and speech have never been absolute, but they have always remained strong enough to shape the contours of a national narrative, one that casts the Party as the protagonist in a tale of national rejuvenation. Brave Chinese journalists or academics can be pesky in undercutting parts of that narrative, but the distribution sources and perpetrators all remain within striking distance of Party authority. Newspapers can be shut down and professors can be jailed.

When they emerged, the internet and social media posed the greatest test yet because they challenged both of these mechanisms of control. What happens when police can't seize the means of distribution? And what happens when the sources of information either are so diffuse they can't be controlled or are physically outside of China's national borders? From the Party's perspective, these propositions are unacceptable. Control over the internet—the content posted and the companies that host it—remains an issue of paramount importance.

But control isn't the only goal. China's leaders and its companies are banking on technological innovation and commercial applications to help fuel the next decade of growth in China.

The engines that powered China's three-decade economic boom— cheap exports, rapid urbanization, and a massive infrastructure build-out— are sputtering. Rising wages are undermining China's export powerhouse, and a spending splurge on basic infrastructure and housing has reached saturation. If China hopes to pole-vault into the ranks of developed countries, it needs dynamic new sources of growth to spur domestic consumption and bump it up the production value chain.

For that, China's leaders are banking in large part on a flourishing tech sector. China's technology juggernauts are the grease in the wheels of the country's new consumer economy. The companies themselves continue to post astonishing profits, but their importance goes far beyond that. The auxiliary jobs they create in logistics, sales, and services are providing a major boost for an economy struggling to wean itself off heavy industry.

Alibaba—the Chinese online shopping juggernaut—is fanning the flames of consumption by placing the world's largest shopping mall in the palm of people's hands. That shopping is also fueling a logistics revolution that employs millions of drivers in trucks, in cars, and on three-wheel trikes. Baidu and Tencent, the Chinese internet juggernaut behind WeChat, are opening whole new on-demand O2O (online-to-offline) service industries: nail technicians that show up at your door, grandmas who'll cook you an extra meal for cash, and live-streaming stars who sing for money from fans. China's rapid rise in the field of artificial intelligence could reenergize China's manufacturing sector with robots and unsnarl traffic in China's cities with autonomous vehicles.

Accessing all those material benefits, while keeping its grip on power, has required the Chinese government to perform a tricky balancing act: absorbing ideas and talent from Silicon Valley while also ensuring that any company operating in China is squarely under the Party's control.

For their part, American technology companies looking to enter China face ethical and financial dilemmas. Silicon Valley is both an industry and an ideology. Its juggernauts rake in massive profits but declare themselves to be mission- and value-driven. Google long used the straightforward "Don't be evil" as its ethical ethos and made it the company's mission "to organize the world's information and make it universally accessible and useful." Facebook, meanwhile, wants to "give people the power to share" and "make the world more open and connected."

By acting as the gatekeeper to the country's billion-plus consumers, the CCP possesses tremendous power to demand concessions in exchange for access. For American and European automakers, those concessions have included forming joint ventures and sharing technology with local companies. For information technology companies, that means agreeing to strict censorship requirements and granting the Chinese government access to source code and data on Chinese users.

Those onerous government demands would be laughed at in many smaller markets, but the allure of the Chinese consumer base is simply too great. Totally abstaining from the market would be analogous to European automakers simply giving up on selling cars in America after World War II.

Even if one ignores the profit motive and takes these companies' mission statements seriously, the dilemmas are no less thorny. When Google's search engine provides Chinese users with censored search results—including top-notch English-language sources that aren't found on Baidu—is it helping to make information more universally accessible, or lending legitimacy to powers that seek to control it? If Chinese Facebook users can't share political opinions on the platform, but they can find and communicate with friends overseas, is the world a more open and connected place?

It's a classic dilemma in dealing with unscrupulous or authoritarian governments: should you opt for messy engagement or take the moral high ground? Do you refuse to engage with people and companies in that country, hoping that your abstention sends a message and leads to fundamental change down the road? Or do you continue to work within the rules set up, pushing for change where you can and hoping that greater engagement and exposure contributes to incremental progress?

This dilemma—messy engagement versus moral high ground—confronts not only technology companies, but also American universities that want to open campuses in China, film studios that want their movies shown there, and even governments that fear publicly confronting the Party on sensitive issues would mean a break in transnational ties.

And these are not abstract or academic questions. A Chinese journalist spent eight years in prison after Yahoo cooperated with a government investigation into his email account. Cisco has faced a class-action lawsuit in California over the company's alleged complicity in supplying software tools that could track users and aid the brutal suppression of Falun Gong practitioners.

Beyond the financial bottom lines and ethical breaking points of Silicon Valley companies, the evolution of Chinese cyberspace holds tremendous importance for the future of the internet itself. Technologists and ordinary citizens have long envisioned the internet as a global digital commons, a place where information and ideas flow freely, unburdened by the constraints of the physical world and its outdated political institutions.

But the Chinese government has shown that a combination of cutting-edge censorship technology and old-school authoritarian intimidation can effectively bring the internet to heel. Today, China's ability to wall off its domestic internet, while also fostering wildly successful technology companies, serves as both a warning for internet freedom advocates and an inspiration for other authoritarian regimes.

China is one of the few institutions with the clout and cohesiveness to shape the evolution of internet governance. The United States used its post–World War II dominance to create a new economic order built around free trade and stable exchange rates. Today, China is deploying its leverage over Silicon Valley to rewrite the rules of the internet, coaxing the world's most influential technology companies to play along with its conception of "internet sovereignty."

For years, the question on everyone's mind was, How will the internet reshape the Chinese government? Today, the question persists, but the subject and object have reversed: How will the Chinese government reshape the internet?

The revenge of internet geopolitics hasn't been limited to issues of censorship and market access. Trade wars, hacking attacks, and territorial spats have put the national U.S.–China relationship through the wringer, dragging it from the realm of strategic competition to outright rivalry. And as those tensions escalate, technology has taken center stage. Politicians in Washington, D.C., have begun to treat the nation's technology ecosystem in a way that more closely mirrors their Chinese counterparts: as a core component of geopolitical strength, something to be leveraged, regulated, and protected from rival nations.

That global technological retrenchment is putting heavy strains on the multidimensional ties between China and Silicon Valley, ties that were slowly nurtured by people like Li Zhifei. But can two ecosystems so deeply interwoven really be wrenched apart? And what happens to innovation and national security when the global tech landscape is divided against itself?

HUMBLE BEGINNINGS

When Li Zhifei was born, China was closer to the monomaniacal reign of Mao Zedong than it was to connecting to the global internet. After Mao's death in 1976, China began taking its first tentative steps toward "reform and opening," the set of policies that gradually opened up a space for private enterprise amid China's command-and-control economy. Those policies would put China on the path to being a global technological force, but the country had decades of catching up to do. While Steve Jobs was marketing early Apple computers out of a Cupertino, California, garage, Chinese leaders were still squirming over whether farmers should be allowed to sell vegetables for profit.

It wasn't until 1994 that China saw its first connection to the global internet, the result of a partnership between the Stanford Linear Accelerator and

Beijing's Institute of High Energy Physics.[1] Even that first academic connection was not without controversy: while the U.S. Department of Energy supported the partnership, the Department of Defense was leery about the implications of bringing China onto the global network. A compromise was reached when it was agreed that China could be brought online—as long as an email first went out to everyone on the internet warning them of the onboarding of the People's Republic.[2] The following years marked China's first internet boom. College chat boards and internet cafés sprang up, and with them the breathless anticipation of a new age dawning. Bill Gates's book on the future of computers and the internet became a sensation in China. Actual internet access was limited to a tiny fraction of China's population, but Chinese media insisted that China's traditional greeting—"Have you eaten?"—was fast being supplanted by a more modern question: "Have you been online?"

In its early years, China's internet ecosystem begged, borrowed, and stole from Silicon Valley. Many of China's early internet giants were founded by Chinese students returning from the U.S., funded by American venture capital money, and inspired by Silicon Valley culture. Of the three Chinese internet companies that were the first to list on the Nasdaq, two of them had deep roots in the United States. The first major Chinese-language search engine was named Sohoo, a thinly veiled tribute to the Silicon Valley company that defined the field, Yahoo. (The company later changed the spelling of its English name to "Sohu.") Sohoo was the brainchild of Charles Zhang, a Chinese-born physicist with a PhD from MIT. Zhang launched his first internet company in Beijing with funding from friends in the U.S., and after a meeting with Yahoo founder Jerry Yang, Zhang switched his focus to creating a search engine, taking on funding from Intel's venture arm to make it happen.

Few people did as much to spread the early gospel of Silicon Valley in China as Eric Xu, a Chinese-born PhD in biology at Texas A&M. Xu was working at a biotech start-up in Silicon Valley when he decided to create a documentary showcasing the Silicon Valley ecosystem for Chinese audiences. Xu interviewed U.S. entrepreneurs, programmers, and investors, introducing Chinese viewers to concepts like start-up culture and venture capital. When the time came to interview Jerry Yang, the Taiwan-born and

U.S.-raised whiz kid behind Yahoo, Xu brought along his friend Robin Li, a Chinese-born and U.S.-educated software engineer in the Valley.

"I got inspired," Xu said in an interview with *Bloomberg Businessweek*. "I'm sure Robin got inspired, too, seeing an ethnic Chinese who created such a powerful company."

Xu's film, *A Journey into Silicon Valley*, was broadcast on China's main state media channel, giving millions of Chinese their first glimpse into a region, culture, and business ecosystem that would reshape the world. At a screening of the film at Stanford, Robin Li's wife approached Xu and told him that she wanted her husband to be an internet entrepreneur. Soon after, Xu and Li together founded Baidu, the Chinese search engine that would fight tooth-and-nail with Google and go on to become one of the most powerful technology companies in the country.

NAILING JELL-O TO THE WALL

While Xu spread the gospel of Silicon Valley in China, the Valley's own techno-utopians were proselytizing a lofty vision of what the internet would become. They envisioned cyberspace as a world wholly detached from the stodgy political order of the twentieth century, and framed the internet as an almost organic sphere beyond the fumbling grasp of hapless bureaucrats. That philosophy crystallized in the 1996 essay "A Declaration of the Independence of Cyberspace," a manifesto by John Perry Barlow, a former lyricist for the Grateful Dead and founder of the Electronic Frontier Foundation. The manifesto was initially a response to the United States' Telecommunications Act of 1996, but it spun a much larger prophecy about the fate of the global web.

> Governments of the Industrial World, you weary giants of flesh and steel, I come from Cyberspace, the new home of Mind. On behalf of the future, I ask you of the past to leave us alone. You are not welcome among us. You have no sovereignty where we gather. . . . I declare the global

social space we are building to be naturally independent of the tyrannies you seek to impose on us. You have no moral right to rule us nor do you possess any methods of enforcement we have true reason to fear.

China's Public Security Bureau had other ideas. As internet access grew, what began as sporadic shutdowns of controversial student message boards in China quickly coalesced into a more comprehensive set of controls. By 1997, authorities already had a relatively well-functioning filtering mechanism that came to be known as the Great Firewall. All Chinese internet traffic to the outside world had to pass through a limited number of physical cables, and searches or requests to access websites containing "sensitive" keywords could simply be turned back at the border. In its early incarnations, the Firewall blocked many Western news sources and a smattering of overseas Chinese human rights sites.

Those mechanisms of control were crude, and many in the technology community viewed them as the last gasps of an archaic political system on its last legs. And it wasn't just wild-eyed techno-utopians who saw China's efforts to control the internet as doomed to failure. President Bill Clinton captured the zeitgeist of the era in a typically down-home metaphor:

"In the new century, liberty will spread by cell phone and cable modem.... We know how much the internet has changed America, and we are already an open society. Imagine how much it could change China. Now, there's no question China has been trying to crack down on the internet—good luck. That's sort of like trying to nail Jell-O to the wall."

China's political system may have survived the fall of the Soviet Union and the turmoil of Tiananmen Square, the thinking went, but it wouldn't survive the internet.

BOOM TO BUST IN BEIJING

American observers often framed the Chinese internet as a tool for the liberation of information, but in the late 1990s many of China's first-wave internet entrepreneurs were focused on cashing in at U.S. stock markets. The same hot air that inflated the U.S. dot-com bubble had spread to Beijing and was ballooning expectations for overnight internet riches. During the year 2000, Chinese portal sites Sina, Sohu, and NetEase all listed on the Nasdaq to much fanfare. That same excitement spread to Li Zhifei, who fresh out of college joined China MobileSoft as a software engineer, hoping that his own millionaire-making IPO was around the corner.

The timing was perfectly wrong. By the summer of 2000, Silicon Valley's dot-com boom was coming unraveled, and it wasn't long before investors soured on China's tech giants. Stocks for all three plummeted, with Sohu and NetEase sinking so low that the Nasdaq's own rules on minimum values threatened to boot them unceremoniously from American capital markets. China's first internet gold rush fell apart as quickly as it had come together. It had been inspired by Silicon Valley culture, funded in part by American venture capital money, and driven by returnees from American universities and Silicon Valley companies. The Chinese internet had shown its first hints of promise, but in the context of the global internet it was still a backwater. For now at least, the real action, real money, and real innovation was in the U.S.

And so Li Zhifei headed across the Pacific. In 2004 he enrolled in the computer science PhD program at Johns Hopkins University, in Baltimore. There he would dig into machine-learning algorithms and lay the foundation for a career on the cutting edge of artificial intelligence.

Li and his cohort were part of a new generation of Chinese students in the U.S. The generation that came before him was largely composed of elite PhDs, most of whom wanted to stay in the U.S. long-term, preferring the middle-class life of an immigrant engineer in America to the barely controlled chaos of entrepreneurship in early-reform China. But Li and his cohort were different, and so was the China they left behind. The rough edges of 1980s China were slowly being smoothed out, and the first seeds of the country's start-up culture had been planted. Chinese tech wasn't ready for the prime time yet, but there was potential there.

"When I decided to go to the U.S. the main reason was I wanted to broaden my vision and get advanced training," Li told me. "But my real goal was to come back to China to do a start-up."

As Li soaked up algorithms and international best practices, the battle lines were being drawn for the earliest head-to-head competition between the giants of Silicon Valley and their scrappy Chinese competitors. The first of these skirmishes to break into all-out warfare would pit the global behemoth eBay against local upstart Alibaba.

LOCAL DAVIDS AND FOREIGN GOLIATHS

Looking back with fifteen years of hindsight, it's hard to mentally reconstruct the David-versus-Goliath nature of this showdown. In the intervening years Alibaba has become the glitzy golden boy of China's internet economy, while eBay has lost most of its shine and fallen far behind Amazon. But at the time, this outcome seemed like the longest of long shots. eBay was one of the most valuable internet companies in the world and a darling of U.S. media. Alibaba was instead a local curiosity—a company with a catchy name and a goofy founder.

Jack Ma gained fluency in English as a kid by standing outside a local hotel and offering to lead foreigners around his hometown of Hangzhou's famed West Lake district. He went on to become an English teacher at a local college and discovered the internet on a failed business trip to the U.S. in 1995. He spent the next few years stumbling through a couple early internet start-ups, including creating the "China Yellow Pages" for international sourcing of Chinese goods. In 1997, a temporary job at a government ministry gave Ma the chance of a lifetime: to take Yahoo founder Jerry Yang on a tour of the Great Wall. At the time Yang was the golden boy of Silicon Valley, and his company stood alongside eBay as one of the giants of the early internet. But Silicon Valley's colossal stature in China didn't intimidate Ma—it inspired him. He and Yang hit it off, chatting about the growth and future of the web. That momentous trip was captured by a single photograph, of Yang and Ma sitting on the brown stone steps, smiling at the camera. Within two years, Jack Ma had launched his next start-up: Alibaba.

Alibaba began as a platform for international purchasers of Chinese goods, but when eBay decided to enter the Chinese market in 2002 with its auction-style sales, Ma created the Taobao platform to compete head-on for customers in the auction market. At the outset, it looked like the mighty eBay would steamroll Jack Ma's little start-up. But the former English teacher from Hangzhou turned that power imbalance into an advantage, waging a multiyear guerrilla war against the American company.

eBay began its China venture by buying up the top Chinese e-commerce company at the time, EachNet. EachNet had been founded by Shao Yibo, a Chinese national math champion with two degrees from Harvard and funding from Silicon Valley. But instead of leveraging EachNet's local know-how, eBay gutted it. The Silicon Valley giant remade EachNet's original (and successful) user interface in the parent company's image. It sent in foreign managers to run its China operations and insisted on routing all China traffic through one global platform, slowing down the site as traffic bounced back and forth across transpacific cables.

By contrast, Ma sought every opportunity to localize. His team created a home page that was packed with links and text—irritatingly crowded to Western eyes, but somehow appealing to Chinese users. He built new payment methods that held money in escrow until the receipt of purchased goods, a move designed to assuage the fears of Chinese users who were still new to both credit cards and e-commerce. He tacked on messaging functions that allowed buyers and sellers to communicate in real time.

But Ma's real coup came from business model innovation. As a company listed on the New York Stock Exchange, eBay was under pressure from bankers to show returns, and so it charged multiple types of fees on every transaction in China. Knowing that his company lived and died with growth of the Chinese market, in 2005 Jack Ma pledged to keep his platform free of fees for three years. It was a big gamble, a pledge to forsake short-term gains in hopes that he could expand the market, win user loyalty, and find a way to cash in later. eBay's China operations mocked Ma with a condescending statement, chiding that "free is not a business model," but Jack would get the last laugh.

Alibaba was gaining momentum with Chinese users and funding from allies abroad. Ma scored a major coup that same year when Jerry Yang handed over Yahoo's China business and $1 billion in exchange for 40 percent of Alibaba.[3] That deal had its origins in another walk that Yang and Ma took, this time in Pebble Beach, California. It would turn into the single best financial decision by an American internet company in China.

After four years of losing money and market share to the scrappy start-up, eBay CEO Meg Whitman invited Jack Ma to Silicon Valley to try to broker a deal. But with the American giant on the ropes, Ma refused to negotiate. In 2006, eBay retreated from the China market. It was the first time a Chinese internet company had gone head-to-head with its American rival and won.

"Nobody was betting on the little guys," said Kaiser Kuo, host of the *Sinica Podcast* and former head of international public relations for Baidu. "It seemed like having a big American brand behind you was magic. It really never seemed like the local Davids were going to beat the foreign Goliaths— it just never seemed possible. But then it started to happen left and right."

WWW.GOOGLE.CN

eBay's challenge in conquering China was that of a powerful colonial army facing a ragtag guerrilla insurgence. Google's conundrum was even more complicated—like a game of multidimensional chess played against three wildly different but equally intransigent foes: local competitor Baidu, the Chinese government, and its own much-hyped ethical code. Any move that Google made against one of these foes compromised it along another dimension, leaving the company tangled in a web of moral, political, and business tradeoffs.

Google launched its formal China presence—Google.cn—in 2006. But long before Google.cn went live, the company's U.S. site—Google.com—had already been the subject of fan adoration, government blocks, DNS poisoning, and competitor imitation. Google engineers first made a Chinese-language version of the site in the year 2000, offering unfiltered search results in Chinese to users in mainland China. When those users clicked on links to pages that were blocked in China, the Great Firewall would interrupt the connection, but the mere presence of those links among the search results offered a glimpse of what lay on the other side of the global internet.

Accessibility, speed, and accuracy were all issues. Google.com would flicker in and out of availability for users in China. Speed on the site suffered from bottlenecks as traffic squeezed through cables crossing the Pacific Ocean. And, initially at least, the search giant struggled to accurately parse the intent of users searching in Chinese. But beyond reliability issues, Google faced a malicious environment in China from the start. The Great Firewall would cut users' connections to Google for several minutes if a banned term was searched, making it appear as if the problem was with Google. Some Beijing residents reported being inexplicably redirected to Baidu when they tried to log on to Google. And in September 2002, Google.com was suddenly completely blocked. Google employees hinted that the block came at the instigation of a rival company, but there was no smoking gun and no explanation. After two weeks, the block was lifted just as suddenly and mysteriously as it had appeared.

By the end of 2002 Google had managed to win a healthy 25 percent share of the Chinese search market, all without having set up on-the-ground operations in the country.[4] That impressive growth stemmed from Google's popularity in more international cities like Beijing and Shanghai. But over the next three years, internet connectivity spread to the hinterland, and the company's market share stagnated. Meanwhile homegrown Baidu marketed aggressively and came to own almost half the national search market. Google knew that to compete it would have to build a local presence in China, and that meant coming to some agreement with Chinese authorities on censorship.

MORAL METRICS AND EVIL SCALES

Complicating that task was one of Google's oldest corporate philosophies: "Don't be evil." The Chinese government demanded strict content censorship, and in order to operate a China-based search engine Google would have to be complicit in that censorship. At the same time, what good could the company do if it was permanently blocked and became inaccessible to ordinary Chinese people? "Don't be evil" seemed simple enough, but Google's core mission—"to organize the world's information and make it universally accessible and useful"—posed a more complex question. Did presenting 1.3 billion Chinese people with information that was censored—but still potentially wider in scope, and more useful, than the information available on Baidu—fulfill that mission or forsake it?

Even more disturbing than information control was the potential for complicity in real-world repression. In 2004, Yahoo had disclosed to the Chinese government the emails of a Chinese journalist, Shi Tao, an editor at a business newspaper in central China. Shi, who had been active in the 1989 Tiananmen Square protests, had used his Yahoo email address when he forwarded to human rights activists in New York the government censorship mandates for how Chinese media should cover the fifteenth anniversary of the Tiananmen protests. Chinese authorities investigating the leak demanded information on the offending accounts from Yahoo China, and the company handed it over. Shi was convicted of leaking state secrets and would spend the next eight years in a Chinese prison.

Nightmare scenarios like the case of Shi Tao—and the fundamental question of whether to collaborate in censorship—divided Google's leadership. Cofounder Sergey Brin was a child refugee from the Soviet Union and well acquainted with the "evil" of authoritarian regimes bent on information control. Cofounder Larry Page and CEO Eric Schmidt took a less personal approach, one that the author of Google history *In the Plex* compared to the "moral metrics" of a spreadsheet in which losses (complicity in evil) were weighed against profits (information expansion). In the end, those complex moral calculations apparently yielded the same result as a purely profit-driven approach: Google would enter China.

At the World Economic Forum in Davos, Switzerland, Schmidt explained the decision to enter the country in simple utilitarian terms.

"We concluded that although we weren't wild about the restrictions, it was even worse to not try to serve those users at all. We actually did an evil scale, and decided not to serve at all was worse evil."

Leading Google China would be Dr. Kai-Fu Lee, a Taiwan-born, U.S.-trained AI scientist and pioneer in speech recognition. (I later worked with Dr. Lee on his book about artificial intelligence in the United States and China.) Lee had worked at Apple in Silicon Valley and previously founded Microsoft Research Asia in Beijing. He was now put in charge of both building a Chinese engineering operation and engaging with the government.

One core difference from Google's earlier Chinese search engine was that it would move censorship in-house: instead of showing all results and letting the Firewall do the blocking, Google now needed to keep blocked sites from search results before they ever appeared to the user. The Chinese government issued no explicit guidelines on which sites were banned, so Google came up with an engineering workaround: they programmed computers based within the Chinese Firewall to dial up millions of websites, and when they found one was blocked, they added it to a list of those that would not show up in search results. In a gesture toward transparency, the company added a one-line disclaimer at the bottom of any page with censored results: "In accordance with local laws, regulations, and policies, some search results do not appear."

Chinese government officials hated the public reminder of censorship. One industry insider told me Chinese officials compared it to arriving at someone's house for dinner and saying, "I will agree to eat the food you've made, but I don't like it." Still, the government did not outright ban the notice, and Google competitor Baidu soon added it as well.

Prior to entering China, Google had dominated almost every market it officially entered. But from the beginning, China was a different story. Google had to play catch-up in terms of market share and its core technology, all while balancing the demands of the Chinese Communist Party and indignant American politicians. Jun Liu, Google China's lead engineer, told the author of *In the Plex* that he was "shocked" to learn how advanced Baidu was, and how far behind Google lagged in surfacing relevant search results for hot topics in China. Google engineers spent years overhauling search algorithms to compete with Baidu.

But members of the Google team often felt as if they were fighting with one arm tied behind their back. Any significant changes to Google China products had to be cleared with leadership at the Silicon Valley headquarters, a review process that often took weeks or even months. That was meant to ensure that actions remained in line with Google's own ethical codes, and also to ensure Google Search maintained a consistent product across all markets—essentially, the opposite of localizing.

But Chinese users were unique in their online habits. One example came in the way they read and clicked around a page of search results. Using focus groups and eye-tracking software, the Google China team was able to map out how Chinese and American internet users interacted with a page of search results. Americans tended to focus on the top two results, quickly finding the most relevant information, clicking on it, and leaving the page. Chinese users were different: their eye movements and clicks were all over the place, lingering on the page longer and exploring many of the links on it. Dr. Kai-Fu Lee would later describe these divergent habits to me with an analogy: American users treated Google Search like the yellow pages, and Chinese users treated it like a bustling bazaar. The Americans opened the yellow pages, found what they needed, and moved on. Chinese users wanted to peruse the aisles, picking up and shaking dozens of products before making a purchase.

The difference clearly called for a local adaptation: when users clicked on a link, it shouldn't navigate them away from the search results page, but rather open a new window for each link clicked. That way the users could continue shopping at the bazaar while checking out all the offerings. Baidu had already made that adaptation and was gaining users for it. But when Google China asked headquarters for permission to the do the same, it encountered resistance. It took months of transpacific bureaucratic infighting to get that simple change made, slowing the company's momentum and costing it users in the process.

"BAIDU UNDERSTANDS CHINESE BETTER!"

But Baidu wasn't competing with Google solely on who could best meet the information needs of Chinese users. It also appealed to those users on a far more gut-level emotion: patriotism.

As with most American ventures abroad, the Americans involved were very clear on who the good guys were: the Americans. This seemed especially obvious to American tech companies in the heavily censored world of the Chinese internet: they were purveyors of truth and openness, the underdogs in a righteous struggle against the forces of authoritarianism. Except none of this was quite as obvious to Chinese people. For many Chinese users, if there was a moral dimension to Google's entry into China, it was played on a different axis entirely: the arrogant imperialists versus the hometown heroes.

Baidu doubled down on that narrative with perhaps the most infamous advertisement in Chinese tech history. In a two-minute spot that was leaked online, a cocky white American in a tuxedo and top hat engages in a battle of wits against a clever Chinese poet dressed in traditional garb.[5] The American begins the battle surrounded by fans and with an adoring Chinese woman in a blond wig hanging on his arm. But as the Chinese rival shoots off progressively more complex Chinese tongue twisters, the American grows frustrated and stumbles over the language. Members of the crowd soon abandon the American in the top hat, rushing over to the Chinese poet's side. When this hometown Chinese hero plants a kiss on the wig-wearing woman, the American begins spitting up blood and collapses on the cobblestones. The spot ends with the crowd standing over the vanquished American, calling out in unison: "Baidu understands Chinese better!"

Between 2006 and 2010, Google fought an uphill battle against Baidu, the Chinese government, and Chinese people's perceptions. It dramatically improved its search relevance but also struggled to win new users in the small cities and towns where Baidu marketed aggressively. It won tentative approvals from Chinese authorities but often found itself caught between pressures for transparency from headquarters and increased demands for censorship from the Chinese government. For its part, Baidu dealt with many of the same tensions over censorship and frequently found itself on the receiving end of government reprimands over content. But as a homegrown company, it was still seen as more controllable and worthier of promotion than its American rival. By late 2009, Google had won 35.6 percent of the Chinese search market, a respectable chunk but well below Baidu's 58.4 percent.[6]

"A NEW APPROACH TO CHINA"

In the end, it wasn't low-blow marketing or direct demands on censorship that drove Google out of China. It was a far-reaching cyberattack known as Operation Aurora. Beginning in the summer of 2009, hackers within China launched a series of attacks that penetrated dozens of technology companies, including Google, Yahoo, and Adobe. The hackers made off with valuable source code and hacked into the Gmail accounts of human rights activists, including the account of a twenty-year-old Tibetan activist at Stanford during my final year there.

Operation Aurora proved to be the final straw. On January 12, 2010, Google published a blog post titled "A New Approach to China." In the post, Google's chief legal officer outlined the nature of the attacks and said that after four years of operating in the country, Google had changed its mind on China. The experiment of playing by the government's rules for the sake of increasing information had failed. Google would stop censoring its search results. Instead, it would attempt to negotiate with Chinese authorities in hopes of reaching a compromise that would allow them to continue operating in the country on Google's terms.

That very public airing of China's dirty laundry on hacking and censorship caught Chinese authorities off guard, putting internet restrictions that were often invisible to the average Chinese person on very public trial. On most days, that person could go about their online life without too many reminders that their own government prevented them from accessing widely available information. But the American company's reversal now rubbed those restrictions in the face of over a hundred million Chinese people who regularly used Google Search and woke up one day to find it gone. Government-controlled media labeled Google a tool of American imperialism, but those accusations initially fell flat with the many internet users loyal to the site.

"[Chinese officials] were really on their back foot, and it looked like they might cave and make some kind of accommodation," Kaiser Kuo, the American China watcher and podcast host who would later head international public relations for Baidu, told me. "All of these people who apparently did not give much of a fuck about internet censorship before were really angry about it. The whole internet was abuzz with this."

The tension had observers questioning who could hold out longer in the standoff. China had blocked purely social sites like Facebook and Twitter, but would the government really cut the country off from the single best portal to global news, research, and communication? Did Google need China more, or did China need Google more?

Ironically, it would be a show of support for Google by one of the world's most powerful people that undercut its chances of striking a deal in China. Ten days after Google announced its intention to stop censoring, Secretary of State Hillary Clinton delivered a major speech on internet freedom at the Newseum in Washington, D.C. In that speech, she referenced the Google case, condemned censorship, and described U.S. government efforts to fund and create tools to help people in other countries circumvent their own governments' internet restrictions. She compared the "virtual walls" of countries like China to the Berlin Wall, the fall of which precipitated the demise of America's last great rival. That rhetorical connection between Silicon Valley companies and the collapse of rival governments seemed innocuous—maybe even inspiring—to American audiences. But it rubbed many Chinese listeners—both Party loyalists and ordinary people—the wrong way.

"There definitely was sympathy for Google after they made this announcement, because Google really was a better product at the time than Baidu," Bill Bishop, a China-focused digital media entrepreneur and founder of the *Sinocism China Newsletter*, told me. "But as soon as Hillary made her speech, things really shifted because no one believed it was independent. They looked at Google as an agent of American imperialism—that they were working with the U.S. government."

In the wake of that speech, the Chinese government showed no willingness to compromise with Google. In March of 2010, Google announced it would be redirecting all traffic from Google.cn to its Hong Kong website, Google.com.hk. That move effectively shifted the burden of censorship back onto the Great Firewall. Users who searched for sensitive terms would see the results, but the Firewall would prevent them from navigating to them. Executives hoped this compromise would keep other Google products accessible on the mainland, and a temporary détente was reached: Google could operate out of Hong Kong, but the Firewall would continue to block access to forbidden sites.

Over the ensuing years, many analysts still held out hope that the Chinese government would be forced to relent once it saw the damage to its business and innovation environment. Google chairman Eric Schmidt laid out the philosophy in a 2012 interview with *Foreign Policy* magazine.

"I personally believe that you cannot build a modern knowledge society with that kind of [censorship], that is my opinion," Schmidt told the magazine. "I think most people at Google would agree with that. The natural next question is when [will China change], and no one knows the answer to that question. [But] in a long enough time period, do I think that kind of regime approach will end? I think absolutely."

But instead of retreating, Chinese authorities progressively ratcheted up restrictions on the company. Just three months after Schmidt's interview, all Google services were temporarily blocked during China's once-per-decade leadership transition. In 2014, the government made those restrictions permanent with a total block of all Google services, including business essentials such as Gmail, Google Maps, Google Docs, and Google Scholar. Charlie Smith, the pseudonymous cofounder of China censorship tracker GreatFire.org, described that block as one of the major turning points in China's approach to internet controls.

"When the authorities blocked everything Google it took us by surprise, as we felt Google was one of those valuable properties [that authorities couldn't afford to block]," Smith wrote to me.

An archaic, Leninist political system had gone toe-to-toe with the most important company of the early twenty-first century, and—for now at least it—it had won. Conventional wisdom held that China couldn't thrive without companies like Google, and the CCP intended to prove the conventional wisdom wrong. But first it would have to tame, cultivate, and finally harness its own freewheeling internet.

"DO NOT QUESTION, DO NOT ELABORATE"

In its showdown with Google, Beijing had demonstrated its willingness to wall off the country's domestic internet from the outside world. But what about homegrown threats?

That challenge came in the form of Sina Weibo, "the Twitter of China," a microblog platform whose users were slowly eroding the CCP's monopoly on information. Weibo (pronounced "Way-bwo") was created in 2009 and immediately exploded in popularity. Users chatted about all the inane details of celebrity gossip and their own meals. But Weibo was also quickly emerging as a kind of digital town square, a home for freewheeling public conversations about corruption, pollution, and international affairs. The platform allowed users to post in relative anonymity, and the lightning-fast pace of new posts often outstripped the censors' ability to delete them.

But Weibo truly became a national political force on the night of July 23, 2011. That was the night when a high-speed train traveling through a rainstorm outside the city of Wenzhou smashed into another train that was stalled on the tracks. The collision demolished multiple train cars on impact and sent four more tumbling off a sixty-five-foot viaduct bridge into a field below. Forty people died, and 192 more were injured in one of the worst accidents in the history of high-speed rail.[7]

The government immediately attempted to deploy its standard narrative for both natural and man-made disasters: an unavoidable tragedy, followed by heroic efforts of Chinese rescue crews to pull survivors from the wreckage. An internal government censorship directive sent to Chinese media outlets gave them no room to maneuver: "Do not question, do not elaborate."

But Weibo wrestled the power to set that narrative out of the CCP's hands. Camera-phone photos, probing questions, and corruption allegations abounded on the platform. Why had the rescue crews sought to bury one of the train cars before a full investigation was done? Why was a two-year-old girl found alive hours after the search was called off? The high-speed train crash had morphed into a metaphor for the lurking costs of China's break-neck pace of economic development. It prompted Chinese people to ask, If our health and safety becomes the collateral damage of 10 percent GDP growth, is that growth really worth the cost? In-house censors on Weibo raced to delete all the offending posts, but they couldn't keep up with the constantly evolving narrative.

Questions ricocheting around Weibo emboldened Chinese reporters to challenge the official narrative. Press conferences turned into interrogations, and even anchors on state-run CCTV ripped into the government's response. Badgered incessantly about the gaps in the government's official explanation of events, one spokesperson for the Ministry of Railways simply threw up his hands: "Whether or not you believe it, I believe it." The sentence instantly turned into an internet meme, crystallizing the image of a government flummoxed by free-flowing information.

From the CCP's perspective, the international backdrop was ominous. The Wenzhou train crash occurred near the height of the Arab Spring, as social media fueled grassroots movements toppling governments across North Africa and the Middle East. Early in 2011, dissident websites run by overseas Chinese had called for a "Jasmine Revolution" in China, inaugurated by a protest outside a McDonald's in Beijing. Inorganic and with no clear focal point, the protests flopped—the "crowds" that gathered outside McDonald's were made up almost entirely of foreign journalists armed with cameras, with a guest appearance by the United States ambassador to China, Jon Huntsman.

But the fallout of the Wenzhou train crash demonstrated that organic, homegrown discontent could catch fire online. It may not yet threaten the Party's grip on power, but it clearly loosened its grip on the national narrative. For those who had long argued that government controls on the internet were futile, this appeared to be the proof: the Jell-O was not sticking to the wall, no matter how many nails they hammered in.

CHINESE NOOGLERS

As Google was exiting China, Li Zhifei was entering Google. In May 2010, Li began his first day of work at the company's famed headquarters, the "Googleplex," in Silicon Valley. New Google employees are called Nooglers and outfitted with a goofy baseball hat with colored stripes and a plastic spinning helicopter top. Alongside Li in that day's crop of Nooglers was Mike Lei, a Chinese-born graduate of Tsinghua University. After earning an electrical engineering PhD from the University of Washington, Mike worked on speech recognition at Microsoft and SRI International, a research lab spun out of Stanford University. Mike is a geek in the purest sense of the word, someone who gets increasingly animated the more technical the subject. He and Li hit it off. Decked out in their Noogler hats, Li went to work on machine translation, while Mike deepened his study of speech recognition.

Around them at the Googleplex were thousands of other Chinese-born programmers and researchers. (Google received over 1,200 visas for foreign workers in 2018, a large chunk of those for Chinese nationals.)[8] Listening to the chatter at Google cafeterias, it can feel like Mandarin is the official second language of the company. That welcoming environment for Chinese folks goes well beyond the Googleplex. The entire San Francisco Bay Area is to Chinese nationals what Shanghai is to Americans—a foreign city where you can still live in a cocoon of food and friends that make you feel at home.

The engineering focus of Silicon Valley's tech companies is also well suited for international transplants. Notoriously numbers-driven, Google is an easy place for nonnative English-speaking engineers to plug into the system and churn out valuable code. Mike and Li thrived in this environment: Li won recognition for his work in machine learning, and Mike was the lead author on one of Google Research's most influential papers of 2013. Talented Chinese engineers like them can put in the hours, bank a great salary, and in a few years' time land a green card that allows them to put down roots on American soil.

But for Chinese-born entrepreneurs who want more, the land of the free can feel surprisingly limiting. Silicon Valley loves to tout immigrant founders like Elon Musk, but many Chinese in the Valley describe hitting a "bamboo ceiling" when trying to launch their own ventures. A thick Chinese accent can be a major hurdle when it comes time to pitch investors. The hard skills of engineering may be international, but soft skills often don't translate as easily across borders.

"It's easier for me to do a start-up in China than in the U.S.," Li told me. "Starting up requires raising money, building a team, and knowing your customer. All of those things are really difficult for foreigners in the U.S."

Li also cited more subtle cultural divides that can hamper Chinese entrepreneurs in a Silicon Valley culture that thrives on inflated claims and relentless self-promotion.

"For Chinese people, if they do a project that's really a ten out of ten, when they tell other people about it they'll say that it's really just an eight. We're more conservative and we don't want to brag about ourselves."

The VP of product at Li's company Mobvoi, Lin Yili (surname Lin, given name Yili, pronounced "E-Lee"), graduated from Tsinghua University and worked at Volkswagen before attending Harvard Business School. But despite his impeccable résumé and nearly unaccented English, Lin still felt that a social disconnect in America would hold him back.

"When we go to bars with my classmates in business school, there's all that small talk: what shows did you watch growing up, what's the reputation of your hometown. With that gap, it's hard to have a real connection with someone," Lin told me. "All my friends, my resources, my networks are all in China. If I stay in the U.S., basically I'd have to start from zero again. I could probably get a decent job and have a middle-class life, but it's hard to really do some fun stuff."

At the same time, China's technology scene began exerting an ever-greater pull on its prodigal sons and daughters in Silicon Valley. Many of these budding programmers left home in the mid-2000s, while China's technology ecosystem remained primitive. Angel investing was virtually unheard of, venture capital was scarce, and major corporations were more likely to steal your ideas than acquire your start-up. Recruiting top-notch grads was difficult. Parents who remembered the all-consuming hunger of life in Mao's China would shudder at the idea of their children joining a start-up. A steady gig at a state-owned steel company—providing the pro-verbial "iron rice bowl" of lifetime employment—was the preferred route. China's multidecade blitz of economic growth had been powered by cheap exports and a massive infrastructure build-out. The robber barons of this gilded age were real estate developers, steel magnates, coal bosses, and the corrupt officials who took bribes from all of them.

"Just a few years ago lots of stuff in China was still very primitive," Lin told me. "Lots of businesses . . . were not really driven by technology, by product, by your knowledge. Five or ten years ago it was driven by connec-tions, by who you know. Back then if you went to America and came back, what you learned there wouldn't necessarily be useful. The time there might even affect you negatively."

But by 2012, that was shifting. Chinese authorities had countered the fallout of the global financial crisis of 2008 with an earth-shaking construc-tion stimulus. That massive infusion of cash into markets led to an equally massive hangover in heavy industry: a glut of overcapacity in coal and steel that pulled the rug out from under those markets. Real estate prices, which had grown by double digits for more than a decade, faltered. Rising wages in Chinese factories were pushing some low-cost manufacturers to Southeast Asia. Desperate for new sources of fast cash, Chinese investors began plowing their money into the hottest sector around: the internet.

"That easy money, dirty money has already been saturated," Lin remarked to me on the bus ride to Mobvoi's hackathon. "Now if you're doing something new you need to have some vision, you need to be driven by technology."

Crucially for start-ups, the component parts of a funding ecosystem were coalescing. American venture capital launched many of China's earliest internet juggernauts, but now that first generation of Chinese founders was paying it forward, providing seed funding and mentoring to a new generation of entrepreneurs. The "big three" internet companies known as BAT (Baidu, Alibaba, and Tencent) also played a role. Flush with cash and eager to arm themselves against competitors, these companies began to shed their reputation for stealing ideas from start-ups and began acquiring those start-ups instead. Those acquisitions became the payoff for other early investors in these start-ups, further fueling an explosion in Chinese venture capital.

In the eyes of many investors, China had the customers, but Silicon Valley had the talent. Angel investors like Bob Xu began flying directly to San Francisco to host dinners for Chinese engineers in the Valley. There they would encourage Chinese Googlers or Facebook programmers to return to the motherland, offering to fund whatever start-up they founded before even seeing a product or business plan—the Silicon Valley credentials were enough. For ambitious Chinese, returning home meant a radical upgrade in status. By moving home, they instantly transformed from the nth Chinese Googler in Silicon Valley into a member of a much smaller and more elite cohort: ex-Googlers in China.

Stories of billion-dollar start-ups founded by friends began trickling back to the Valley's Chinese community. Chen Peng, a Stanford PhD and data scientist at Google, described the feeling of watching one of his Chinese friends from Stanford take his company public on the New York Stock Exchange for over a billion dollars.

"It's just crazy that happened to one of my friends, and as you can imagine that really excited a lot of us," Chen told me. "It's just one example of what you can do if you bring your skills, experience, and knowledge to China, where you understand the culture, you understand the people, and there is a big market potential. With all of the things combined you have a lot higher chance of breaking out."

SHANGHAI START-UP

Li Zhifei wanted to break out. In the fall of 2012, he quit his job at perhaps the world's most prestigious company and headed to Shanghai. He had $1.6 million in funding and the bare bones of a product—a Siri-esque tool that could answer basic questions posed to it in Chinese. To handle the business side of the start-up, he recruited Li Yuanyuan (surname Li, given name Yuanyuan; we'll call her Yuanyuan to avoid confusion with Li Zhifei). Yuanyuan had met Li while she was doing her master's at the University of Maryland and he his PhD at Johns Hopkins. When Li approached her about cofounding Mobvoi, she didn't hesitate.

"If he decided to drop Google and drop everything in the United States, I don't think I need to spend too much time thinking about it," she told me.

They set to work building a product and a team in Shanghai's Lujiazui district. Cramming into a high-rise apartment, Li and Yuanyuan brought on interns and hired an *ayi*, a Chinese "auntie" who cooks and cleans for a household. Juggling language algorithms and business licenses, the team watched through their apartment window as migrant workers tacked new stories onto the massive Shanghai Tower outside, a slick spiral building on its way to being one of the world's tallest.

Apple had launched Siri in 2011 and debuted its Mandarin-language version in mid-2012 to mixed reviews. Google's voice-activated assistant, Google Now, launched that same year and was named Innovation of the Year by *Popular Science* magazine. But the Google-powered system was blocked in China, leaving China's non-iPhone users without a disembodied voice to argue with. Li and his team looked to fill this gap, producing a voice assistant that could run on Chinese Android phones and answer questions like, "Where is the nearest hot-pot restaurant?" The bare bones of the product had been built by Li, but he and Yuanyuan initially had trouble attracting talented programmers to a no-name start-up.

"We struggled a bit with hiring until we found the magic recipe: put 'Google' in the title of all the posts," Yuanyuan told me. "We'd say 'ex-Googler is hiring,' and this worked so much better than writing a hundred-character description in Chinese."

After a year in Shanghai, Li and Yuanyuan decided that the atmosphere in a glitzy commercial city like Shanghai just didn't feel right. They pulled up stakes and moved the company to Beijing.

CHINA VERSUS "FAKE NEWS"

Beijing was the heart of China's tech scene, but it was also the seat of a government in the midst of a crackdown on social media. Weibo users had flexed their muscles following the Wenzhou train crash, and the authorities were flexing back. After Xi Jinping took over leadership of the CCP in late 2012, he wasted no time in inaugurating a new approach to internet governance. The man he picked for the job was Lu Wei (surname Lu, given name Wei; pronounced "Lou Way"), a feisty propaganda official with a flair for publicity. Lu kicked off his campaign by striking out at some of Weibo's biggest personalities.

In early 2013, Lu hosted private dinners in Beijing to which he invited the platform's so-called "Big V's," verified users with millions of followers. Some politically minded Big V's—real estate developers, social commentators, and celebrities—were sparking conversations and shaping debates that rubbed the Party the wrong way. At the dinners, Lu tried to both ingratiate himself to these influencers but also send a signal: cool it with the criticism. When that didn't work, he threw one of them in jail. Charles Xue, a Chinese-born investor turned United States citizen, had been broadcasting his sometimes-impolitic views to twelve million Weibo followers, and so in August of 2013, he was snapped up in Beijing on charges of soliciting a prostitute. But Xue's confession broadcast on national state-run TV made clear his real crime: sounding off on Weibo. In an interview from behind bars, Xue said he retweeted news without verifying it, and that his legions of followers made him feel like an "emperor of the internet." Xue's detention sent shivers up the spines of other Big V's, a tactic captured in the Chinese idiom "killing the chicken to scare the monkey."

The government complemented that highly personal crackdown with one of the world's first laws against spreading "fake news." In 2013, China created criminal penalties for "spreading rumors" online: anyone who sent out a false social media post that received 500 reposts could be sentenced to up to three years in prison. Just weeks after Chinese courts announced the penalties, a sixteen-year-old boy in western China was arrested for spreading rumors about police misconduct in a local suicide. One former in-house censor at Sina Weibo described the impact on users: "The effect was felt immediately. The amount of original posting dropped rapidly. Users not only withdrew from serious commentary, but became reluctant to post about what they heard or saw in their daily lives, because any information not confirmed by government authorities could potentially be deemed as creating or spreading rumors."[9]

To outside commentators, it looked as if the Chinese internet was being neutered. To the Chinese government, the local internet was finally getting "cleaned up."

"The internet is like a car," Lu Wei told the World Economic Forum in 2014. "If it has no brakes . . . once it gets on the highway you can imagine what the end result will be. And so, no matter how advanced, all cars must have brakes."

Could the Chinese internet really thrive when it had the Chinese government constantly pumping the brakes? Li Zhifei and other ambitious returnees from Silicon Valley were going to find out.

GOOGLE SEEDS IN A CONCRETE JUNGLE

I first spoke with Li over Skype in early 2014. I'd been interviewing Chinese tech workers in the Bay Area, and several had cited him as an inspiration to return to China. Mobvoi had recently raised $10 million in Series B funding, and Li was upbeat about the prospects for his company and China's technology scene.

"Coming back was the right move," he told me. "Now when something happens in the U.S. we get that information almost immediately. It's about the speed of information transfer and that pool of people who have come back."

He invited me to visit Mobvoi's headquarters the next time I was in Beijing, and in early 2015 I headed out to a gray office park in the Zhongguancun tech corridor of northwest Beijing.

Zhongguancun is often called the "Silicon Valley of China," a talent-dense hub where Chinese engineers, entrepreneurs, and venture capitalists rub shoulders. And if you just tally up their component parts, Zhongguancun and Silicon Valley share a lot: Home to multibillion-dollar startups? Check. Stocked with talented software engineers? Check. Abutting the best universities? Check. Overflowing with venture capital money? Check.

But seen from street level, the two tech hubs are worlds apart. Silicon Valley's endless office parks strive for the platonic ideal of workplace productivity: spacious green "campuses," colorful slides to take you between floors, free in-house massages, and cafeterias serving up grass-fed steak and brain-boosting kale juice. The environment, the companies, and the culture all coddle you.

Zhongguancun smacks you right in the face. Shove your way out of the Zhongguancun subway stop, and you emerge onto a traffic intersection big enough to host an NFL game. Twelve lanes of bumper-to-bumper traffic on Beijing's Fourth Ring Road cross under or feed into Zhongguancun Road. At street level, a sea of bikes, tuk-tuks, and electric scooters muscle their way through traffic, and onto sidewalks, when the spirit moves them.

Car horns and hawkers of used cell phones compete for the highest decibel count. Offices are often cramped and low-lit, smelling of instant noodles and chicken-foot snacks. Like the rest of Beijing, the sky above Zhongguancun is often the same color as the pavement below, and the two are about equally as clean.

It's in this urban Chinese jungle that Li Zhifei is trying to create a Google-inspired oasis, a company that grafts the best of Silicon Valley's culture onto Chinese markets free for the taking.

I head up an office-park elevator to Mobvoi's headquarters, where I am greeted by Yuanyuan and Li. They walk me across the open-office-plan floor, where around fifty employees squint at computer screens or fiddle with gadgets. Google Glass went on sale a year earlier, but with so many Google functions blocked in China, the fancy hardware was severely handicapped. Mobvoi is working to fill that vacuum, creating its own Chinese-language voice recognition software for the Silicon Valley hardware. Li encourages me to try on a pair, and I use a few simple Chinese commands to take a picture of Mobvoi's coders at work.

Li, Yuanyuan, and I sit down in a glass-walled office in the back. There we sip loose-leaf tea while Li shows off the company's Siri-esque app, Chumenwenwen (the name roughly translates to "head out, ask around"). I shoot a series of Chinese questions at the app—Will it rain tomorrow in Beijing? Where's the nearest Sichuan restaurant?—and mostly get back the answers I am looking for. It isn't perfect, but neither is Siri, especially when you only speak Chinese.

Putting the app down, we chat about the Zhongguancun start-up scene and what Li learned from his time in the Valley.

"At Google, to me the most important was the culture: how a high-tech company in Silicon Valley operates, innovates, and competes," he tells me.

Yuanyuan has headed up the operations and business side since Mobvoi's founding in that Shanghai apartment. She describes the difficulty of recreating that company culture with some programmers who have never experienced it firsthand. As a result, Mobvoi leans heavily on "sea turtles" (haigui) who studied or worked overseas and returned to the motherland.

Sea turtles make up much of the senior leadership of the company, and at times 20 percent of the total staff.

"We love *haigui*," she tells me. "We feel that people with a dynamic background work harder. They don't calculate, 'Okay, this is my working hours.' They treat this as a start-up experience, and that's an experience that they really want to have. Those people are more flexible—they're problem solvers. They don't care about 'What's my job description?' They don't play politics."

As I'm getting ready to depart, Yuanyuan invites me to join the team for an off-site event they're planning: a hackathon designed to build out apps for their wearable devices. It sounds like a perfect chance to watch Mobvoi at work, and I tell her that I'm in.

On my way out of the office, I notice two plates of colored glass shaped like arrows and built into the floor. One points toward the work space and has the word "California" printed across the arrow. The other arrow reads "Silicon Valley" and points toward a pair of plush red chairs nestled in a corner near the front desk. This little relaxation station is Li's nod to the nap pods and play areas strewn around Google campuses. A couple of reclining chairs wouldn't pass muster with employees in Mountain View, but here they at least signal an aspiration. I ask Li what is up with the glass arrows in the floor.

"Ah." He looks at me with a smile. "They're supposed to remind our people of the Silicon Valley culture of working hard, and also the California culture of being relaxed and having fun."

"But why does 'California' point toward the desks and 'Silicon Valley' toward the comfy chairs?"

"Oh, well, the construction workers who installed them couldn't understand the English words, and so they accidentally installed them backward."

———

Heading out through the building's glass doors, I plunge back into the current of bodies and bicycles surging north toward the subway. Hawkers, hackers, and pickpockets hunting for iPhones all cram onto the pedestrian sky bridge that spans Zhongguancun Road. It's almost rush hour, and the subway ride back across town is guaranteed to be a suffocating crush of humanity.

Halfway across the sky bridge I push sideways through the stream of foot traffic to get to the railing that faces south, toward the heart of Zhongguancun. It's a far cry from the sunny climes of the San Francisco Bay and the multibillion-dollar companies that treat a talented coder like a firstborn child. In China, Google has been hacked and blocked, forcing it to run south toward the freedom and (relatively) fresh air of Hong Kong. But out here between the smog and the concrete, a seed spliced with Google genes has found fertile soil. And it's growing.

BACK TO THE HACKATHON

Three weeks later, my stomach is lurching as the bus screams around switchbacks on the way out to Mobvoi's smartwatch hackathon. The destination is Wulingshan, a resort nestled against a pristine blue lake two hours northeast of Beijing. We've left the city's smog and traffic behind, but the bus driver still finds plenty of reasons to plant his meaty palm on the vehicle's horn.

Li and Yuanyuan sit up front. Next to them is Mike Lei, the fellow Noogler who Li met at Google orientation. After four years working on voice recognition in Mountain View, Mike moved back to China to join Mobvoi as chief technology officer. The three of them have charted an ambitious agenda for the next twenty-four hours. They've split their coders, designers, and product managers into teams of three or four, each tasked with producing a functioning mock-up of a smartwatch app. These apps will populate the app store for Ticwear, Mobvoi's smartwatch operating system. The Apple Watch will go on sale at noon today, and Li wants Mobvoi to have a head start on other local start-ups when it comes to defining the local smartwatch ecosystem in China.

As Mobvoi employees file off the bus at the resort, it's time first for a

Chinese-style icebreaker: massage trains. Programmers and PR reps array themselves in rows and proceed to squeeze the shoulders, pound the back, and gently rub the earlobes of the person in front of them. Li plants himself right in the middle of the massage train, getting and giving it just like any other member of the team. If this were Silicon Valley, HR and legal reps would be biting their fists and waiting for a lawsuit resulting from this level of employee-on-employee intimacy. But out here at Wulingshan it appears to be taken in good, goofy fun.

Once the massages are finished and the luggage dropped off, everyone heads down to a conference room. There, Lin Yili, the Harvard grad turned VP of product, delivers a presentation on the goals of the hackathon ahead. Part product analysis and part pep talk, Lin's presentation breaks down smartwatch competitors and outlines the specific use cases where smartwatches can supplement or replace smartphones.

I've sat through many a presentation or product unveiling at traditional Chinese companies. My Chinese friends often dismiss these bureaucracy-meets-marketing presentations with a three-word descriptor: *jia da kong*—"fake, big, empty." China has spent millennia mastering the art of bureaucratese, a virus that has been transmitted from its political establishment to the leadership of many of its largest companies. Presentations by executives somehow manage to be simultaneously dramatically overhyped, dreadfully boring, and totally devoid of content. It's a symptom of a legacy system in which success was based less on the strength of one's ideas and more on access to vast amounts of government-controlled resources: public land, bank loans, foreign currency, etc. The content of these speeches is more a game of abstract signaling than actual transmission or exchange of ideas.

But this is different. When Mobvoi's leadership talks to employees, they trim the fat. It's all about user experience, product-market fit, and execution. It's a leadership style that I've only witnessed a handful of times in China, mostly at tech start-ups and often by those who have spent time outside the country.

Here it seems to hit the mark. When Lin finishes up, Mobvoi employees splinter into their groups and dive into brainstorming sessions for their apps. Engineers in China and the U.S. are still exploring what exactly a smartwatch is good for. Is it a mini smartphone on your wrist? Or just a more advanced Fitbit to monitor your health? The Mobvoi teams reflect that ambiguity: some go for straightforward voice-activated push notifications ("Tell me when the Beijing air pollution index goes above 150"); others have the watch extract and analyze data from the user's body movements and phone calls.

While the teams huddle in the lobby and hotel rooms, Mobvoi management gathers around a MacBook in the conference room. The Apple Watch has just gone on sale, and Yuanyuan is refreshing the purchase page on Apple's site, trying to get through and buy a few different versions for Mobvoi's engineers to experiment with.

"Wow. . . only that gaudy gold version has sold out here in China?" she says with a groan. "That's kind of terrifying."

Chinese conspicuous consumption aside, Li thinks the debut of the Apple Watch will be a boost for his own efforts. Mobvoi has already created its own operating system for smartwatches, and it's knee-deep in a secret design process for its own smartwatch, Ticwatch, which will debut later this year.

"Apple is incredibly good at market education," he tells me as Yuanyuan clicks Purchase on a few Apple Watches. "It's creating the market, and that's a really good thing. If it sells well that's going to be good for us. If the market isn't big enough then there's no use in us having a large market share."

I head back upstairs to type up my notes and take in the view. The hackathon is being held in a luxurious resort, the kind of place that wealthy Chinese come to escape the constant fight-or-flight mindset imposed by life in Beijing. The view from the hotel room balconies is a full panorama of blue water, rugged mountains, and blue skies. Gazing out at the lake and thinking of the coding blitz that lies ahead, one of the engineers quietly grumbles: "Such a nice hotel, such a nice room, and we can't even sleep in it."

As the hackathon drags into the evening, teams hole themselves up in their rooms, breaking only to boil water for instant noodles and coffee. I leave them to it, crashing for the night while most of the apps are still just flowcharts on pads of paper.

When I head down to the dining hall the next morning, most teams are either working through breakfast or asleep at the table. Li comes down and joins me for a plate of boiled vegetables and fried rice. He's less tired but just as anxious as the coders that surround him. He invites me to take a walk with him by the lake while we wait for the final presentations.

As we stroll along the water, Li begins to question whether Mobvoi has really been able to imprint that Google DNA into the team he's building. Comparing Chinese-trained coders and his colleagues at Google, he sees a gap.

"They're still far behind. It's because of Chinese university education. Classes are still taught in that broadcast method, with the teacher standing at the front and lecturing. If you look at Stanford computer science classes, a lot of their projects are just like the hackathon we're doing now."

Shelving that bit of self-doubt, Li heads back inside for the presentations. Li, Yuanyuan, Mike Lei, and Lin Yili array themselves in the front row as judges. First up is a team that lost its main engineer to a night of drinking. The presentation is a train wreck—a sketch of an idea for an app, no more developed than what you'd come up with over a round of beers with friends. A few pointed questions from the judges knock the legs out from under the idea, and the team is dismissed from the stage. The judges clearly are not happy with the results.

But from there on, the ideas quickly improve. One group presents a smartwatch companion for PowerPoint presentations, giving presenters a timer and outline of their talk on the watch face, and the ability to change slides with a flick of the wrist. Another group turned the watch faces into chameleon-like glow sticks that change color when the user dances in the dark. Winning some of the highest marks from the judges is a simple cosmetic function: an app that changes your watch face to the album cover of whatever song you're listening to. Nothing built overnight is quite ready for prime time, but as we pour out of the conference room the judges are clearly excited by the foundations their teams laid down.

"These really opened up the space for us to imagine what a smartwatch can do," Lei says to me.

Relieved and a little delirious from sleep deprivation, everyone grabs their luggage and piles back onto the bus. We head to a nearby village for a celebratory barbecue of Chinese favorites: lamb skewers, grilled eggplant, and chicken hearts. Yili works the grill while Li surveys his troops. He's wearing a jacket given to him by his former employer, with the green Android robot logo stitched into the fabric over his heart. After half an hour, a spring rain sends everyone clambering back onto the bus, and we nap all the way back to Beijing.

3

TOWARD THE NEW
TECH LANDSCAPE

When Li Zhifei's team of smartwatch hackers rolled back into Beijing in April of 2015, they were returning to a city in the middle of a technological renaissance. Beijing and the other hubs of China's start-up ecosystem—Shanghai, Hangzhou, Guangzhou, and Shenzhen—buzzed with an excitement and techno-optimism that matched or surpassed Silicon Valley. Not only were Chinese tech start-ups crowned with dizzying valuations and IPOs, they were fundamentally restructuring life in urban China.

The ripples of that revolution flowed all the way across the Pacific. Where Chinese start-ups had once blindly followed Silicon Valley trends, they were now exploring new models for e-commerce, social media, and online-offline integration. At the same time, Chinese investors began flooding Silicon Valley with venture capital, inflating valuations and rubbing up against Valley venture capitalists accustomed to being the big fish in their local pond. And the Chinese Communist Party continued its role as gatekeeper to the country's lucrative market. The same Silicon Valley giants who had spurned—or been spurned by—China years ago began begging to be allowed back in. What those companies are willing to do for access—censor content, share data, and divide the internet along national boundaries—will determine not just the fate of their own corporate souls, but the very structure of the global internet.

But China's rapid rise—often leveraging people, money, and ideas sourced from Silicon Valley—was also sowing the seeds of a backlash. Washington, D.C., had long been the odd man out in Silicon Valley's dance with China, and the leaders of the free world were not happy about it. As the Trump administration took over, that anger was reaching a tipping point, one that would break the stalemate of Silicon Valley's China paradox and push the relationship into uncharted—and perhaps dangerous—territory.

A DIGITAL CAMBRIAN EXPLOSION

For the first twenty years of its existence, the Chinese internet had largely nibbled around the edges of mainstream society. It was a playground for the technologically savvy, an outlet for the politically engaged, and a novelty for adventurous Chinese shoppers. Those bursts of high-impact activity—like the Weibo uproar following the Wenzhou train crash—offered tantalizing glimpses into possible futures for China, but the internet had not yet soaked into the fabric of everyday life for most Chinese people. The vast majority of conversations, purchases, appointments, and payments were all made the old-fashioned way: in person.

In 2014 that all began to change. These changes had been brewing for years, even decades, but the year 2014 sparked a digital Cambrian explosion of Chinese internet services and start-ups—a dramatic diversification of what you can do using the internet and who is actually doing it. Suddenly a whole slate of services and exchanges moved from the physical world into smartphones, first catching up to the United States and Europe, and then branching off into apps and business models not seen anywhere else. For two decades China had followed in Silicon Valley's footsteps. By 2014, China was exploring new territory.

Nothing played a bigger role in spurring China's digital Cambrian explosion than WeChat. Disguised as a simple chat app, WeChat has morphed into a digital Swiss Army knife for life in China, one that blurs the line between the online and offline world. The WeChat app (called Weixin, or "micro-message," in Chinese) was created in 2011 by Tencent, an internet juggernaut that already owned QQ, the largest Chinese messaging platform for desktop computers. In its early years, the app mainly served as a convenient way to send text messages, pictures, videos, and voice messages. WeChat quickly took off among Chinese smartphone users, and by 2013 connecting on WeChat became standard social protocol anytime you met someone new.

But in 2014 the app added a function that would change everything: money. During Chinese New Year 2014, WeChat allowed users to send each other digital "red envelopes," a traditional way of giving cash to relatives (or bribes to corrupt officials) during holidays. Wanting to get in on the red envelope fun, tens of millions of users entered their bank account details to the app, and Chinese commerce would never be the same.

Having amassed a huge user base and the ability to have them transact within the app, WeChat capitalized by cramming a dizzying array of new functions into the app: the ability to hail a taxi, pay your utility bills, reserve a hotel room, donate to charity, top up your phone minutes, buy plane tickets, and even invest in financial products. For decades, access to public services in China—doctor's visits, train tickets, social security payments, etc.—was metered out in one way: by standing in a very long, very slow line. In the span of a couple years, WeChat moved a huge chunk of those transactions into the phone, trimming some of the fat off slow-moving public-sector bureaucracies.

The app then took another major step into the physical world by allowing any real-world business to accept payments simply by scanning a code within the app. The vast majority of Chinese businesses had never embraced credit cards, and as of 2015 the national consumer economy still ran on cash. But when WeChat introduced digital payments at physical stores, that changed almost overnight. Not to be outdone, Tencent rival Alibaba added scan-to-pay functions to Alipay, and soon national chains like McDonald's and Starbucks were offering instant payment through smartphones. The cashless movement quickly began filtering down to all levels of society: street food vendors, bicycle repairmen, and even beggars soon began accepting money via WeChat and Alipay. Every month WeChat tacked on new real-world functions, and the app gained an almost gravitational pull to it, sucking in more and more dimensions of Chinese life: social, professional, bureaucratic, and commercial.

But China's digital Cambrian explosion spread far beyond WeChat. Ubiquitous mobile payments lit the spark for thousands of start-ups specializing in online-to-offline (O2O) services—anything in which digital activity translates to real-world purchases. Population-dense, stocked with cheap labor, and generally a pain in the ass to move around in, Chinese cities proved to be the perfect petri dish for on-demand services. Food delivery was an obvious first move, but soon everything from manicures to dog-walking services was instantly available with a few clicks on a cheap smartphone. The streets of Beijing began teeming with delivery men on electric scooters, dropping off bags of steaming-hot noodles or organic groceries, all ordered through WeChat and a constellation of new apps that were cropping up by the day. This round of technical and business innovation was seeping into the very pores of Chinese society. Mobile payments and O2O services were not merely enriching the technological elite—the gains in efficiency and new business opportunities were driving changes at every level of the socioeconomic ladder.

Silicon Valley futurists had long fantasized about a world of frictionless payments and the seamless integration of communication and commerce, and a combination of Chinese protectionism and indigenous innovation was yielding just that. In 2015 Connie Chan, a partner at prestigious Silicon Valley venture capital firm Andreessen Horowitz, introduced WeChat to the Valley in a long-form article titled "When One App Rules Them All." The piece went viral, jolting many in the Valley awake to the presence of truly innovative apps on the other side of the Pacific pond.

China had entered full-fledged start-up fever, and two events in 2014 threw even more fuel on the fire: Alibaba had the largest initial public offering ever on the New York Stock Exchange, and Chinese premier Li Keqiang issued an official call for "mass entrepreneurship and mass innovation."

Silicon Valley prides itself on a counterculture ethos that scoffs at traditional sources of authority and disrupts inefficient "legacy" industries. But in much of China, the opposite holds true. The Chinese tech community may look to Silicon Valley for inspiration, but mainstream Chinese society still places great stock in official rankings and government directives. The former give some signposts in a chaotic marketplace, and the latter can still make or break an industry. So when in the span of one month China's number two politician and the New York Stock Exchange both gave ringing endorsements of Chinese tech, the country's love affair with technology companies kicked into another gear. Living in Beijing, I began receiving messages from young Chinese friends in far-off provinces.

"Matt, can you introduce me to any start-ups in Beijing? The product isn't important—it just needs to be a start-up."

"NAME ME ONE INNOVATIVE PRODUCT"

To be clear, this wasn't supposed to happen. China had spent the previous five years shutting the door to the global internet and neutering political conversations on social media by imprisoning the rabble rousers. Thought leaders in Silicon Valley and Washington, D.C., had long argued that China's internet controls were destined to suck the life out of its tech ecosystem and stunt its economy more broadly. One of the most vocal advocates of this position was none other than Vice President Joe Biden. Speaking to students at the U.S. embassy in 2012, Biden confidently predicted that "innovation can only occur where you can breathe free."

Speaking at the 2014 commencement ceremony for the U.S. Air Force Academy in Colorado Springs, Vice President Biden doubled down:

> I used to give commencement speeches in the nineties, and the line some
> of you will remember was . . . that Japan was going to eat our lunch,

that Japan was the future. We also used to be told that China—and it's true—is graduating six to eight times as many scientists and engineers as we have. But I challenge you, name me one innovative project, one innovative change, one innovative product that has come out of China.

Vice President Biden had understandably never heard of WeChat, but he no doubt soon would. The Chinese Communist Party has been defying predictions of its demise for decades, and by the time of Biden's speech it appeared to have pulled off the same trick with its domestic internet. In hindsight, the logic of Silicon Valley's argument isn't exactly airtight: Why would restrictions on political speech prevent Chinese people from ordering fried rice on their smartphones? Or as Kaiser Kuo, host of the *Sinica Podcast* and former head of international communications at Baidu, put it to *The Washington Post*:

"There's this strange belief that you can't build a mobile app if you don't know the truth about what happened in Tiananmen Square. Trouble is, it's not true."

BAT SIGNAL IN THE VALLEY

That excitement wasn't limited to wide-eyed entrepreneurs and small Chinese start-ups. Flush with cash and confidence, China's biggest internet companies—Baidu, Alibaba, and Tencent, a.k.a. BAT—were now casting their gaze toward Silicon Valley. These companies had maintained a low-key presence in California for years. Tencent has operated a small office in my hometown of Palo Alto for a decade, a discreet Spanish-style building sitting opposite the downtown police station. Alibaba and Baidu had similarly kept up little corporate outposts in the area for a handful of overseas employees. But beginning in 2013, Baidu, Alibaba, and Tencent dramatically ramped up their activity on U.S. soil: investing in American start-ups, poaching American talent, and establishing R&D centers next door to their American peers.

Making the biggest splash was Baidu. In May of 2014, the company announced that it was bringing on Andrew Ng, one of the most respected AI researchers in the world, to head up a new research lab in Silicon Valley. Ng was uniquely positioned to head up a cutting-edge, cross-cultural research team. Born in the United Kingdom to parents from Hong Kong, Ng then grew up in Singapore and Hong Kong. After earning his PhD at Berkeley, he helped pioneer work on deep learning at Stanford and eventually led the Google Brain project, which constructed an AI "neural network" that taught itself to recognize cats using YouTube videos. That was all before Ng cofounded Coursera, an online education platform valued at around $800 million.[1]

Ng's choice of Baidu for his next adventure got the world's attention and shifted the conversation about China's tech juggernauts. What did it mean that a world-leading researcher like Ng—the kind of player who could have his pick of plum jobs at any of the Silicon Valley juggernauts—chose to work for a Chinese company? Ng told me that almost immediately after the announcement the cold calls and emails began pouring in, with AI researchers from around the globe asking about joining the new Baidu lab. The location of that lab was also rife with symbolism. A decade earlier, Baidu had gone to war with Google to protect its home market from foreign takeover. Now worth $60 billion, Baidu had hired the man who launched one of Google's most promising projects. Baidu chose to set Ng up with a research lab less than one mile from Google's own Sunnyvale campus.

Shortly after he joined Baidu, I asked Ng about what drove his decision, and whether he'd be filling the new lab with Chinese or American researchers. He said that Baidu's ability to harness massive amounts of data while remaining extremely "nimble" made it the best place for him to conduct AI research. And while everyone else fretted over which nation was ahead in the race for AI talent, Ng's intercontinental upbringing and engineering mindset made those questions feel irrelevant to him.

"My focus is on bringing the best people in: the most skilled, talented, dedicated, mission-focused people. And that group of people happens to come from all walks of life and all different parts of the world," he told me.

"[In terms of their nationality,] I don't really think about that. My head doesn't work that way."

Baidu's new research facilities were just the beginning. Alibaba would go on to announce new labs in both Silicon Valley and Seattle, and in 2017 Tencent divulged plans to bring on former Microsoft scientist Yu Dong to lead its own new Seattle lab. Explaining the location, Tencent founder Pony Ma bluntly said it was about poaching U.S. talent from its U.S. neighbor.

"Lots of Microsoft people aren't willing to leave Seattle, so we just set up [our lab] next door," Ma said. "There's nothing you can do. That's how talent is."

But talent was just one piece of the puzzle. Baidu, Alibaba, and Tencent also wanted to get in on Silicon Valley start-ups at the ground floor. Between 2012 and 2015, the number of investments or acquisitions by BAT (plus e-commerce site JD.com, the J in the new acronym "BATJ") multiplied by a factor of almost five. The cumulative value of the funding rounds that BATJ participated in (including money put in by other investors) rose from $355 million in 2012 to $3.8 billion in 2015. Tencent led the way with over fifty investments during those years, while Alibaba clocked in second with around twenty deals.[2]

The flurry of BAT activity reflected frenzied competition back home. Bombastic founders like Jack Ma would occasionally claim that they wanted to compete with American companies on U.S. soil, but in reality, they know that making inroads with American consumers isn't in the cards, for now at least. Instead, they're looking to invest and acquire American start-ups to arm up for the battle in China's own markets. Every shift in the tech landscape—desktop to mobile, the rise of artificial intelligence—threatens to scramble the BAT leaderboard. A decade of ruthless and rapid-fire competition has instilled in them a near-neurotic fear of missing out on the *next big thing*. And so they've come to Silicon Valley looking to buy that thing before their competitors do.

The Chinese newcomers made a name with their speed and willingness to pay. Thiru Arunachalam, cofounder of a remote-control app maker named Peel, got a taste of both in 2013 when Alibaba crashed a Series C funding round for the company. According to an account in *Forbes*, just four days before Arunachalam planned to close the round, Alibaba suddenly entered the picture with an offer to invest a cool million[3]. When Peel demurred—it was just too late in the game to add more investors—Alibaba came back with an offer to pump $5 million into the round. That proved too good to resist, and Peel brought China's biggest e-commerce player on board as an investor. In less than a day, the money had landed in Peel's accounts.

"They were the last people to talk to us but ended up being the first to wire the money," Arunachalam told *Forbes*. "They moved like a big start-up."

But that speed has come with sloppiness. Behind closed doors, Silicon Valley venture capitalists say that BAT—particularly Alibaba—has overspent for underperforming start-ups. They blame that spending pattern on an excess of exuberance stemming from Alibaba's soaring profits and massive 2014 IPO, and a lack of discipline within an investment team that was empowered but not well guided. Tencent has been lower-key but earns higher marks from professional investors in the Valley, while Baidu is just dipping its toes in the water.

THE ROGUE CHINESE VC ARRIVES

Whatever discipline these corporate investors may have lacked, they looked like sages of strategy compared to the other main source of Chinese money in the Valley: the fresh-off-the-plane rogue Chinese venture capitalist (VC). Some of these investors were early employees at major tech firms, but many came from traditional industries such as real estate or restaurants. With their home industries slumping and start-up fever spilling over into society at large, they began trying to elbow their way into the next hot sector.

A typical profile is a Chinese man—yes, mostly men—who spent a decade building a family business from the ground up—say, a high-end karaoke chain. After taking the company public in Shanghai, his investment office picked winners in a variety of other Chinese industries: hotels, hot-pot restaurants, maybe even a CrossFit gym. Now assured of his abilities as both a karaoke entrepreneur and a deeply discriminating investor, he decides to bring that wisdom to bear on start-ups exploring machine learning and the internet of things. He may have some ambitions to leverage the technology in his own business, but these notions are usually vague at best. Much of that hot money ended up in Zhongguancun and other Chinese tech hubs, but the more daring—or foolish—among these rogue VCs headed straight for Silicon Valley.

Stories emerging from these ventures can be cringe-inducing. Without established professional networks in Silicon Valley, these investors were listening to pitches from anyone they could get in touch with. For many Chinese investors awed by the dorm-to-IPO mythos of Silicon Valley, mere proximity to institutions like Stanford and Google was enough for them to crack open the checkbook.

Rui Ma, a former partner at 500 Startups in China and an active angel investor in both countries, has worked for years to educate and connect people from both technology ecosystems. As the wave of Chinese venture capital washed over the Valley, she watched it take on increasingly amateur incarnations.

"In 2016, really everyone I knew had a fund," Rui Ma told me. "I literally know four grad students at Stanford that told me they hosted some group of rich people, and by the end of the trip [the rich people] were like, 'Here's some money to invest in other Stanford students.'"

For these wealthy Chinese investors, the lessons learned from their own industries on the mainland leave them ill-prepared for the world of venture capital. Chinese real estate markets had conditioned investors into an almost Pavlovian expectation of immediate returns. These markets have only existed for around twenty years, and during most of that period they produced nothing but ever-increasing values. Investments often come with (legally dubious) guarantees of returns in just one to two years, functioning more like interest-earning loans than money at risk. Nothing could be further from the art of venture investing in the Valley, with its high-risk–high-return model, and long horizons for payouts on even the most successful investments.

"Some of those people are professional investors, but they have no understanding of tech or different asset classes, and they're not familiar with funds," Ma told me. "I just found it very difficult to talk to them. They were just not knowledgeable."

That ignorance about asset classes didn't seem to bother the investors themselves. From 2011 through 2015 the number of deals involving investors from Greater China (including Hong Kong and Taiwan) multiplied by a factor of almost ten. By 2015, total financing from those rounds (including money put in by other investors) skyrocketed to nearly $10 billion, around one-seventh of total investment in U.S. venture-backed companies.[4] Those numbers are almost certainly an underestimate, both because much venture funding goes unreported, and because of the loosey-goosey nature of much Chinese funding.

"Chinese money doesn't ask a lot of questions," Hans Tung, managing partner at GGV Capital and a longtime cross-border VC, told me. "They are so enamored with the brand and the reputation—their standing in Silicon Valley—that [start-ups] can encourage the Chinese funds to pay a high price just to have access as an investor."

Chinese arrivals may be itching to join the club, but Silicon Valley hasn't always been eager to welcome them in. Players around the Valley say that both start-ups and fellow investors look with some suspicion on the new arrivals. Renowned venture capitalist George Zachary described to *TechCrunch* how three consecutive funding rounds went awry when Chinese investors switched up the terms at the last minute. After term sheets were signed and other investors turned away, the Chinese side suddenly demanded a better deal, often in exchange for the dubious promise of helping the company enter China.

Another hard-to-shake stereotype for Chinese investors is the idea that they're "dumb money." For start-ups, taking on venture investment is about more than just cash—it's about bringing on a trusted adviser, someone who can make introductions and help guide the company through its next stage of growth. But without a track record or networks on U.S. soil, Chinese players are seen as a pure-cash play.

"People usually feel like [taking Chinese money] is a last resort," Tung told me. "They feel like, if you want to get the Chinese money it's because you need them to pay up on a price that U.S. VCs won't."

A TSUNAMI DRIES UP

By late 2016, Chinese funding in the Valley had experienced five years of near-exponential growth, and the trend lines were all pointing upward. Naval Ravikant, founder of seed fund AngelList, predicted a tenfold growth in Chinese funding—"a tsunami of capital" that would wash over the Valley.

And then, it stopped.

Sustained capital outflows from China were draining the country's foreign currency reserves and threatening to force the government to devalue the RMB. Party leadership responded by making it extremely difficult to move money out of the country. These spasms in currency policy are often short-term, or easy to maneuver around with the right connections. But the chill of late 2016 proved far more impactful and lasting. A VC with SAIC Capital, the venture wing of one of China's "Big Four" state-owned auto companies, told me in early 2017 that even that company's rock-solid government connections weren't enough to get capital out of the country.

With a sudden halt to the hysteria, an eerie calm settled over the sector. Chinese capital controls threw cold water on a burst of irrational exuberance by amateur Chinese tech investors. Most Chinese funds had made their investments in very early-stage start-ups, with over 50 percent of investments made in seed or Series A.[5] Without the ability to drown money in more money, this first wave of venture novices was forced to sit back and see what came of these start-ups. Meanwhile, more experienced Chinese investors with preexisting funds in U.S. dollars were able to continue their more meditated investment work for the time being.

Chinese controls had temporarily cut off the money at the source, but it was looming American restrictions on these investments that would put transpacific tech investments into a deep winter freeze. Still, the seeds planted by these early-stage investors continue to germinate in the start-ups that they funded, keeping open the chance that a Silicon Valley unicorn will have been born of Chinese funding.

"It's just a matter of time, unless you're consistently stupid or consistently unlucky," Ma told me. "As long as you have capital and you're playing the roulette wheel over and over and over again, you'll hit something."

THE AGE OF INTERNET SOVEREIGNTY

At the same time that China's rogue venture capitalists were flooding Silicon Valley with cash, Chinese authorities began trying to export an ideology: "internet sovereignty" or "cyber sovereignty," a country's inviolable right to control internet content within its borders. As a concept, internet sovereignty was an intellectual label for describing the de facto reality of life in China: unless you got a VPN, the Chinese government decided what you could and could not see on the internet.

Those controls had originally been born out of fear: fear of social unrest sparked by social media, fear of free-flowing information that undercuts the CCP's legitimacy. But as China's domestic internet gained strength, China's leaders gained confidence. They were no longer on the defensive, ducking the question every time censorship was raised. Instead, they now began describing these once ad hoc restrictions as a full-fledged ideology, inviting world leaders to learn from their example in defending national sovereignty in cyberspace. That international evangelism around internet sovereignty marked a new phase in China's relationship to the global internet.

Leading the charge was Lu Wei, Xi Jinping's internet czar and the man who orchestrated the crackdown on Weibo Big V's. A career bureaucrat in the state-controlled news and propaganda apparatus, Lu became the inaugural head of the Cyberspace Administration of China (CAC) in April 2013. It proved to be auspicious timing. Just one month later, a twenty-nine-year-old contractor for the National Security Agency named Edward Snowden boarded a plane bound for Hong Kong. Over the next three years, the slow drip of documents about NSA surveillance and the building of back doors into U.S. technology undermined the American government's good-boy image in global technology. It also provided the rhetorical raw material for China's arguments about the intimate connection between national security and "information security." With America's reputation suffering, Chinese leaders stepped into the void.

THE WORLD COMES TO WUZHEN

In November of 2014 Lu Wei played host at the inaugural World Internet Conference in Wuzhen, a sleepy southern Chinese town crisscrossed by canals. The conference slogan was "An interconnected world shared and governed by all." In reality, it marked China's first concerted play at getting major global players to endorse cyber sovereignty. It was also the international coming-out party for Lu Wei, and China's internet maestro was in his element.

"He's very confident and very definitely a politician," one attendee told *The New York Times*. "He's a smoker, he drinks, he's up late, he's up early, he's a workaholic. He's like a ringmaster, trying to be at the center of everything and juggling a million things at once, and he's pretty good at it."

Still, results for the conference were mixed. Though the conference did draw some executives from top internet companies like Facebook and LinkedIn, it failed to attract major heads of state or many big-name CEOs from Silicon Valley. The one representative of the American government scheduled to attend, a midlevel official from the State Department, reportedly did not show up.

Worse, though, was the bungling conclusion to the conference. Chinese authorities desperately wanted attendees to officially endorse cyber sovereignty, but they were not yet confident enough to truly submit the concept to open discussion and debate. Instead, after days of bureaucratic speeches and hollow pronouncements, at eleven p.m. on the night before the closing ceremony, organizers slipped a document under the door of attendees' hotel rooms. Called the "Wuzhen Declaration," the document purported to be a set of principles that represented the "consensus" of the participants. Among the nine principles enumerated, number two called for all countries to "respect Internet sovereignty." It defined the term as "each country's right to the development, use and governance of the Internet," and called on all to "refrain from abusing resource and technological strengths" to violate those controls. The organizers said that if any participants hoped to make revisions to the document, they should contact the organizing committee—before eight a.m. the following morning.[6]

It was a ham-fisted attempt to trick attendees into inadvertently endorsing internet sovereignty. Western participants protested, and after a testy closed-door meeting, Lu stormed off, leaving the conference without his declaration.

At the first World Internet Conference, Lu Wei had failed in getting attendees to endorse "internet sovereignty." Lucky for him, what Silicon Valley leaders are willing to *say* is far less important than what they're willing to *do*. And some of them appeared willing to do almost anything.

FEISIBUKE

On October 22, 2014, Mark Zuckerberg strode into a midsize lecture hall at Tsinghua University. The school is China's premier engineering campus, and Zuckerberg had just agreed to join the board of its business school. As part of that announcement, Mark had agreed to sit down for a public question-and-answer session with students and faculty. Just the presence of a Silicon Valley legend like Zuckerberg was enough to put the crowd on the edge of their seats, but no one was prepared for what would happen when Zuckerberg opened his mouth.

After the Chinese moderator introduced him in English, Zuckerberg turned toward the assembled students: *"Dajia hao"*—"Hello, everyone." Many visiting businesspeople and politicians will kick off their speeches with a word or two of mangled Mandarin, and the token gesture of cultural humility almost always earns (undeserved) applause. With Zuckerberg it was no different: the audience cheered his effort, minor as it may be. But then he kept going.

"I'm really happy to come to Beijing. I love this city," he said in halting but totally understandable Mandarin. "My Chinese is terrible, but today I'll try to use Chinese, okay?"

With each passing sentence, the whoops and gasps from the crowd grew louder. Every time he paused or sounded stuck the audience laughed, believing that he had finally hit the wall of his fifty-word vocabulary, but he didn't.

Zuckerberg had apparently spent four years secretly studying Chinese, and the results were impressive. The speech may have been chock-full of platitudes and executed with painfully bad pronunciation, but it was also a very public performance of giving face to China. Language often acts as a proxy signal for global power. For decades, Chinese students were browbeat into memorizing the mother tongues of the world's two superpowers: Russia and the United States. Reversing roles and watching Americans struggle to speak (read: butcher) a few words of Mandarin often signals a certain level of respect for Chinese counterparts.

And now in 2014, one of the most important figures of the early twenty-first century thought China was important enough to dedicate thousands of hours of his own time to learning its language. When the moderator asked why he studied Chinese, Zuckerberg stumbled through an endearing story:

> There are three reasons. The second one . . . The first one! My wife is Chinese. Her family speaks Chinese, and her grandma only speaks Chinese. I want to speak with them. Last year, one day, me and Priscilla decided to get married, so I told her grandma, using Chinese. She was really surprised.

For reasons number two and three, Zuckerberg cited the fact that "China is a great country," and that learning Chinese is extremely hard, the kind of challenge he likes to give himself.

But Zuckerberg left one major reason for his Chinese studies off the list: he desperately wants the Chinese government to unblock Facebook. The social network has been banned in China since 2009, when a spate of deadly ethnic riots in the western Chinese region of Xinjiang spooked the CCP into blocking Facebook and Twitter and completely shutting off the internet in Xinjiang for ten months. The end was sudden, but not entirely unexpected for an international platform built for sharing information, photos, and opinions. Chinese internet users summed up Facebook's fate by giving the company a new Chinese name based on a transliteration of its English name: *feisibuke*, literally, "other than death, there was no possibility."

The following year, Mark Zuckerberg began studying Chinese.

THE CEOS FOLLOW THE SEA TURTLES

Zuckerberg wasn't alone in his quest to woo Chinese authorities. While BAT and Chinese venture capitalists arrived in California, the leading lights of Silicon Valley returned the visit in China. Following in Zuckerberg's footsteps, many titans of Silicon Valley—Uber founder Travis Kalanick, Google CEO Sundar Pichai, Apple CEO Tim Cook, and LinkedIn's Reid Hoffman—began making regular pilgrimages across the Pacific to court Chinese leaders.

The tone of these visits marked a sea change from just a few years prior. When Google exited China, analysts were confident that Beijing would come around—China *needed* Google, and it would eventually either compromise with the company or fade into technological irrelevance. But in the intervening five years, something had shifted. China had successfully shut out the foreign internet giants *and* turned its domestic internet into a commercial behemoth, the single largest market in the world for smartphones, e-commerce, and cutting-edge online services. By 2015 China already had 650 million people online, and its internet penetration rate was still only 50 percent.[7] Just bringing internet penetration up to the U.S. level of 75 percent would mean adding another 325 million users—greater than the entire population of the United States. Those users would be shopping, reading, and watching online videos at a rate that far exceeded people in other parts of the globe. The upside was simply too great to ignore, and executives who had once turned their back on China now found themselves begging for a second chance.

"DID YOU FEEL THE ROOM SHAKE?"

China's internet czar gave them a good chance to do so just weeks after the Wuzhen conference. In late 2014, Lu Wei traveled to America's two technology capitals—Silicon Valley and Seattle—and then on to Washington, D.C. On the West Coast, he visited the headquarters of Facebook, Apple, Amazon, and Microsoft, among others. The PR departments for the companies involved were not eager to publicize the meetings, but members of the Chinese delegation snapped some grainy camera-phone photos that leaked to the Chinese press. The images are striking. Apple's Tim Cook is seen greeting Lu Wei like an old friend, beaming while Lu wags a joking finger at him. Amazon founder Jeff Bezos was photographed midguffaw at a joke made by the internet czar, with a Chinese banner welcoming Lu Wei to Amazon hanging behind them both.

But Zuckerberg topped them all. He personally toured Lu around Facebook's headquarters (speaking Mandarin, of course), including a visit to Zuckerberg's own desk, where Lu took a turn sitting in the CEO's chair. Pictures from the event show Lu beaming while he stares down at something: there sitting atop Zuckerberg's spray-painted desk lies a copy of *The Governance of China*, a 515-page tome collecting the speeches and statements of Chinese president Xi Jinping. *Foreign Policy* magazine described the book as "a mix of stilted Communist Party argot, pleasant-sounding generalizations, and 'Father Knows Best'-style advice to the world." Facebook's founder disagrees. According to Chinese media reports, Zuckerberg told Lu that he bought the book for himself and his colleagues: "I want to make them understand socialism with Chinese characteristics."

That gushing hospitality didn't extend to the second portion of Lu's trip. After spending time on the West Coast, he flew to Washington, D.C. Visiting the NSA, Lu reportedly received stern lectures on Chinese hacking and government controls on the Chinese internet. Elusive dreams of access to Chinese markets had bought friendship and compliance out of the American tech elite. The American government was a much tougher customer.

But when Lu made his trip, the key U.S. decision makers on internet sovereignty were not in D.C.; they were in Silicon Valley. The CCP's self-appointed role as the gatekeeper to China's internet has given it tremendous leverage over individual companies, allowing it to drive a wedge between those companies and American policy makers.

That wedge was on dramatic display during President Xi Jinping's 2015 visit to the United States. Xi had been invited to the White House by President Barack Obama, but his first stop was in Washington State rather than Washington, D.C. At Microsoft's Seattle headquarters, Xi summoned CEOs from the premier U.S. tech companies, including Apple, Facebook, Airbnb, and Amazon. And they all came. Zuckerberg chatted briefly with Xi in Mandarin, while Lu Wei continued his backhanded-charm offensive. Also in attendance were top Chinese tech executives, such as Jack Ma and Tencent founder Pony Ma. After perfunctory speeches, the executives, Lu Wei, and Xi gathered for a group photo. The combined market cap of the companies in the photo came to $2.5 trillion.

The event was convened under the auspices of the eighth U.S.–China Internet Industry Forum, but the real motivation was clear: to give the U.S. tech elite a chance to kiss the ring of Xi Jinping. It was an impeccable piece of economic muscle-flexing—one that reportedly irritated the Obama administration. It was a sign that China's economic pull reached right to the core of America's twenty-first-century trophy companies. These companies may have been born in the U.S.A., but the world leader with the most to offer them at that moment was the president of the People's Republic of China. Describing the moment when Xi entered the room, Apple CEO Tim Cook asked: "Did you feel the room shake?"

FIRST CHILDREN AND FACEBOOK CENSORSHIP

Mark Zuckerberg certainly did. Shortly after the Seattle meeting, President Xi visited the White House for a state dinner. Zuckerberg and his wife, Priscilla, pregnant with the couple's first child, were right there with them. Speaking with Xi, Zuckerberg reportedly asked if the Chinese president would do him the honor of giving a Chinese name to his unborn child. In an early sign of where this cross-cultural brownnosing would get Facebook, Xi declined Zuckerberg's request, calling it "too great a responsibility."

But Zuckerberg would not be deterred. A month later he returned to Tsinghua for an encore performance. This time he delivered a twenty-minute speech laying out Facebook's origin story and what makes for a successful start-up. The speech was a hit, another coup of public face-giving. Then came the "smog jog." On a day when Beijing's pollution levels hovered at the level of "hazardous" by American air quality standards, the Harvard wunderkind cheerily bounded through the streets of Beijing. A photographer captured the Facebook founder midstride, grinning as he passed between the Forbidden City and Tiananmen Square. The background of the photo is tinged by a lung-straining haze, but Zuckerberg was unfazed. He posted the photo to his own Facebook page with the caption, "It's great to be back in Beijing!"

For all the grins and language goofs, Zuckerberg's courtship of China came with a darker side. Just eight months after the "smog jog," *The New York Times* reported on Facebook efforts to build a new censorship tool for use were it to enter the Chinese market. The tool would give a third party, likely a Chinese partner or government agency, the ability to "geo-fence" content (blocking specific content in certain geographies), monitoring and suppressing posts from appearing in news feeds within a certain geographic area. Geo-fencing would by no means be unique to Facebook entering China; companies like Google and Facebook have long removed content from their platforms in certain regions to comply with local laws, for example, bans on Nazi iconography in Germany.

But the censorship required by Chinese authorities would be orders of magnitude greater, and the moral swamp Facebook waded into much murkier. Building a geo-fenced product that lived up to the standards of the CCP would mean micromanaging, and frequently severing, millions of nodes of connectivity: the Facebook pages of all major Western media outlets, conversations between friends in and outside China, silly viral videos and posts by democracy activists alike. It would be akin to creating an entirely different universe of information, a "Facebook with Chinese characteristics." It would also be the highest-profile endorsement yet of internet sovereignty. If the largest social media platform on earth bought into the ideology, why shouldn't everyone else?

Development of the tool was controversial within Facebook, and several employees working on it reportedly quit the company outright. Murmurs about the censorship software grew so great that in July 2016 Zuckerberg addressed the issue directly during a company all-hands. He didn't offer specifics on Facebook's plans for entry but did offer a glass-half-full moral argument for accepting censorship in exchange for market access: "It's better for Facebook to be a part of enabling conversation, even if it's not yet the full conversation."

GOOGLE GETS BACK IN THE RACE

While Zuckerberg performed a very public courtship, Google took a lower-key approach to rapprochement with the mainland, preferring to operate behind the scenes. On its first attempt at winning Chinese markets, Google had gone it alone and suffered a stinging defeat. On its second go-around it wanted some help. The question was from where, and at what cost.

In late 2014 reports surfaced that Google was looking for a partner to bring its Google Play app store for Android back to China. The first potential partnership to make headlines was a tie-up with Huawei, a hardware company that produced routers and cell phones, one suspected of maintaining close ties to the People's Liberation Army and the CCP. Maybe Google and Huawei felt a certain kinship with each other—while Chinese authorities blocked access to Google, the U.S. Congress told telecoms not to work with Huawei over national security concerns. United by their troubles abroad, Google and Huawei reportedly reached an agreement to have the Google Play app store preloaded on Huawei phones sold in China.

Banking on the fact that app stores are far less politically sensitive than search results, the company likely thought Google Play was an easy, apolitical doorway back into China. They were wrong. Apps for *The New York Times*, YouTube, and censorship watchdog organizations are intolerable to Chinese authorities. That presented Google with the same thorny choice it faced when it entered the market and exited in 2010: are you willing to participate in censorship in order to access the market? This time around, Google made it clear it was willing to play ball. By 2015, technology news website *The Information* reported that Google had promised Chinese authorities it would follow government directives when it came to policing the app store. That represented a retreat by Google and another major act of acquiescence to the doctrine of internet sovereignty.

But approval from Chinese authorities never materialized, and the agreements went nowhere. Over the next three years, that hype cycle about Google's return would repeat itself several times. Credible reports in the tech press would announce that Google was "near an agreement" with Chinese partners or the government to bring its Google Play store or Google Scholar back to China. Those reports cited major players in the Chinese tech space as potential partners—Huawei, Xiaomi, NetEase—but government approvals never came through.

Instead, it was a Google alumnus who would give the company its first real footprint in Chinese markets since its exit. In September 2015, both Mobvoi and Google were in talks with Motorola about partnerships on the second-generation Moto 360 watch. In the rest of the world, Moto 360 ran on Google's Android Wear operating system, but with Google Search blocked in mainland China, any watch reliant on it would be useless there.

That dilemma sparked triangular negotiations between the three companies, and representatives from Google decided to pay Mobvoi a visit. They tested the reliability and accuracy of Mobvoi's voice search technology, and they found it up to snuff with Google standards.

"When they engaged us, they found out how easy it was to work with our team, especially the engineering part," cofounder Li Yuanyuan told me. "It has the Google genes. The way we think about things and make decisions are quite similar. The values are quite similar."

The two companies formed a strategic partnership to bring Android Wear to China for the first time. Just three weeks after the Google teams first arrived at Mobvoi, the Moto 360 launched in China, using the Android Wear operating system but swapping out Google Search for Mobvoi's own voice search technology.

One month after the launch, Google doubled down on its partnership with Mobvoi by investing in the company. Google poured an estimated $40 to $45 million into the company (exact figures weren't disclosed), the first direct investment by the parent company into a Chinese start-up since it left the country.[8]

Three months later in Beijing, I watched as Li Zhifei took the stage at a Beijing convention center alongside Google vice president David Singleton, head of Android Wear. Together they announced that Mobvoi was launching an officially sanctioned app store for Android Wear, a proxy that would for the first time allow most Android smartwatch apps into China. Singleton was glowing in his praise of Mobvoi.

"Working with the Mobvoi team has been a real pleasure," he remarked. "They are a smart, user-focused team that exemplify everything exciting about the ecosystem here."

Four years after Li Zhifei left Google for mainland China, the start-up he had founded in the shadow of Google's absence from China was becoming the bridge between his former employer and his home country. It was an arrangement born out of Silicon Valley's China paradox: flows of people, money, and ideas between the two ecosystems were at an all-time high, but companies and products largely stopped at the border.

ENTER THE DRAGONFLY

In the months and years after that press conference, a parade of Silicon Valley juggernauts all made their runs at the Chinese market. Uber duked it out with local rival Didi Chuxing, waging a prolonged war of subsidies before abandoning the market in exchange for a 20 percent stake in Didi. LinkedIn had long censored content in exchange for market access but continued to struggle in a country that funnels professional networking through WeChat. Airbnb looked to use Chinese traveling abroad as a back door into the country and had some success in high-end home rentals. But local rival Tujia swamped the Silicon Valley player in quantity of listings and adapted the model to China's glut of empty homes by offering full-service rentals for absent landlords.

By early 2018, the Chinese tech landscape was littered with the remains of American tech giants: some blocked, some beaten, and some barely hanging on. Many analysts speculated that Silicon Valley might finally be ready to give up its quixotic quest for China's one billion customers.

And then, investigative news outlet *The Intercept* dropped a bombshell: Google was secretly planning to reenter China with a fully censored search engine. The company had already built the app and demonstrated it for Chinese officials. Not only would it censor search results, but it would also require users to sign in, track their location, and grant unilateral access to the data to an unnamed Chinese partner. The project name: Dragonfly.

Google had been nibbling around the edges of the Chinese market for years, trying to squeeze its app store, Google Translate, or Google Scholar back into the market. In doing so, Google was implicitly signaling its acceptance of certain censorship requirements, such as removing VPNs that circumvent the Great Firewall from the app store. But bringing back Google Search—and tracking user data for a Chinese partner—would entail a whole new level of cooperation.

The project was deemed so sensitive that knowledge of it was restricted to just a few hundred people among Google's workforce of nearly 100,000. Unfortunately for corporate leadership, one of those few hundred people was sufficiently outraged at the idea of Google acceding to Chinese censorship that they handed over top-secret internal documents on Project Dragonfly to *The Intercept*.

Google CEO Sundar Pichai was reportedly leading the charge, visiting Beijing in December 2017 and meeting with one of Xi Jinping's closest advisers. Pichai reportedly viewed the meeting as a "success," and over the ensuing months Google rolled out a series of new China ventures: an AI research lab in Beijing, an investment in a Chinese gaming start-up, and a patent-sharing alliance with Tencent. The search app was intended to be the cherry on top but was still awaiting approval from Chinese regulators.

That approval was going to be hard to come by. Google's first departure from China had deeply embarrassed the CCP, airing its dirty laundry out for both Chinese users and the international community. Timing for Project Dragonfly was particularly bad: just three months after Pichai's visit to Beijing, President Trump launched the trade war that dragged U.S.–China relations into the gutter.

But Google leadership remained ready should the call come. In July of 2018, Google's search chief reportedly told the Dragonfly team that they had to be ready to launch the product at any time, like if "suddenly the world changes or [President Donald Trump] decides his new best friend is Xi Jinping."

Human rights and internet freedom activists were outraged.

"It's almost the final nail in the coffin, isn't it?" Charlie Smith, pseudonymous cofounder of GreatFire.org, a site that both tracks and circumvents Chinese internet censorship, wrote to me. "At the moment, if any foreign internet company wants to operate in China, the authorities just simply have to say, Apple and Microsoft self-censor, so you do, too. If they add Google to that list, then what hope is there for any other company?"

Chinese people who I spoke to about the ventures were more ambivalent, or even positive. After news of Project Dragonfly broke, I posed a question in Chinese to my friends on WeChat: "If Google reentered China with a search engine that 'complies with national laws and regulations' [read: censored], would you use it?"

I got back a mixed bag of answers. Some said that if Google complied with censorship, there wouldn't be any reason to use it. Many complained about the clutter of ads on Baidu and the poor quality of search results for any international content. A couple friends said they'd have to do some comparison searching and then decide. But the single most common response was some version of "Of course I'd use it!"

It's a set of answers that sent me back to the question Google leadership agonized over as far back as 2005: does offering a censored—but higher quality—search engine do more to expand information horizons, or limit them? Is it "worse evil" to engage with an authoritarian regime or ignore it?

America has a history of debating and deciding these ethical questions in the public sphere: through our freewheeling media, Supreme Court rulings, and clunky legislative process. But when it comes to global internet governance, tech companies have effectively brought this process in-house. The key decision makers shaping the global internet are not directly responsible to American voters, or even their own government. They're responsible to stockholders and board members, or simply guided by the founder's own idiosyncratic vision for the way the world should be.

But even start-up founders with billions in the bank can be seduced by the promise of a billion new users. And they can stumble when they bring the world-conquering hubris of Silicon Valley to a country and a government that refuses to be conquered. Bill Bishop, a digital media entrepreneur with extensive experience in Silicon Valley and China, has watched as that hubris ran into a brick wall in China.

"I know people in Silicon Valley are really smart, and they're really successful because they can overcome any problem they face," he told me. "But I don't think they've ever faced a problem like the Chinese Communist Party."

THE BACKLASH BEGINS

Over the preceding decade, the Chinese government had pulled off an unexpected hat trick: taming political speech on its own domestic internet, bringing the giants of Silicon Valley to heel, and turning itself into a technology superpower. For the powers that be in Beijing, the state of Chinese technology was cause for celebration.

But that triumphalism was also breeding a backlash in Washington, D.C., one that would change the course of technology and geopolitics. What had long been a one-sided fight (strict controls in China, but open technological borders in the U.S.) was rapidly turning into a reciprocal struggle. Politicians in Washington, D.C., had watched China transform from an internet backwater into a formidable competitor—often by leveraging talent and technology incubated in the U.S.—and they began looking for ways to batten down the hatches.

No longer should money, talent, and technology be allowed to flow freely between Silicon Valley and China. The American government began to assert its right to police these borders, a move it hoped would protect America's technological edge from slipping away. At the same time, companies and bureaucracies in both countries redoubled their focus on game-changing technologies like artificial intelligence and quantum computing, each believing that leadership in these fields would translate into far-reaching commercial and geopolitical power. The stage was set for a rapid escalation in tech tensions and competition.

The precise contours of this geopolitical struggle are constantly evolving, but the broad dimensions have become clear. In ranking "Global Tech Cold War" as one of its top geopolitical risks of 2018, the Eurasia Group outlined three core dimensions of the tensions: disentangling tech ecosystems, competing for third-country markets, and taking leadership in frontier technologies. Disentanglement entails the slow wrenching apart of the ties that have bound these two ecosystems together: Chinese investment in Silicon Valley, cross-border research networks, and tech talent like Li Zhifei. Third-country competition is about transposing the battles between Silicon Valley and Chinese companies out of the U.S. and China and into new markets: Vietnam, Brazil, India, and Mexico. Finally, frontier technologies represent the most forward-looking of these three dimensions: a recognition that the technological future is up for grabs, and for the first time, China is in the running. How these dimensions play out will shape the future of not just these two tech ecosystems, or even these two countries, but an entire global community that finds itself increasingly at the mercy of the very technologies that we have created.

DISENTANGLEMENT

The quest for technological disentanglement began in the twilight years of the Obama administration, around the same time Mobvoi and Google were deepening their partnership. After years of freewheeling cross-border technology deals, the U.S. government began to reassert its right to block Chinese investments and acquisitions of technology companies. In 2016, President Obama stepped in to block multiple Chinese acquisitions targeting semiconductors, the microchips powering computers, cell phones, and intercontinental ballistic missiles. That wariness toward Chinese technology takeovers carried into the Trump administration, with rejections of deals for a U.S. semiconductor company, as well as an Alibaba affiliate's bid to take over money-transfer company MoneyGram.

Raising the alarm here was the Department of Defense's Silicon Valley beachhead, the Defense Innovation Unit Experimental (DIUx). In a highly influential report commissioned during President Obama's final year in office, DIUx argued that Chinese investment in Silicon Valley was a Trojan horse, a tool for accessing "the crown jewels of U.S. innovation." The report described Chinese VC investments as part of a multidecade, government-sponsored technology transfer scheme and argued that the U.S. government's system for reviewing these deals was sorely in need of an update. It was a line of argument that would be echoed as justification for the Trump administration's trade war: China was executing a multipronged campaign to acquire U.S. technology, and America needed to do something, anything, to fight back.

The DIUx report was ahead of the curve in certain respects. Some Chinese government-backed VCs were operating in Silicon Valley with virtually zero oversight into their investments or their goals. Several recent Chinese acquisitions of U.S. technology companies, particularly semiconductor producers, were part of a concerted Chinese government effort to upgrade the country's technology stack. And the existing mechanism for reviewing those investments, the Committee on Foreign Investment in the United States (CFIUS, often pronounced "Si-fee-us"), was proving to be too crude an instrument to deal with twenty-first-century technology deals.

The report also missed the mark on some fronts. It painted all cross-border investment with the same brush, misidentifying international VC firms with operations in China as "Chinese funds," and insinuating that almost any investment coming out of the country was part of one master plan to make off with U.S. technology. Those assumptions didn't match what I observed on the ground in Silicon Valley: a gaggle of mostly private investors who couldn't get into funding rounds for the best U.S. start-ups. Many of these newly minted VCs lacked a coherent plan for investing their own money, let alone for guiding the technological upgrading of their home country.

But what the DIUx report lacked in nuance it made up for in influence, alerting large parts of the defense establishment to transpacific technology dynamics that had long flown under their radar. It circulated widely within defense and policy circles, and Senator John Cornyn cited it as the inspiration for his bill that would overhaul CFIUS: the Foreign Investment Risk Review and Modernization Act (FIRRMA). CFIUS had been formed in 1975 and charged with reviewing whether foreign acquisitions of U.S. firms threatened U.S. national security. It had for decades been a relatively sleepy bureaucratic entity, reviewing few deals and blocking even fewer.

FIRRMA sought to breathe new life into CFIUS as a way to confront China's technological rise, dramatically expanding the scope of deals it would review and the criteria on which it would evaluate them. In terms of scope, it no longer required that a deal involve a takeover of a U.S. firm, but instead brought many Chinese VC investments and U.S.–China joint ventures under the CFIUS microscope. In terms of criteria, it expanded the definition of "national security" from its traditionally narrow scope (e.g., does the acquired company make components used in missiles?) to a much further-reaching definition: "whether the transaction is likely to reduce the technological and industrial advantage of the United States" relative to countries such as China. That quick rhetorical move—equating technological prowess with national security—captured a core tenet of the new technology rivalry: private-sector technologies that Silicon Valley long viewed as nonpolitical would now be treated as national security assets, to be both protected and regulated by the government.

FIRRMA was passed as part of a broader defense authorization bill for 2019 and will take effect once CFIUS turns the bill's language into concrete regulations. Even before taking effect, FIRRMA has already severely curtailed Chinese activities in the Valley, drying up investments and nixing partnerships with U.S. companies involved in areas such as artificial intelligence, advanced robotics, and microchips.

But the push for technological disentanglement could go much deeper than cutting off flows of money. As FIRRMA takes effect, defense and policy circles murmur with discussion of the need to sever cross-border research networks, such as Chinese labs in Silicon Valley or the U.S. tech giants' research facilities in China. The Trump administration's restrictions on Chinese student visas—and threat of an all-out ban—look to disrupt the flow of people and ideas, preventing Chinese students from acquiring too much know-how on U.S. soil and then bringing that know-how back to China. These are the students that Senator Marco Rubio characterized as "weapons" in the Chinese government's campaign to "steal & cheat their way to world dominance." They're also ordinary people like Li Zhifei, who learned from the best in the U.S., applied those skills for a few years to helping an American company like Google, and then went back to his home country because that's where he had the best chance of creating a game-changing start-up.

In many ways, D.C.'s push for technological disentanglement is nudging it closer to the position that the Chinese Communist Party has long held: a country's technology industry is part and parcel of national power, something to be fostered at home and shielded from foreign influence. That approach has worked far better than anticipated in China, and many see its adoption as a long-overdue correction in the U.S., a move away from an overly laissez-faire approach to technology that allows other countries to take advantage of American openness.

But it also raises new questions about the nexus of innovation and competitive advantage in the twenty-first century. Which country loses more if you prevent the best and brightest Chinese students from studying in the U.S.? What are the true sources of America's long-term strength in technology? And what happens when technical innovation becomes part of a zero-sum geopolitical contest?

THIRD-COUNTRY COMPETITION

While Beijing and D.C. move to reassert national interests on the technology industry, private companies are taking the battle overseas. After years of running into brick walls in each other's home markets, leading companies from China and the U.S. are now fighting it out in places like Brazil and India, where hundreds of millions of people are coming online for the first time. The result is a series of private-sector skirmishes that can be seen as proxies for the influence of each country's technology ecosystem.

American and Chinese tech companies are taking two different approaches to this proxy competition. U.S. technology firms tend to go it alone: when they enter a foreign market, they bring their home product and their home brand to the country. They seek to beat the local competition and win the entire market for themselves. Chinese firms have instead largely chosen to back a leading local start-up in each market: investing and sharing technology with the companies trying to drive out the American juggernauts. If the local start-ups win, the Chinese company will get a percentage of the spoils via their stake and also have an ally in charge of a key market. It's a strategic divide born out of the U.S. and Chinese tech communities' divergent histories. Early U.S. tech companies largely romped across global markets (except for China), and they assume that American dominance will continue. For the Chinese companies, their defining battle was the fight on their home turf against these foreign companies, a contest that drove home the advantages a scrappy local start-up can have over a global juggernaut.

So far, India has proven to be a hotbed for this kind of proxy competition. Alibaba has poured hundreds of millions of dollars into Indian e-commerce and digital payments companies attempting to beat Amazon. Tencent, the company behind WeChat, has invested $175 million into Hike, a local messaging app seeking to dethrone Facebook-owned WhatsApp. And Didi Chuxing, the ride-hailing company that drove Uber out of China, took a stake in Indian start-up Ola, hoping that it can repeat that feat. All of these partnerships have gone beyond mere financing, with the Chinese company offering technical support, personnel exchanges, and advice on operating in a billion-person market. Explaining his alliance with Tencent, Hike founder Kavin Bharti Mittal pointed to similarities extending from product to demographics.

"These guys have built what we're trying to build," he told *The Wall Street Journal.* "India's economy and population has many more similarities to China than the U.S."

At this point, it's too early to declare winners in these proxy competitions. The U.S. firms have huge war chests and a strong track record of global conquest. They also offer users something that neither local start-ups nor their Chinese backers can: the chance to link into truly global networks. But the Chinese-funded start-ups have their own advantages: the ability to relentlessly localize the product and to move quickly without waiting for the go-ahead from headquarters.

Depending on how that competition shakes out, we could well see the emergence of divergent technological blocks: American companies would lay claim to the U.S., Europe, and most developed countries, while Chinese companies could end up owning their home market and exerting influence across large swaths of the developing world.

FRONTIER TECHNOLOGIES

The third prong of China–U.S. technological competition involves frontier technologies: AI, 5G networks, and quantum computing. These technologies hold the potential to reshape the geopolitical balance of power—economic, cybersecurity, and military—and each country brings a different set of strengths and weaknesses to them. For a better picture of these strengths and weaknesses, let's zoom in on the technology that's making the most waves in both countries today: AI.

Ironically, it was Google that gave China its Sputnik moment for AI: a dramatic wake-up call that led the country to double down on its pursuit of the technology. That moment came in 2016 when Google AI affiliate DeepMind pitted its product AlphaGo against Lee Sedol, one of the world's top players of the ancient Chinese game of Go. Artificial intelligence had long ago conquered Western chess, but the breathtaking complexity of Go—with more possible positions on the board than there are atoms in the universe—made it into something of a Mount Everest for AI researchers.

Google leadership likely hoped AlphaGo's mastery of a revered Chinese game would burnish its brand in the country, helping pave the way for the company's triumphant return. But the greatest legacy of AlphaGo may end up being its impact on China: jump-starting China's own AI ambitions.

When AlphaGo beat Lee in a best-of-five series, the matches barely registered in the U.S. In China, they caused a sensation. More than sixty million people in China watched the matches online, granting them a real-time window onto the power of AI.[9] That excitement kicked up another level in 2017, when AlphaGo defeated China's own world-champion Go prodigy in the city of Wuzhen, home to China's World Internet Conference.

Within two months of the matches in Wuzhen, China's State Council had released a massive national plan outlining the country's ambitions in AI, calling for China to become "the world's primary AI innovation center" by 2030. The plan acted as a signal for local officials around the country: AI was the next big thing, and they were to do what they could to accelerate adoption. Those officials began adapting public infrastructure, subsidizing private investment, and procuring products, all in an attempt to stimulate their local AI industry.

By the end of 2017, Chinese VC funding for AI start-ups would surpass the U.S.[10] Companies like Alibaba were partnering with local governments to create AI-powered "city brains"—systems using AI to improve efficiency of public systems such as traffic lights—and some ambitious Chinese mayors were turning their cities into playgrounds for testing self-driving cars. The technology also took on an expanding role in the state's surveillance apparatus, with facial recognition software attempting to create an AI-powered panopticon that blanketed Chinese cities with its gaze.

In China's western region of Xinjiang, home to the country's Muslim Uighur ethnic minority, the government has brought surveillance to an entirely new level, creating the first true AI-fueled police state. Following a spate of terror-related stabbings that authorities attributed to Uighur extremists, the government began deploying high-tech checkpoints and facial recognition systems across the region: at mosques, gas stations, and small village alleys. Information gathered from those systems helped feed into one of the largest ethnic internments in the world: outside estimates claim up to one million Uighurs have been sent to "reeducation camps," where they are indoctrinated with Communist Party messages and, according to some who escaped, tortured.[11] Uighurs could be sent to the camps for many reasons: contacting a family member abroad, growing a beard, failing to act sufficiently patriotic, or the police discovering a VPN during a digital scan of a Uighur's smartphone.

The extreme campaign of religious and cultural repression has also taken on many low-tech forms, with non-Uighur Chinese citizens sent to live with Uighur families as "big brothers"[12] (read: civilian surveillance officers). But the power of AI to spot a face in the crowd or recognize a voice has dramatically expanded the scope of possible surveillance by eliminating the need for human eyes and ears to monitor each feed. In April 2019, *The New York Times* revealed a vast and previously secret system using facial recognition to spot Uighur faces outside of Xinjiang, the first known instance of a government intentionally using artificial intelligence to racially profile its own population.[13] Taken together, the situation in Xinjiang constitutes one of the darkest corners of the technology landscape, a glimpse of what can happen when AI is paired with unchecked political power. It also represents one of the major strands in the Chinese government's attempt to weave artificial intelligence into the fabric of Chinese society.

It's not as if the American government or companies were sitting back, letting China seize the lead in AI. DeepMind was able to deliver that Sputnik moment precisely because it was already so far ahead of its peers—Chinese or otherwise—in cutting-edge research. American universities and corporate labs still enjoy a near-monopoly on top research talent in AI. As part of the ChinAI project at the Paulson Institute's MacroPolo, my colleague Jeffrey Ding found that 126 of the 182 AI researchers publishing at the most elite conference of 2017 (~1 percent acceptance rate) were working at U.S. institutions.[14] The United Kingdom came in a distant second with around twenty-five researchers, while China was in seventh place with just two researchers working at Chinese institutions.

But examined from another angle, that talent distribution appears much flatter. If you look at where these elite researchers completed their undergraduate degrees (a rough proxy for where they grew up), the United States still led with fifty, but China came in second with twenty-five. The deltas between these statistics (50 to 126 for the U.S., 25 to 2 for China) represent the gains and losses from highly skilled immigration. For the Chinese government, those numbers also likely represent a population of potential "sea turtles" that they hope will bring their talents back to China.

The U.S. government has also sought to capitalize on America's rich pool of talent, forging partnerships with top American companies to bring AI to bear on government functions. So far, the results have been mixed. In 2017, the U.S. Department of Defense entered into a contract with Google for AI software that could analyze drone footage and potentially improve targeting on drone strikes. The contract was small by tech standards, but many saw it as a foot in the door for wider cooperation between the Valley and the Pentagon. That is, until Google's employees got involved. When details of the contract leaked, over 4,000 Google employees signed a petition demanding that Google never build "warfare technologies." Dozens of Googlers resigned in protest, and within a few months the company announced it would not be renewing the contract. That kind of employee revolt is almost unimaginable in China, but it is becoming increasingly commonplace at American tech giants that have fostered their own versions of pseudodemocratic civil society within the company.

China and the United States enter the age of AI like a study in contrasts. While the U.S. leads in game-changing research, China shows strength in practical applications. Where American companies draw data from diverse users around the globe, China's AI giants have a wealth of relatively homogenous data at home. And while Silicon Valley sometimes actively rejects entanglements with the U.S. government, Chinese companies often work with local officials to bring large-scale AI projects to life.

China's prowess in AI is also challenging American technologists and policy makers to rethink the connection between policy and innovation. A relatively light-touch approach has served the U.S. well during the internet revolution, turning Silicon Valley into a global mecca for software engineers and ambitious entrepreneurs. But real-world applications of AI—driverless cars, automated stores, and intelligent cities—have a much larger physical footprint, one that often requires the government adopt, or at least adapt to, the technology. In that context, how will the American government's relatively hands-off approach compare with the Chinese government's active embrace of the technology?

But as AI systems become more capable and more omnipresent, U.S.–China competition could raise questions far deeper and more troubling than today's geopolitical arm wrestling. Today, AI systems have the power to do extraordinary things when they are trained to perform a single, narrow task (e.g., winning at Go, or recommending a song). But a single narrow AI system doesn't yet have the general intelligence of humans that allows a single brain to perform the full range of complex human tasks: conducting innovative research, raising a child, or writing a bestselling novel. Estimates of when we might be able to build powerful AI systems up to these complex tasks—often called "artificial general intelligence" (AGI) or "high-level machine intelli-

gence" (HLMI)—vary widely. The most aggressive estimates from some top
AI scientists come in at under ten years, while median estimates from surveys
of researchers have projected around forty years until HLMI.[15]

Whatever the timeline is for HLMI or AGI, its arrival would pose profound questions for humanity—questions that could be further complicated by a tense U.S.–China relationship. Such AI systems could be put
to almost limitless uses—curing disease, automating jobs, or designing
complex cyber-weapons that cripple an entire country. What happens if
the United States and China are engaged in spiraling competition to build
ever more intelligent machines, AI systems that we might not know how
to control? Many familiar with the field—from elite AI researchers such as
Stuart Russell to the late astrophysicist Stephen Hawking—fear that if not
designed with foolproof safety mechanisms, such superintelligent systems
could potentially threaten the very existence of humanity.

Given the potential risks from AGI systems, the move toward disentanglement of the two technology ecosystems raises serious questions. Should
the U.S. government attempt to silo America's top scientists, walling off
new AI breakthroughs from China? Or would we be made safer by an open
dialogue around AI safety, one that shares international best practices across
research teams and borders? Can two superpowers that find themselves at
geopolitical loggerheads work together to confront a larger global threat?
And can the "sea turtles" of the Transpacific Experiment—the students,
researchers, and technology entrepreneurs crisscrossing the Pacific Ocean—
play a role in mitigating these threats?

THE FIVE-WAY INTERSECTION

My last visit with the Mobvoi team occurs in 2017. Tech tensions are
gathering momentum in Washington, D.C., but those geopolitical machinations feel far away as I head to today's event: a press conference in
Beijing to announce a new joint venture between Mobvoi and Volkswagen's China branch. Volkswagen will put $180 million into the venture,

and together the two companies will be developing applications of Mobvoi's machine learning software for cars: rearview mirrors that respond to voice commands, routing information that can be summoned through a smartwatch and transferred straight to the vehicle.[16] The event is held at a technology park abutting the city's art district, in a chic two-story event space with concrete floors and high white walls. Black Volkswagen cars and SUVs sit parked on the ground floor, alongside block letters spelling AI MEETS AUTO.

Entering through the building's tall glass doors, I don't recognize Li at first glance. It has been three years since I first met him on a grainy Skype call, and two since I listened to his team debating the merits of stinky tofu on the hackathon bus. I've never seen him dressed in anything but hoodies, T-shirts, or the branded jackets of his past employers. But today he wears a black suit jacket, black pants, and brown leather shoes. His hair is combed down, and his white collared shirt buttoned up. Around him, the rest of the Mobvoi leadership is dressed in elegant black dresses and shirts, mingling with Volkswagen execs and members of the press. Li and his team look all grown up.

On the wrist of cofounder Li Yuanyuan is the latest edition of the Ticwatch, the sleek round-faced smartwatch that Mobvoi built from the ground up. It runs on the company's own operating system and, thanks to Mobvoi's partnership with Google, supports the China-compatible version of the Android Wear app store. Mobvoi had begun selling the watch overseas, raking in $2 million of preorders through a Kickstarter campaign and getting positive reviews in tech media. Soon they will begin selling the watch directly through Amazon. Chinese tech companies in the U.S. still struggle to shake the stigmas of censorship and "copycat" products, but Mobvoi's leadership is determined to make the company a global player.

"We're not going to emphasize that we're a Chinese company, but we're not going to hide it either," Li told the *Financial Times*.

An announcement over the event space's sound system calls everyone upstairs for the press conference and official launch of the joint venture. A suave young Chinese television personality emcees the event, switching back and forth between English and Chinese as he introduces Volkswagen executives and Mobvoi leadership. Each side takes turns praising the other company and pontificating about the way artificial intelligence will shake up the global car industry. The string of investments and partnerships with Google has pushed some folks to frame Mobvoi as a vessel for Google's reentry into China. But this tie-up with Volkswagen pushes things in a different direction. It reasserts Mobvoi's status as an independent company but also feels like an inkling of things to come: Chinese tech companies branching out globally, beyond the Silicon Valley–Beijing axis.

Downstairs after the press conference, I congratulate Li and his team on the partnership and head out into the warm Beijing evening. The air is a bit muggy and a bit smoggy, but spring has arrived and the city is emerging from its winter cocoon. Young Chinese people flood out of the technology park and the neighboring arts district, with groups of geeky twentysomethings chattering among themselves while hailing cars and ordering takeout on their phones. I have some time to kill, so I grab a cold beer from a streetside stall and set off walking back toward the center of the city.

It has been just five months since my last trip to Beijing, and the texture of the city has already changed. Roads, bike lanes, and sidewalks are suddenly jammed with a rainbow of brightly colored bikes, the product of China's hot new tech trend: bike-sharing. Flocks of rusty old Flying Pigeon bicycles were a hallmark of a bygone Beijing, but as the city's population and average income skyrocketed, young people abandoned two-wheeled transport for the status and convenience of cars. Now, in the span of a few months, a handful of Chinese start-ups threw that trend into reverse, blanketing cities with bikers (and piles of abused or discarded bikes). The bikeshare companies here differentiate themselves by color: orange and silver bikes for industry leader Mobike, bright yellow for challenger Ofo, and the rest of the palette for the dozens of other start-ups trying to carve out their niche.

These start-ups pioneered a dockless model for bike-sharing, in which you use your phone to unlock thousands of bikes scattered across the city by scanning a code on the handlebars. Unlike the docked bike programs that popped up in U.S. cities, these bikes can be picked up and left anywhere. Simple as that sounds, it quickly revolutionized urban transport here by giving Chinese urbanites a flexible option for short trips, or to cover the first or last mile to and from public transport. The colorful bikes have effectively created millions of new transit routes by stitching together the clunkier lines of legacy systems.

Ripples from this transportation revolution have already begun spreading across the Pacific. Just three weeks before Mobvoi's press conference, Silicon Valley–based LimeBike raised tens of millions of dollars with the mandate of copying that dockless bike-share model in the United States. LimeBike was founded by Chinese-born, U.S.-trained entrepreneurs and took on funding from Chinese VCs in the Valley, as well as the prestigious Andreessen Horowitz. While Chinese pioneers like Mobike and Ofo were taking their first tentative steps overseas in Singapore and London, American-born LimeBike was adapting to local conditions. Facing uncooperative ordinances that banned the dockless bikes in U.S. cities, the company shortened its name to Lime and pivoted into dockless electric scooters, inspiring its own slate of American copycats in the process.

On this Beijing street, I walk through a wave of shared bikes and wander toward a tangled five-way intersection. It's the kind of intersection that used to stop me dead in my tracks when I first arrived in China: a knot of poorly marked roads crowded with vegetable carts, taxis, and trucks spewing diesel, all fighting for every inch of space and snarling traffic for blocks. Traffic is still backed up for blocks, but the swarms of orange, yellow, and blue bikes flow around the stopped cars like water around rocks midstream. I hop up on a ledge in the southeast corner to get a better view and stand there transfixed. With each change of the lights, a new wave of colorful bikes pours into the five-way intersection, flowing in from every direction and out through another.

4

IS MICKEY MOUSE
AN AMERICAN?

Waking up as ambiguous orange sunlight fills the room, I'm caught in the familiar daze of the jet-lagged traveler: a total inability to remember where I am or figure out whether it's sunrise or sunset outside my window. I scan the room for clues and slowly piece it all back together. A half-opened suitcase reminds me of the three airports I moved through to get here. The kitschy paintings of rice paddies hanging on the walls locate me in a cheap Chinese hotel. The calls of breakfast hawkers on the street below tell me it's morning.

I'm on the outskirts of Shanghai, where the glass skyscrapers give way to cornfields and the chic urbanites are replaced by an earthier crowd of farmers, fruit sellers, and off-duty construction crews. I often wander the fringes of China's urban sprawl to catch sight of the culture clashes produced when you have urbanization by osmosis: the lifelong rice farmers who suddenly find themselves living atop an ocean of concrete, or the rural entrepreneurs who build a massive karaoke complex in a sleepy village, betting that sooner or later the city will come to them.

But today I'm here to explore a different kind of cultural negotiation. This stretch of land is home to one of the most ambitious and expensive experiments in bringing a wholesome slice of Americana to the Chinese middle class: Shanghai Disneyland. Fifteen years and $5.5 billion in the making when it opened in 2016, the Shanghai location represents what Disney CEO Bob Iger called the "greatest opportunity the company has had since Walt Disney himself bought land in Central Florida."[1]

That opportunity is about much more than ticket sales and concession stands. It's about priming the cultural pump of what is soon to be the largest market for movies in the world. Between 2010 and 2018, the Chinese box office more than quintupled to $8.9 billion, making it the second largest market in the world behind North America.[2] While China's industry has chalked up double-digit growth, North America's numbers have largely stagnated or gone negative. Many Hollywood blockbusters that bombed at home have been bailed out by Chinese moviegoers, and major franchises like *Transformers* and *The Fast and the Furious* regularly earn more in China than their home market. During the first quarter of 2018, Chinese movie receipts surpassed North America for the first time.

It's a monumental shift in the center of gravity for the industry, one that has sent Hollywood executives and A-listers on pilgrimages across the Pacific. They come in search of greater access to China's tightly controlled markets and expertise that can help them "localize" films like *Captain America* for Chinese audiences. That same quest for profits has also lured Chinese moguls, who got rich off traditional industries like real estate, into the business of culture. What they lack in experience they're trying to make up for in cash. These titans of China's traditional economy plowed billions into financing movies, building theme parks, and acquiring Hollywood studios.

Together these odd couples of American artists and Chinese tycoons have pursued the new Holy Grail of global entertainment: a movie that can cash in big at the box office in the United States and China.

AT THE GATES OF THE MAGIC KINGDOM

I want to check in on Disney's progress toward that Holy Grail, so I haul myself out of bed, slurp down a bowl of Chinese porridge, and hop on a shared bike that will take me through fields of corn and to the gates of the park.

By the time I reach the entrance, I'm already soaked in sweat from the ninety-three-degree temperatures. But the excitement at entering a "Magic Kingdom" seems to have inoculated the Chinese preteens swarming around me from the oppressive August heat. They surge through the turnstiles, impervious to the pleas of parents struggling to keep up.

Strolling up the park's main boulevard, I watch as grinning Chinese kids flash peace signs while taking pictures with Goofy. Among the millennial crowd, attentive Chinese boyfriends hold purses on one shoulder while taking posed-to-appear-candid photos of their girlfriends gazing philosophically toward the park's trademark castle. We're only a minute into our time at the park, and Disney already appears to have cast its spell on the crowds here.

My wandering mind is jolted back to reality by a Chinese boy of around eight years old, who is standing next to me and pointing an accusing finger my way: "*Laowai!*"—"Foreigner!" Having lived in interior China, I'm used to unsolicited declarations of my nationality. But this time the observation triggers a question for me: In this kid's mind, are Disney's beloved characters also *laowai*? Is Mickey Mouse an American?

Disney has opened a number of language schools in China that use its original movies as English teaching materials, but the Mickey that millions of Chinese kids watch on screen cracks jokes and pulls off his hijinks in Mandarin. At the park here, Mickey and Minnie regularly make appearances in traditional Chinese garb and speak to children in their native tongue.

Language skills and wardrobe changes are one thing, but I want to know if Chinese kids think that Mickey Mouse is a *laowai*, a visitor from a foreign land. So I take out my phone and shoot a WeChat message to my former coworker Helen, an English teacher in the central Chinese city of Xi'an. I ask her to pose the question to her young students: "Is Mickey Mouse Chinese, or is he an American?"

THE STAKES

Silly as it sounds, a version of that core question—who claims, controls, and profits from global culture in the twenty-first century?—has been at the center of a high-stakes tango between Hollywood and China. That's because the impact of movies goes much deeper than dollars and RMB. Popular cinema is one of the most potent sources of "soft power"—the ability of a country to attract and influence others through culture and public perception. Hollywood's role as the undisputed heavyweight champion of global culture gifts the United Sates with deep wells of soft power, a kind of cultural capital that helps subsidize the United States' foreign policy initiatives around the globe.

For the Chinese Communist Party (CCP), that American control over global culture generates deep anxiety. China's top leaders have warned that "international hostile forces" are using cultural products as a Trojan horse to "infiltrate" and westernize China. They fear that Chinese youth will end up under the spell of American values, worshipping all things foreign and contemptuous of their country's own culture. It's a problem that many leaders in developing countries worry about, but one that the CCP obsesses over. To combat the nefarious influence of these Hollywood blockbusters, the CCP places strict limits on the content and number of foreign films shown in China, hoping to funnel China's ever-growing audience toward domestic films and traditional values.

But if China wants to develop a thriving domestic film industry—and keep box office receipts rising—it can't afford to shut out Hollywood entirely. The draw of American movies and the know-how of Hollywood studios continue to buoy China's own film industry. These competing desires—for cash, better production quality, and control over culture—locked Hollywood and China in an awkward tango, with both sides fighting over who leads and who follows.

That dance has taken several forms. In its early incarnation, Hollywood and China embraced each other with open(ish) arms, each seeing in the other boundless possibilities and a certain mystique. Geopolitics soon put the kibosh on those feel-good vibes, forcing both sides to embrace the "co-production" model. Hollywood studios partnered with big-money Chinese backers, pledging to insert Chinese elements into American blockbusters in exchange for access to the Chinese market. But behind the scenes, Chinese tycoons and Hollywood producers wrestled for control, and the products of these arranged artistic marriages often looked more like international marketing campaigns than organic films. Some succeeded, some flopped, but none showed these cultural powerhouses a way forward.

In their place, we've seen the emergence of a new equilibrium, one in which the more culturally specific a product is, often the broader its appeal becomes. When Disney does Disney, it can succeed in Shanghai. When Ang Lee creates a deeply Chinese film like *Crouching Tiger, Hidden Dragon*, it can capture the imagination of American audiences. And when Chinese filmmakers produce screwball comedies tailor-made for Chinese audiences, they have a shot at winning mass appeal, at least at home if not yet abroad. It's a process that's playing out in real time in Hengdian, a rural town south of Shanghai that aspires to build "the Hollywood of China" the old-fashioned way: by literally building full-scale, carbon-copy replicas of China's most famous monuments to use as film sets. Today, Hengdian (pronounced "Hung-dyen") boasts its own Forbidden City, the palace of the first Qin Emperor, and Mao Zedong's World War II cave hideout, all crawling with film crews and thousands of extras. That mammoth engineering effort has turned the town into a mecca for starry-eyed Chinese actors and a tourism hub for a cheap look at the greatest hits of Chinese history.

It's a far grittier approach to creating movie magic than what's done in Hollywood, and it's one that's testing out a counterintuitive theory about what it takes to build a thriving film industry. What if it isn't about personal freedoms or inspired artists? What if it comes down to throwing together a critical mass of the raw physical ingredients: grandiose sets, decent cameras, plenty of money, and a hell of a lot of people? Gather enough of that stuff in one place, the theory goes, and eventually you're bound to create something that people want to watch. That's similar to the approach that worked for China in nurturing traditional manufacturing industries and even helped fuel the country's booming internet economy. But do the lessons learned from building the factory of the world really apply to something as ethereal as art? And can a rural town in southern China ever truly compete with the glitz and glamour of Los Angeles?

For answers to those questions, and a peek into the future of global cinema, we'll have to travel from Hollywood to Hengdian and back again.

SPIELBERG ON THE BUND

The modern-day Hollywood–China story had hopeful beginnings. During the 1980s, China and Hollywood enjoyed a brief romance, one that showed what was possible when you matched the storytelling magic of California with the massive scale of China and the drama of Chinese history.

That brief opening came in the wake of Mao Zedong's disastrous Cultural Revolution (1966–76), when China almost completely sealed itself off from the outside world. During the Cultural Revolution, any association with foreign culture—or even "feudal" Chinese culture from the pre-CCP era—could turn into a death sentence. The only acceptable cultural products were those mindlessly exalting the heroism of the working masses or Mao's own dogmatic ideology. Films, when they were allowed to exist at all, were shown purely for utilitarian ends: education and indoctrination.

After the death of Mao in 1976 and the ascent of Deng Xiaoping, Chinese leaders and citizens slowly began looking again to the outside world. The Chinese government began sending some top students and scholars for training at American universities and invited overseas investors to set up shop in select coastal cities like Shenzhen. Conservative factions within China's own government warned against the dangers of these capitalist cultural influences, but Deng dismissed their concerns with his characteristic brand of folksy wisdom.

"If you open the window for fresh air, you have to expect some flies to blow in," he famously remarked.

China also hesitantly opened the door to a small number of Western films. At the center of that process was Janet Yang. Born in Queens, New York, to parents from mainland China, Yang moved to Beijing in the early 1980s to work as a translator and editor at a state-run publishing house. That work required disentangling the turgid language of Chinese political texts, but it also exposed her to the first wave of Chinese films to emerge from the wreckage of the Cultural Revolution. The on-screen images were a revelation to a young woman who had grown up watching films in which Asian actors were either excluded or relegated to roles as walking stereotypes.

"I'd never seen Chinese people in a dramatic film," she told me. "It reminded me of what I missed out on my entire life. I never, never thought we could do this. I never thought people that look like us could be on camera."

At that time, a new crop of Chinese filmmakers was emerging, exemplified by directors like Chen Kaige and Zhang Yimou, members of the first class to graduate from the Beijing Film Academy after the Cultural Revolution. These visual storytellers would go on to mesmerize international audiences with quietly rich depictions of life in the Chinese countryside. Chen's 1984 debut film *Yellow Earth*, with stunning cinematography by Zhang Yimou, turned heads in the international art house crowd. Janet Yang credits it with changing her life.

When she returned to New York, Yang began importing thirty-five-millimeter prints of Chinese films to screen at U.S. theaters and film festivals. In 1985, she parlayed that into a role representing three major Hollywood studios in China. These studios saw potential in China's massive population, but the Chinese partners were quick to lower expectations when it came to profits.

"They had to educate us about Chinese distribution," Yang said. "They told me, 'Go to the countryside and look at how films are screened there. They're hanging on a sheet, and people pay with an egg and sit on a brick.'"

Given those limits on the purchasing power of your average Chinese moviegoer, Yang began by introducing films from deep in Hollywood's back catalogue: *Roman Holiday, Spartacus,* and *In the Heat of the Night.* The world's largest country and its preeminent cultural powerhouse were back on speaking terms.

That dialogue kicked up to another level in 1987. That was the year that Steven Spielberg arrived in China to film *Empire of the Sun,* a sweeping historical epic set in World War II–era Shanghai. The film starred a young Christian Bale and featured John Malkovich and Ben Stiller. Yang was recruited to lay the groundwork for the three weeks of in-country shooting.

It was an unprecedented effort, one that required government approvals all the way up to the State Council, China's equivalent of the U.S. president's cabinet. It would be as if shooting a Chinese film in New York required the secretary of state to sign off on it. Yang worked her contacts and nixed some shots involving prostitutes or beggars, knowing that they would raise red flags for the Chinese side. In the end, the government didn't just approve the film; it mobilized massive resources for the crucial scene: a sequence in which Christian Bale is separated from his parents amid the chaos of Japan's invasion of the city.

"The whole city of Shanghai shut down while we were shooting," Yang recalled. "We had five thousand extras in period costume. They came from work units. They came from the military. They came from police. They came from wherever we could get them. We just said, 'This is what we need.' And they said, 'Okay, we're going to have to use this factory and that factory' and so on. You would never do that today. It was crazy."

While Spielberg worked his magic in Shanghai, famed Italian director Bernardo Bertolucci was filming *The Last Emperor* in Beijing, another historical drama on an even more massive scale. Bertolucci's British producer, Jeremy Thomas, secured the unprecedented privilege of filming in Beijing's Forbidden City, and the Chinese government called on the country's military to help supply 19,000 extras.

"This is the first [Western] film about modern China, and China is one of the stars of the movie," Thomas told the *Los Angeles Times*. "It was really a $25-million cultural and business joint venture."

At the 1988 Academy Awards, *Empire of the Sun* and *The Last Emperor* combined for seventeen nominations.[3] While Spielberg's team didn't take home any hardware, *The Last Emperor* won all nine of its categories. That same year, Zhang Yimou's directorial debut, *Red Sorghum*, won the top prize at the Berlin International Film Festival. For Janet Yang and others bridging China and the West through film, the possibilities for collaboration seemed endless.

"Everybody was thinking, 'Oh my God, China is really opening up to very good movies with really respectable directors. Imagine what can happen now.'"

SHUTTING OUT THE FLIES

What actually happened next was the Tiananmen Square massacre of 1989, when the People's Liberation Army killed thousands during the brutal suppression of a student-led democracy movement. In the wake of that tragedy, culturally conservative factions in the Chinese government seized the initiative. They blamed the protests on the nefarious influence of Western culture, a force that manifested itself in the rock music the students adored and the Goddess of Democracy statue they built, an art piece with a striking resemblance to the Statue of Liberty. China had opened its windows to the outside world, but now its leaders decided the disease borne by the cultural "flies" was far more dangerous than Deng had anticipated. China went into a period of cultural retrenchment, and the courtship with Hollywood was put on ice.

China's own filmmakers continued to produce internationally acclaimed works of art, but they rubbed up against limitations at home. Chen Kaige's 1993 masterpiece *Farewell My Concubine* won the Palme d'Or at the Cannes Film Festival but was first banned and then released with cuts to portrayals of same-sex intimacy and the Cultural Revolution. Zhang Yimou received multiple Academy Award nominations but found several of his films banned at home.

Hollywood actors and studios were getting the same treatment. The major studios managed to get a limited number of blockbuster films released in China during the 1990s, but in 1997 the relationship soured once more. That year, China's Ministry of Radio, Film, and Television blacklisted three major studios for their work on three films that portrayed China in a negative light: *Seven Years in Tibet, Kundun,* and *Red Corner. Seven Years in Tibet* and *Kundun* dealt with the Dalai Lama—a persona non grata in mainland China—while *Red Corner* told the story of an American businessman framed for murder by the Chinese state. In announcing the studio ban, the government declared that the films "viciously attack China [and] hurt the Chinese people's feelings."

It was a power move by a country that appeared to have limited bargaining power. As Chinese film scholar Stanley Rosen has pointed out, receipts from China at the time were still roughly on par with those from Peru, with U.S. studios taking in less there than in countries like Malaysia, Thailand, or the Philippines.[4] And yet China held firm on the ban, and the studios took the lesson to heart: if you wanted access to China's nascent market, there were red lines that weren't to be crossed, even for movies marketed solely to American audiences. The ban may not have had an immediate impact on the studios' bottom line, but it set down rules of engagement that would reshape what people around the world could and could not see depicted on the silver screen for decades to come.

That's because Hollywood and the Chinese government may have been at odds on the Dalai Lama, but they agreed on one thing: someday, the Chinese box office was going to be very, very big.

SEIZING THE MEANS OF PROJECTION

Wang Jianlin would seem like an odd man to lead the global revival of Chinese film. A trim five foot six inches tall, Wang speaks softly in a high-pitched voice and sports a widow's peak that would make a Bond villain proud. He spent seventeen years of his young life in the People's Liberation Army and another thirty years building high-rises and massive malls around China as the chairman of the Wanda Group. Known to his legions of employees simply as "Chairman Wang," he developed a reputation for militaristic discipline within the Wanda Group and ruthless business instincts with his competitors. His multibillion-dollar property empire has made him the richest person in Asia for several years. The political connections that helped him build that empire have made him the subject of multiple rumors that he has been detained in high-level corruption investigations.

But for decades Chairman Wang showed an unusual gift for reading the political tea leaves in China and turning those prophecies into gobs of money. During the 1990s and 2000s, Chairman Wang's Wanda Group both rode and fed China's epic urbanization boom. The Wanda Group displayed an uncanny knack for securing development rights to government land on the cheap, filling that land with the company's trademark offering: Wanda complexes, densely packed mixed-use facilities combining shopping malls and high-rise apartments. The mayors got a boost to their city (and maybe their personal) GDP, and Wanda got the land on which to build an empire.

Chairman Wang is the kind of man who can sniff out opportunity like a shark smells blood, and in 2012 his nose led him to Hollywood. After twenty years as little more than a footnote on Hollywood's balance sheet, the Chinese box office was exploding. Between 2004 and 2010, Chinese film receipts grew by an average of 38 percent per year.[5] Hollywood insiders began predicting that the Chinese box office would surpass the United States by 2018 and double it by 2025. Suddenly every Hollywood studio was scrambling for an angle into the Middle Kingdom, and Chairman Wang was happy to oblige.

He capitalized on this frenzy by buying himself into the role of China's unofficial ambassador to Hollywood. He forked over billions of dollars for American movie theaters and production companies, promising to both spread Chinese culture abroad and grant American studios access to China's booming market. He flew celebrities like Leonardo DiCaprio and Nicole Kidman to China to walk his red carpets and raked in investments from the relatives of China's leaders. In the coastal city of Qingdao, he promised to spend $8 billion to build an industrial-scale movie studio and theme park that would become "the Hollywood of the East."

And yet, for all that spending, Chairman Wang himself shows almost no interest in the films themselves. Speaking to reporters, he can name-check a few famous actors and spout a couple clichés about the "magic" of film, but he otherwise steers clear of anything having to do with the creative process. Chairman Wang says he only goes to the movies once a year, to take his ninety-year-old mother out for a special treat.

In that aversion to messy questions about the creative process, Chairman Wang embodies one of the central tensions of China's film industry: the country wants to become a source of vibrant global culture, but it has pursued that goal primarily by buying up filmmaking hardware.

He kicked off that process in 2012, when he set out to buy the biggest chain of movie theaters in the world. One former Wanda employee told me that Chairman Wang approached the process with typical dryness: he asked an employee to print out a list of the world's largest movie theater chains, went down the list until he found the biggest privately owned company, and decided he would make it his own. That company was AMC Entertainment.

At the time, Wanda was virtually unknown in the United States, and negotiations with the American theater chain were on and off for over a year. But after AMC was forced to abandon its own plans for a public listing, Wanda finally sealed the deal. In May of 2012, Dalian Wanda Group acquired AMC Entertainment for $2.6 billion, the largest-ever overseas purchase by a private Chinese company at the time.[6] Chairman Wang had planted a flag in the U.S. film industry, and he was just getting started. In the ensuing years, AMC would buy out rival theater operators until it became the largest movie theater chain in the world, and Chairman Wang would set his sights on buying a leading Hollywood studio.

"His whole business philosophy is, 'I work with number one. I don't work with number two, and I don't actually work with anybody else. I want number one,'" an ex–Wanda employee told me. "He acts as though everything is his playground: the world, business deals—he just juggles them with perfect ease. But behind the scenes, it's a fucking grind."

HARDWARE AND SOFT POWER

Wang wasn't making these acquisitions in a political vacuum. Chinese president Hu Jintao had kicked off 2012 with a high-profile essay on the dangerous soft power of Western cultural imperialism.

"We must clearly see that international hostile forces are intensifying the strategic plot of westernizing and dividing China, and ideological and cultural fields are the focal areas of their long-term infiltration," Hu wrote.

In assessing China's cultural soft power, Hu was surprisingly blunt: "the West is strong, while we are weak."

Academics assessing soft power often focus on external or international soft power, e.g., what citizens of foreign countries think of a given country. Chinese leaders do have some ambitions in this space, frequently calling on artists to "tell China's story to the world." But for the Chinese Communist Party, the far more pressing problem was internal soft power: how did Chinese people feel about their own country and their own culture?

During the 1980s and 1990s, China's leaders cobbled together a positive answer to that question with a mix of rising standards of living and pumped-up nationalism. But when I moved to China in 2010, that unspoken social contract was showing signs of fraying. Rampant corruption, food safety scandals, and the 2011 high-speed train crash had undermined public faith in the government's competence. Chinese social media buzzed with ordinary people mocking or lashing out against their own government, all at a time when the Arab Spring was demonstrating the power of the internet to overthrow authoritarian governments.

A deep cynicism was seeping into Chinese society, a sense that China's economy may still be booming, but this just wasn't a place you wanted to live. Many families I knew were looking for a way out of the country.

According to one survey of Chinese millionaires, 60 percent were either considering emigrating or already in the process of doing so.[7]

Forced to pick a new home, many of them headed to China's top strategic rival. The United States had a grip on the imaginations of many Chinese people, the result of America's formidable international soft power. Taylor Swift and Lady Gaga blasted through the earbuds of Chinese tweens, and parents schemed for any way to get their children into American schools. China might be these families' past, but they hoped America would be their future.

RUMBLE IN THE BOX OFFICE

That same soft-power strength showed up in the Chinese box office. At the time Chairman Wang purchased AMC in 2012, the three highest grossing movies in the history of the Chinese box office were all Hollywood films: *Avatar*, *Transformers 3*, and *Titanic 3D*. And those record-breaking totals for American films came despite drastic attempts by the Chinese government to limit the success of foreign movies on Chinese soil.

China imposed a strict annual quota on foreign films, allowing the release of just twenty foreign films in the country each year on a revenue-sharing basis (Hollywood's preferred business model). Even for imported films that got a spot in that quota, the Chinese government did its best to kneecap their performance and funnel Chinese moviegoers toward domestic films. It imposed "blackout periods" on screening Hollywood films during the peak seasons of Chinese New Year and summer vacation. And it used control over release dates to pit the premiers of comparable Hollywood films against one another on the same weekend, hoping they would cannibalize each other's box office receipts.

And things appeared ready to go from bad to worse for domestic Chinese films beginning in 2012. An official United States complaint at the World Trade Organization had forced China to expand its quota for foreign films. In addition to a quota of twenty traditional films, China would now have to allow an additional fourteen Imax or 3-D films into the country. Following the expansion of the import quota, Chinese films earned less than 50 percent of the box office for the first time in several years.[8] The head of China's media regulation and censorship body declared it to be a "severe situation."

And it wasn't just culturally insecure bureaucrats who were nervous about the new quota. Filmmakers in China also worried that with even more slick Hollywood productions entering the market, domestic productions wouldn't stand a chance. Janet Yang was attending a festival at the time and found local artists gripped by a deep pessimism.

"Filmmakers in China were saying, 'Oh, we might as well just give up. We might as well just hang up our hats. Hollywood's going to just come and eat us alive. We'll never survive.'"

"A SHARK CALLED WANDA"[9]

If the 2012 purchase of AMC was Chairman Wang's first knock on Hollywood's door, then the 2013 groundbreaking for the "Oriental Movie Metropolis" was his coming out party. Spanning 900 acres in the coastal city of Qingdao and costing $8.2 billion, the complex was slated to include over 100,000 square feet of studios, the largest indoor and outdoor underwater film stages in China, a five-star hotel, a film museum, a movie cineplex, and a theme park to boot.[10] Touting the development as the "Hollywood of the East," Chairman Wang even announced plans to place an homage to the famous Hollywood sign on the scrubby hill overlooking the park.

But dizzying real estate developments are a dime a dozen in China. Making this ceremony special would require some help from Chairman Wang's new friends in Hollywood. His AMC acquisition had put him on the map in Los Angeles, earning him a reputation as a man with billions in the bank and vast networks within China. Now it was time to call on some of that Hollywood glamour to impress the folks back home.

The Wanda chairman gave his team a straightforward task: get three

A-list Hollywood celebrities to come to Qingdao for the announcement. Doing that would require throwing around some cash, and Wanda sent offers of $500,000 to Leonardo DiCaprio, John Travolta, and Nicole Kidman. As some of these celebrities began signing on the dotted line, Chairman Wang moved the goal posts: he now wanted six A-list celebrities. More invitations went out, including to executives from all the major Hollywood studios. (These business folks would have to pay their own way.)

Qingdao—a city best known for churning out the watery, low-alcohol Tsingtao beer—began preparing for an infusion of Hollywood glamour. Wanda hired a small army of young people to act as personal butlers for the foreign guests. The organizers bought an exceedingly wide red carpet and made sure both sides would be lined with Chinese people begging for autographs. A week before the event, Chairman Wang made a $20 million donation to the Academy of Motion Picture Arts and Sciences, the group behind the Academy Awards. The organization's president agreed to come to Qingdao.

Speaking on the day of the event, Chairman Wang confidently predicted that China would soon emerge as the world's largest market for films, with his company serving as China's ambassador in that process.

"Those in the world film industry who realize this first and are among the first to cooperate with China," Chairman Wang told attendees, "will be the first to reap the benefits."

THE AGE OF COPRODUCTIONS

How exactly was a Hollywood studio supposed to cooperate with a company like Wanda? Coproductions. If American and Chinese teams worked together on a movie, the product could be classified as a "coproduction" between the countries, a distinction that exempts the film from the Chinese government's quotas on imported movies. It also allows Hollywood studios to take a 43 percent cut of the box office revenue, far higher than the 25 percent allowed on imported films.[11]

For years, Hollywood had used coproductions as a technical work-around for the quota. They would take on some financing from a Chinese partner to make a purely American film, use that Chinese funding to qual-ify the film as a coproduction, and skirt the restrictions. But by 2013, Chi-nese regulators were demanding "real" coproductions: international movies that incorporated Chinese actors, plotlines, or production crews. These films were meant to give Chinese soft power a shot in the arm by placing the country's own celebrities and scenery at the heart of global blockbusters. China would get itself some much-desired face, and American movies could access the Chinese box office. It sounded like a win-win.

For everyone except the audience, that is. Coproductions were supposed to be a force for transpacific bridge building and cross-cultural creativity. Instead, most of them ended up taking on a Frankenstein-esque quality: including elements of American and Chinese culture, but at home in nei-ther one. They were birthed from an entirely inorganic process, one driven by the pursuit of profit and national pride rather than any allegiance to the story itself. Stephen Galloway, executive editor of *The Hollywood Reporter*, described the coproduction process as "the yoking together of heterogeneous forces to create a bastard child that no parent could love."

Instead of building real cross-cultural narratives from the ground up, many Hollywood studios simply took their all-American blockbusters and stuck the required "Chinese elements" somewhere in the script. Chinese actors would make nonsensical cameos. Plots would suddenly take detours that landed the main characters in a Chinese city. And those characters would take long, slow sips of Chinese beverage brands, making sure the logo faced squarely at the camera.

One of the most cringeworthy examples came from *Iron Man 3*, a movie that was shot as a coproduction but didn't even end up receiving the final designation from the authorities. The film's script had been entirely writ-ten by Disney and Marvel before being sent to the Chinese partner, DMG Entertainment. DMG responded by telling the L.A. team that it would need actual Chinese elements to earn the coproduction stamp, and so a Los

Angeles–based scriptwriter came back with several proposed scenes involving Chinese actors. The two teams finally settled on one that would give maximum face to China in minimum screen time: a Chinese doctor and his beautiful assistant would perform a crucial surgery to save Iron Man.

The surgeon is played by Wang Xueqi, a respected actor if not a household name in China, and the nurse by Fan Bingbing, the most famous actress in the country. As Fan enters Wang's office to announce Iron Man's arrival, Wang just happens to be pouring himself a glass of Yili brand red bean milk from a juice box. Ominous violins creep into the soundtrack while Fan and Wang ponder the gravity of the surgery ahead ("If something goes wrong, the whole world will lose a great hero . . ."). Robert Downey Jr., Gwyneth Paltrow, and Don Cheadle all make dialogue-free appearances, but the entire surgery sequence lasts less than thirty seconds. We're told that the surgery is a success. In less than four minutes of total screen time, China has given the whole world the gift of saving its greatest superhero.

The scene was jarringly out of place in the film, and at the last minute Marvel announced it would release two versions of the film: an international edition to be distributed around the globe, and a Chinese version with "specially prepared bonus footage made exclusively for the Chinese audience." Even Chinese audiences squirmed at the groan-inducing product placement and irrelevant additions. Watching Fan and Wang dip in and out of the story, one Chinese audience member commented, "It's like they wandered onto the wrong set. What is going on?" Instead of giving Chinese audiences a feeling of pride, the added scenes felt like when your parents force another group of kids to invite you out to play. Yeah, you're finally part of the game, but the whole process ends up feeling cheap and humiliating.

But gripes about the added scene didn't damage the film's stellar box office performance. *Iron Man 3* earned a record-breaking $21.5 million in its opening day in China and went on to become the second-highest grossing film of the year with $121.2 million.[12] If adding a couple cringe-inducing scenes was the price of admission to the Chinese market, Hollywood was more than happy to pay up.

"THE PANDER EXPRESS"

In this awkward dance between China and Hollywood, the Chinese government has served as both matchmaker and chaperone: it first forced the two sides into an unnatural partnership, and then strictly policed the results of that union.

Coproductions had to proceed through China's full domestic censorship process, with scripts vetted in advance and representatives from China's media regulator often visiting the set itself and giving notes. Some filmmakers even believed that the censors placed moles within the production team, keeping an eye out in case the production deviated from the approved script. But for some in Hollywood, that constant monitoring by Chinese authorities was actually seen as a blessing: if you brought the censors into the filmmaking process, it reduced the risk of a movie being rejected upon completion.

Films that seek to enter China as foreign imports face a trickier task. China's censorship process can be extremely opaque: some films are given conditional permission to be released in China provided they make certain cuts, while others are rejected without any explanation or opportunity for remedy. That leaves studio executives the task of self-censoring before submission, trying to guess what scenes or bits of stray dialogue might lower their chances of earning one of the limited spots for imported films. It's a process that comedian Stephen Colbert ruthlessly skewered in a segment he called "The Pander Express."

The kitchen of the Pander Express was opened up to public scrutiny when hacked emails by Sony executives leaked to the public. In the leaked files, executives discussed what parts of the Adam Sandler movie *Pixels* might raise red flags. The executives went back and forth over a scene in which aliens blow a hole in the Great Wall of China: would the Film Bureau take offense at the desecration of a national treasure, or would it be permitted because the film also depicts the destruction of the Washington Monument and the Taj Mahal? The emails also suggested cutting dialogue in which the president of the United States and a CIA officer debate whether China might be the perpetrator of an attack using mysterious new technology.

"Changing the China elements to another country should be a relatively easy fix," wrote Steven O'Dell, president of Sony Pictures Releasing International. "There is only downside to leaving the film as it is. Recommendation is to change all versions as if we only change the China version, we set ourselves up for the press to call us out for this when bloggers invariably compare the versions and realize we changed the China setting just to pacify that market."

Sony executives ended up cutting all references to China in the film. For the scene in which leaders debated who was behind the mysterious attack, the dialogue was changed to speculate whether it was Russia, Iran, or even Google. *Pixels* ended up making it into the 2015 import quota, earning $15 million in the country.[13]

But the ripple effects of this kind of censorship stretch far beyond films that the studios hope to release in China. Chinese authorities have shown that they have an expansive view of Chinese interests and a long memory when it comes to slights. The Tibet-focused films of the 1990s were never intended for the Chinese market, and yet they meant the blacklisting of the entire studios behind them. Today, no major studio will participate in a project that could be in any way perceived as casting China in a negative light. Looking at the geopolitics of today, one would fully expect the next Bond villain to be Chinese, but as one industry analyst remarked to me, "We're not going to see a Chinese Bond villain for a very, very long time."

For now, Chairman Wang—with his villainous widow's peak and billion-dollar swagger—would have to do.

THE RED CARPET TO NOWHERE

On the surface, the groundbreaking ceremony for the Chairman's movie metropolis looked like a tantalizing glimpse into our cross-cultural cinematic future, a world of movies without borders. Leonardo DiCaprio—beloved in

China for his role in *Titanic*—flew into Qingdao on his private jet. Nicole Kidman offered a tentative *"Nihao"* to the screaming fans. Executives from Sony and Disney schlepped across the Pacific to discuss coproduction agreements. Officials in China's Film Bureau even came out to mingle with the people whose works of art they would be censoring.

And standing at the center of it all was Chairman Wang, the ringmaster of a global entertainment circus made for the twenty-first century.

But something wasn't quite right. A few probing questions or a peek behind the event's glamorous billboards revealed a dearth of substance and some suspect logic. If Chairman Wang really wanted to get into filmmaking, why did he buy a movie theater chain? Spending on online entertainment was booming, but Chairman Wang had poured billions of dollars into the one part of the film industry that looked ready to die a slow death at the hands of the internet. And if you're going to buy movie theaters, why do it in the United States, a shrinking market for movie tickets, while the Chinese box office is growing at 40 percent each year?

Rumors abounded as to Chairman Wang's true endgame. In 2012, China was going through a once-a-decade leadership transition, a time when many of China's top leaders would step down and a couple major ones would fall on corruption charges. It's a nerve-racking period for many Chinese businesses, but Chairman Wang appeared particularly vulnerable this time around. He had made his early real estate money in the northern city of Dalian at a time when Dalian's mayor was Bo Xilai, a rising political star with ambitions to be China's top leader. But in 2012, Bo was taken down on corruption charges in one of the most dramatic political scandals in recent memory, and anyone who had risen alongside him was suddenly considered suspect. On top of the Bo Xilai connection, an investigation by *The New York Times* found that between 2007 and 2011, Chairman Wang's company had sold shares now worth over a billion dollars to companies associated with the family members of China's top leaders. That tangled web of dark money had insiders asking, Was the AMC deal really about getting into the entertainment business, or was it a convenient excuse to stash a couple billion dollars offshore should a hasty departure from China be necessary?

Others saw a more pedestrian logic to Chairman Wang's entertainment overtures: more real estate. President Hu Jintao's 2012 call to boost China's cultural industries and soft power had sent government officials around the country scrambling for ways to fulfill the big boss's mandate. One easy way to do that was to transfer public land to companies promising to develop "cultural industries," and Chairman Wang was more than ready to take up the banner of Chinese culture if it meant good deals on public land. As Disney prepared to open the gates at Shanghai Disneyland, he pledged to open fifteen to twenty theme parks dedicated to Chinese culture around the country.

"Disney really shouldn't have come to China," Wang told a state-run television station a month before the American theme park opened its gates in Shanghai. "The frenzy of Mickey Mouse and Donald Duck, the era of blindly following them, has passed. . . . Disneyland is fully built on American culture. We place importance on local culture."

One former Wanda employee told me that Chairman Wang merely saw culture as a "shiny, new, politically appropriate wrapper" for buying more land and building bigger real estate developments. It was an attitude reflected in how the Chairman acted during the event. Despite having many of the world's most powerful entertainment figures on hand, Chairman Wang spent most of his time chatting with officials from the local Qingdao government. These were the people who controlled access to the land on which the Chairman intended to build his $8 billion Oriental Movie Metropolis. Construction was already partly under way, but details on tax breaks and land transfers still needed to be hammered out. Parading the likes of Leonardo DiCaprio through Qingdao would be a major boost to the Chairman's bargaining position vis-à-vis government officials, both on the Movie Metropolis and for dozens of other mega-developments he was plotting around China. Chairman Wang's total lack of interest in actually making movies found symbolic expression in the red carpets at the Qingdao event.

"[The Hollywood stars] walked two red carpets in one day, and each red carpet ended with 'Thanks, you may get in your car and go back to the hotel now,'" the former Wanda employee told me. "There was no awards ceremony or movie premier. It was a red carpet to nowhere."

"WHO IS THE CEO OF HOLLYWOOD?"

A shared passion for making money may have brought together Chairman Wang and the Hollywood elite, but similarly sized egos often drove them apart. Both sides would pay lip service to "a new kind of cross-cultural storytelling" and "truly global films," but the reality has been far more fraught. Each side has something the other side wants, and both sides believe that what they bring to the table is more valuable. Yuan Yuan, a producer with experience in both Los Angeles and China, described the coproduction process to me as a battle of wills between two obstinate negotiators.

"Companies in China often say, 'We have money, so you have to do things our way,'" she told me at a café in Beijing. "And then companies in Hollywood come back saying, 'We're Hollywood, so you have to do things our way.'"

Beyond private-sector struggles over control, many China–Hollywood ventures involving the Chinese government have suffered from mutual ignorance about the other side. Many unsuspecting Hollywood executives have watched their projects sink into the abyss of China's bureaucracy, never to emerge again. And many of those Chinese officials—accustomed to the rigid ordering of a bureaucratic org chart—have a hard time grasping amorphous concepts like "Silicon Valley" and "Hollywood." One international businessman described to me a 2008 meeting with China's deputy minister of culture, in which the senior official opened with a simple but totally misguided question: "Who is the CEO of Hollywood?"

On a deeper level, these transpacific cultural partnerships have suffered from a fundamental misalignment of goals, one that can only be papered over for so long. Janet Yang worked as a producer on multiple China–U.S. coproductions, including a Chinese version of *High School Musical*, but found the two sides to be talking past each other.

"There's a lot of mutual projection: China has a Hollywood dream and Hollywood has a China dream. China wants respect—they want their content to be seen."

And Hollywood's China dream?

"Cash."

DREAMS DEFERRED

It took a few years, but Chairman Wang's Hollywood ending slowly came unraveled. He was able to get off one more major acquisition in Los Angeles, a $3.5 billion purchase of Legendary Entertainment in 2016, and financed a handful of films, such as the boxing drama *Southpaw*. But his oft-stated ambition of acquiring one of the five major studios and winning an Oscar went unfulfilled. Paramount Pictures turned down his $4.9 billion bid for 49 percent of the company, and strict new capital controls imposed by the Chinese government in 2017 killed a billion-dollar offer for the production company behind the Golden Globes.[14] In August of 2017, the Chinese central government formally announced a ban on "irrational" overseas investments, specifically real estate, hotels, and entertainment—the Chairman's bread and butter.

It wasn't just the financials that were falling through. The Great White Hope of China–U.S. coproductions also bombed. *The Great Wall*, a monster flick starring Matt Damon and directed by Zhang Yimou, looked like the best shot the two countries had at a cultural and commercial success in both markets. But the film fell flat in both countries, suffering from stilted dialogue and the unshakable sense that it was born out of the logic of a financial spreadsheet. Financed by Universal Pictures and Wanda (through newly acquired Legendary), the movie was the highest-budget production ever shot entirely in China. It ended up losing an estimated $75 million.[15]

"You're trying to appeal to everyone, and you're not compelling enough to appeal to anyone," one executive connected to the project told *The Hollywood Reporter*. "It feels like Esperanto."

The Great Wall felt like the nail in the coffin for the gilded era of China–Hollywood coproductions. Watching the film on opening night at a nearly empty theater in downtown Oakland, it was clear that if I wanted to find a model for Chinese and American cultural exchange that actually worked, I'd need to look elsewhere.

And so I headed to Shanghai Disneyland.

"AUTHENTICALLY DISNEY, DISTINCTLY CHINESE"

The question of Mickey Mouse's nationality is still bouncing around my head as I walk through the Gardens of Imagination and toward the Enchanted Storybook Castle. In spite of the heat, the park feels like a comfortable combination of two familiar settings: a bustling Chinese city and an intricately landscaped American theme park. If I plug my ears and just scan the horizon, I could be in Anaheim. If I close my eyes and just listen to the chatter around me, I could be at my favorite park in Beijing.

But behind that seamless cultural mingling were grueling international negotiations that stretched over a decade. Disney CEO Bob Iger relentlessly lobbied CCP officials from the Shanghai government to the Ministry of Culture and all the way up to President Xi Jinping. The resulting agreement saw Disney making a series of concessions, many of them financial, unheard of in its other global ventures.

The Shanghai government effectively owns a full 57 percent of the theme park via Shanghai Shendi Group, a state-owned enterprise formed specifically for the purpose of partnering with Disney on the venture.[16] Chinese officials had veto power over the rides in the park and used that power to push for more rides that were unique to the Shanghai park. Shendi also maintained ownership over much of the surrounding land, aiming to make the park one part of a larger tourism ecosystem that will drive local economic development.

In addition to profit sharing, Disney leadership pledged to use Disney's platform to "introduce more about China to the world," and to infuse the Shanghai park with Chinese culture. In promoting the project, Iger summed up the philosophy with an oft-repeated slogan: making the park "authentically Disney, and distinctly Chinese."

Some changes were obvious. The park's signature boulevard, a collection of old-timey shops that are a staple of Disney theme parks around the world, has been renamed from "Main Street, USA" to "Mickey Avenue." (Extraterritoriality is a particularly sensitive subject in Shanghai, a city with a history of colonial occupation and foreign territorial "concessions.") Food and concessions were another easy area for localization. The park's Wandering Moon Restaurant is built in the style of a traditional teahouse and is designed "to honor the restless, creative spirit of China's wandering poets." It features local Chinese dishes served for kids on plates shaped like Mickey Mouse's head.

But those delicately negotiated nods to Chinese culture feel far away as I dive into the park's dizzying array of attractions. I explore the Enchanted Storybook Castle (the largest Disney castle in the world) and wait in line for a picture with Captain America, a square-jawed New Yorker about my age. I ride the Winnie the Pooh Honey Pot Spin, take another picture embracing the bear himself, and eat an overpriced lunch of "Puff Ball and Vegetables" at the Tangled Tree Tavern.

"WO JIAO KEVIN!"

Eventually, the broiling Shanghai sun drives me toward an indoor attraction dedicated to the 2002 animated film *Lilo & Stitch*, about a Hawaiian girl who bonds with an adopted extraterrestrial pet she names Stitch. I've never seen the movie or been to Hawaii, and I would guess 90 percent of my fellow attendees are in the same boat. We huddle in a hallway while a smiling Disney guide gets everyone up to speed on the foreign culture and mischievous alien we're about to interact with.

"When Stitch landed on Earth he was in Hawaii, so when he greets you he'll be saying 'Hello' in Hawaiian," she tells the assembled children in

Mandarin. "Does anyone know how to say hello in Hawaiian? *Aloha*. Say it with me!"

"Aloha!" the kids scream in unison.

As we're ushered into a small auditorium, a kindergarten-age boy in front of me is shaking his mom's arm at the elbow, chanting, "*A-lo-ha! A-lo-ha! A-lo-ha!*" while she attempts to type on her phone with the other hand. We take our seats facing a big screen designed to look like the dashboard of a spaceship.

The cartoon Stitch (Chinese name: *Shi-di-qi*) appears on-screen guiding the ship, looking like a mix between a koala bear and a puppy. He greets everyone with an "Aloha" that earns a raucous chorus of the same word from the crowd. The animated Stitch starts to interact with the kids, picking out audience members by their clothing, asking what their name is, and finding some reason to tease them. Regardless of which audience member Stitch has asked the name of, the boy one row in front of me bounces up and down shouting, "*Wo jiao* Kevin! *Wo jiao* Kevin!"—"My name is Kevin! My name is Kevin!"

Stitch asks the moms out on dates, and when cameras facing the audience catch an adult picking his nose, Stitch displays a photo of the perpetrator midpick on the screen of his flight deck. He has everyone in the room cracking up. Kids who ten minutes earlier had never heard of Hawaii or Stitch are now whipped into a frenzy by this big-eared alien.

When Stitch speeds off for some intergalactic mission, we are escorted out through an exit that feeds directly into a shop full of themed merchandise. A pair of middle school girls are bear-hugging big stuffed Stitches, eyes closed and chanting, "Shi-di-qi! Shi-di-qi!" Chinese parents who are notoriously strict with their kids' schoolwork are often pushovers when it comes to spoiling those kids with toys. The shopping bins begin to fill up.

Heading back out to the afternoon heat, my phone buzzes. My former coworker Helen has gotten back to me with some WeChat videos of her young students' answer to my question from earlier. In each one, she points the phone at a couple of kids and poses the question to them in Chinese: "Is Mickey Mouse an American or Chinese?" In one video, a pair of girls look quizzically at each other, pausing for a moment before one slowly says, "American . . ." In another clip, one precocious girl seems to have intuited the politically correct answer: "He's an American *and* he's Chinese. That way the things he creates are equal for people all over the world."

STEAMBOAT WILLIE AND CHAIRMAN WANG

I spend the rest of the afternoon bouncing between rides and respite in the shade, finally getting a much-needed dousing with water during a live performance of "Under the Sea" in front of the castle. Throughout the park I find a few more superficial nods to Chinese culture: Mickey and Minnie in their retro-Chinese outfits, and a set of a wall displays that match a Disney character to each animal of the Chinese Zodiac (Tigger for the Year of the Tiger, Remy from *Ratatouille* for the Year of the Rat).

But the people here didn't pay 300 RMB to look at wall displays of their own culture's zodiac. They came for the magic that Disney has proven itself uniquely capable of conjuring, a particular kind of storytelling alchemy that manages to be commercially lucrative while still feeling organic. Chairman Wang can gripe all he wants about Mickey Mouse and Donald Duck, but the fact is they still reliably put smiles on faces in a way his own company can't.

In many ways, it's an unfair fight. Walt Disney gave Mickey Mouse his debut in 1928's *Steamboat Willie*. His company spent the next five decades building up an unparalleled stockpile of intellectual property, as well as deep in-house knowledge about creating and commercializing lovable characters. During that time, China careened from civil war to invasion to famine to Cultural Revolution. CCP leaders love to reference China's 5,000-year history of rich indigenous culture. What they mention less often are Mao's violent campaigns to beat that culture out of Chinese people, or the fact that the modern People's Republic has had just two generations of artists who have been allowed to create anything for commercial consumption. Given that history, it would be an absolute miracle if China had managed to produce a Disney of its own by this point.

In the meantime, Shanghai Disneyland offers the Chinese government a decent compromise. Sure, opening the door to Disney might let in some foreign cultural "flies," but it also holds plenty of tangible benefits for China. Running a park like this on Chinese soil drives tourism, introduces local creators to industry best practices, puts money in government coffers, and puts smiles on the faces of Chinese kids. That's a deal the CCP is willing to take, for now at least.

———

The sun has gone down, and the oppressive heat of the day is just starting to lift as I follow the families streaming through the exits. Outside the official Disney store, villagers from the surrounding countryside swim against the stream of the crowds, furtively trying to sell knockoff Mickey Mouse ears out of a backpack for one-tenth of the prices inside.

Soaring orchestral music still booms from loudspeakers, and fireworks light up the sky behind us as we trudge toward shuttles and parked cars. Kids who ran into the park screaming this morning are being carried out, sleeping on the shoulders of parents who would love to be doing the exact same thing.

HENGDIAN RISING

The demise of Chairman Wang's Hollywood schemes hasn't meant China's film industry surrendered to Disney outright. Coproductions may have flopped, but domestic Chinese films have largely filled the void. And in place of China's (once) richest man, it's been a scrappy rural town that has carried the torch for Chinese films, putting up some of the most effective resistance to the Americanization of the Chinese box office. That town is Hengdian, a place that has transformed itself from a center for black-market silkworm production into China's gritty hub for homegrown cinema. So, a day after sweating it out at Disneyland, I head off to explore "the Hollywood of China."

For a place that aspires to be the movie capital of the largest country in the world, Hengdian is surprisingly hard to get to. The city has no airport and even lacks a train station. Coming from Shanghai, I take a high-speed train headed southwest to the wholesale trading hub of Yiwu (slogan: "A Big World for Small Commodities") and then wait in a steaming-hot long-distance bus station for the ninety-minute ride out to Hengdian.

The town is located on a flat piece of land between the scraggly green hills of Zhejiang Province, a region with a reputation for producing razor-sharp private businessmen. Hengdian owes its rise to one of those men: Xu Wenrong. In 1975, with Mao still ruling the country up in Beijing, Xu opened an illegal factory for harvesting silkworm cocoons. It was a gutsy move, one that easily could have earned him a stint in a Maoist "reeducation through labor" camp. Instead, it turned out to be the first step on Xu's road to building a billion-dollar conglomerate. As China opened up its economy in the 1980s, Xu's Hengdian Group diversified into dozens of industries: hotels, metals, semiconductors, and much more.

But the company and city took an unexpected turn in 1995. That year, Chinese director Xie Jin was desperately casting about for a place to shoot *The Opium War*, a major propaganda film about China's loss of Hong Kong to British colonialists. The film was scheduled to be released on the day Hong Kong returned to China in 1997, but the director couldn't find any-where to shoot nineteenth-century street scenes. After meeting the director, Xu offered to build those streets from scratch in his hometown. He mobi-lized the city around the effort, scavenging for suitably worn-out stones from surrounding villages and recreating storefronts from Canton of the 1840s.

The shooting and the film were both a success, leading other filmmakers to descend on Hengdian with their own requests for replicas. Lucky for Xu, Chinese film and TV shows constantly retread the same historical terri-tory: patriotic propaganda films about China's World War II fight against Japan and imperial dramas set in a couple of different ancient palaces. Xu poured his fortune into building more historical carbon copies, and Hengdian World Studios was born. Use of the massive replicas is offered free of charge for film crews, with Xu earning money off the stream of tourists who visit the replicas, eat at his restaurants, and stay in his hotels.

"COME TO HENGDIAN!"

Today, Hengdian is an odd mix of big-screen dreams and rural Chinese grit. It aspires to create the fantastical: movies and TV shows that capture the imagination—and disposable income—of over a billion Chinese people. But Hengdian's approach to that process of creation is the opposite of its competitors', both in China and California. People in the U.S. like to tell a feel-good story about the sources of Hollywood's global dominance: it grew out of America's unparalleled personal freedoms and mastery of the art of visual storytelling. While Chairman Wang attempted to buy himself a dose of that movie magic outright, Hengdian is trying to build it brick by literal brick. It's a pitch captured in an English pamphlet I found at Hengdian World Studios, one that feels more suited to a factory town churning out textiles than an incubator for global culture: "Come to Hengdian, with lower cost and less efforts!"

Even if you never set foot on a film set, Hengdian can be a strange place to walk around. Many small Chinese cities haven't yet had their rough edges sanded off, and you'll see things that have long since vanished from cosmopolitan metropolises like Beijing: dentists smoking while working on patients, or twelve-year-olds driving cargo trucks. As a mecca for wannabe movie stars, Hengdian can feel even a little more off-kilter than your average third-tier city.

Walking from the bus station to my hotel, I watch a grown man wearing a black-and-white checkered cape dance in the middle of a five-way intersection, belting out techno-pop karaoke in hopes of getting "discovered." Sitting on the faux-velvet couch of my hotel lobby, I watch a drunk guy with his T-shirt rolled up over his belly pass out next to me, unlit cigarette still dangling from his mouth. Later that evening I'll come across a ribbon-cutting ceremony for a new jewelry store. At the event, female models wearing nothing but paint on their upper bodies are paraded around, while the MC throws red envelopes stuffed with cash into the grasping hands of the crowd.

But for all its strangeness, Hengdian is a city that latched onto the right industry at the right time. The explosion of the Chinese box office, and the proliferation of online TV shows, has ratcheted up demand for everything Hengdian has to offer: premade film sets, tens of thousands of costumes, millions of props, and a whole lot of people willing to work for very little money. Business is booming, and employees from Hengdian World Studios have their hands full juggling the shooting schedules for dozens of crews. When I ask for permission to shadow some film crews, they arrange for me to drop in on some first-century palace intrigue.

OF EMPERORS AND CENSORS

Two thousand and ninety-one years have passed, but the fluttering of a paper fan is still this emperor's best bet at relief from the August heat. Reclining against the walls of a pagoda, twenty-nine-year-old Lu Yi is trying to dry the sweat on his face without smudging his makeup before the next scene. Lu and I were born in the same year (1988) and worked in the same industry (journalism) before his life took a turn toward midlevel stardom. A strong jaw frames his pretty-boy features that Chinese women love in their movie stars, and after leaving his job at a state-run radio station, Lu turned parts in TV commercials in Shanghai into some leading roles in Hengdian films.

Today he is portraying a decadent emperor from the year 74 B.C. who was deposed after just twenty-nine days on the throne. I watch as he strides morosely around the outdoor passageways of the palace, gazing wistfully off into the distance. Around this meditative monarch swirls the controlled chaos of a film shoot, a tangle of microphone wires, conflicting orders, and fussy makeup artists all trying to ensure that the view through the camera lens is without a blemish.

The project is partially funded by the government of Jiangxi Province, where archaeologists recently uncovered the featured emperor's tomb. Their hope is that the movie, set to be released online, can drum up tourism for the site.

Standing out in this genre will be a challenge. Every year Hengdian plays host to several dozen similar TV shows and movies, overwrought historical dramas about tragic emperors, scheming eunuchs, and backstabbing concubines. To a foreigner—even one who understands the language—these shows blur together into one endless stream of overexposed shots and hyperbolic acting played on restaurant TVs across the country. But every once in a while, one of these manages to break through the monotony, winning over tens of millions of viewers with well-crafted plots—or by showing a little extra skin.

Such was the case with the 2014 television series *The Empress of China*, a retelling of the life of Wu Zetian, China's only female emperor. Filmed in Hengdian and starring Fan Bingbing as Empress Wu, the show gave generous screen time to the low-cut costumes of Empress Wu and other imperial consorts. But after just a week on the air, the producers abruptly suspended the show for "technical reasons." Four days later the show resumed broadcasting, but this time with many wide shots cropped to become close-ups showing only the actors' faces. China's censors apparently had second thoughts after initially approving the program and demanded it be pulled until Fan's cleavage was cropped out of the frame.

The episode was both silly and revealing. When Americans think about censorship in Chinese film, it's often in terms of the politically charged films that are banned in China and screened to acclaim abroad. Those limitations are very real, and artists aiming to expose the dark corners of Chinese society often run into a brick wall.

But in a place like Hengdian, the targets of censorship are both more pedestrian and more unpredictable. In the five years I lived in China, the country's media censors nixed a bizarre selection of topics: time travel in TV series, celebrity children on reality shows, same-sex intimacy on screen, and Fan Bingbing's cleavage. During the run-up to the 2016 U.S. presidential election, the authorities also warned against "putting stars, billionaires, or internet celebrities on pedestals."

The common threads uniting those forbidden topics are thin: squeamishness around sexuality (especially anything outside of heterosexuality) and a notion that media regulators must use their power to instill "healthy" and "socialist" values in viewing audiences. It's a vague mission, one that keeps everyone involved guessing. Chinese creators who steer clear of social commentary are usually allowed to see their projects through, but they must accept a certain level of randomness as to what topics may suddenly become taboo.

For now, the crew in Hengdian is far more concerned with getting the required shots in the can so they can break for lunch. The director has stripped off his T-shirt to reveal a tattoo of a tiger on his left breast. A production assistant appears stuck to the hip of the cinematographer, one arm extending to hold a large black umbrella that shades the camera. As the sun nears its peak, my host for the day, a friendly twentysomething guy from Hengdian who studied in Australia, assures me we should move on to the next set. We pile back into a car and crank the air-conditioning as high as it will go.

THE RISE OF THE KITCHEN-SINK COMEDIES

Looking back, 2012 was both the peak of Hollywood's domination of the Chinese market and the beginning of the rise of local Chinese films. That was the year President Hu Jintao delivered his dire warning about Western cultural "infiltration," and also the point when Hollywood blockbusters held the top three spots of all time in the Chinese box office. And things weren't looking up for Chinese filmmakers: many saw that year's expansion in the number of imported films as the final straw that would break the back of the country's nascent film industry.

But from 2012 through 2018, something unexpected happened: six of the seven annual champions of the Chinese box office were Chinese movies.

During that same period, total box office revenue more than tripled, and local films took home over 50 percent of the box office every single year. Those numbers should be taken with a grain (really, a chunk) of salt: China's film industry is notorious for fudging box office statistics and manipulating release dates to give a boost to Chinese movies. Fuzzy math aside, the trend also represents an organic enthusiasm for homegrown films, movies made in the native language and in tune with the tastes and eccentricities of Chinese viewers.

It all kicked off in December of 2012 with the release of *Lost in Thailand*, a low-budget buddy comedy set in the Southeast Asian country of its title. To the handful of Americans who watched the film (it grossed a whopping $57,387 in the U.S.), it looked like a messy mix of slapstick humor and overacting. But Chinese audiences loved it, and the film caught fire. It quickly became the first domestic film to gross over 1 billion RMB. By the end of its run, it had become the highest-earning film ever in China, surpassing *Transformers* and *Titanic 3D* in the process.

Why the gap between tastes in the two countries? For one thing, "comedy doesn't travel." It's an entertainment truism that while action films tend to play similarly across markets, humor is more culturally specific and thus often confined to its country of creation. A string of Chinese box office champions seemed to confirm that trend. The top-grossing Chinese films for 2012–16 were all some variety of screwball comedy, and none made substantial sums outside of Chinese-speaking markets.

But aside from language-specific puns, the movies also had plotlines that felt maddeningly chaotic to Western viewers. They combine slapstick stunts, animated monsters, gross-out humor, and exhausting action sequences. The result is a tangled web of competing plotlines, some of which are hastily resolved and some of which are simply abandoned. It's a kitchen-sink approach to filmmaking and a perfect on-screen manifestation of the zeitgeist that animates Hengdian itself.

Take Hong Kong director Stephen Chow's film *Journey to the West: Conquering the Demons*. The movie was shot here in Hengdian, and in 2013 it overtook *Lost in Thailand* to briefly hold the title of highest grossing movie ever in China. It drew its title from a Chinese legend—a monk and magical Monkey King seeking out Buddhist sutras—but was far from a somber ode to Chinese traditional culture.

Instead, it careened between suggestive slapstick comedy, battles against poorly animated monsters, and frequent dramatic digressions. Sandwiched between the over-the-top action sequences are some real gems of offbeat comedic dialogue and even the occasional bit of social and political satire. But director Stephen Chow appears to feel the need to bracket his best material with animated explosions on either end, stuffing the movie with high-velocity visuals, afraid that otherwise the audience will leave feeling they didn't get their money's worth. The story's central villain is abruptly captured with almost half an hour left in the movie. From there, the story takes a few wandering turns before culminating (spoiler alert!) when an intergalactic Buddha larger than Earth itself appears out of nowhere to smite the new bad guy by pressing his giant palm through the planet's exosphere. By the time the credits roll, I find myself saying, "Really? *That* was the top movie in China all year?"

Hengdian's kitchen-sink comedies might leave Westerners scratching their heads, but they've also helped Chinese filmmakers wrestle ticket sales back from Hollywood. They've given Chinese viewers something to chew on, local filmmakers something to work on, and maybe laid the groundwork for the next phase of Chinese popular films.

SHADOWS AND ECHOES

The journey to the next set has launched us almost two millennia forward in time and taken us a few rungs down on the socioeconomic ladder. Along with its collection of painstakingly reproduced palaces, Hengdian also has a variety of smaller production sets, old temples, or classrooms that can fill in the gaps for more varied productions.

We've come to one such set nestled in the nearby hills, an ambiguous compound of dusty yellow buildings that could be slotted into a few different centuries. The production under way today is a kung fu flick set in the 1930s, a tumultuous period in which various martial arts traditions struggled to adapt to the demands of modern combat. The film is titled simply *Wuzhe*, meaning "Warrior" or "Fighter." But they've picked a different title for it in English: *Shadows and Echoes*.

Production assistants hush us as we tiptoe through the back door of one of the buildings. Soft yellow light pours in from the opposite windows, illuminating wooden buckets and woven baskets positioned around an old-fashioned workshop. A single rope stretches from wall to wall, dangling strings of red peppers and garlic bulbs along the way. At the center of the room stands a sturdy man with close-cropped hair and a slight goatee. He's wearing what looks like a grocer's apron.

Our half of the room is crowded with a camera crew and two young men in blue uniforms. To their left is another man dressed in a black wide-brimmed hat and a matching black floor-length jacket with white cuffs. He is facing away from us with two hands clasped behind his back, but you can sense a certain grace and composure in his posture. One of the production assistants maneuvers around the man, walking around the room and fanning what appears to be dust or smoke into the air to lend some drama to the visuals. Once he has hustled back out of the shot, a man with a walkie-talkie orders the camera turned on, and someone slaps the clapboard.

Suddenly the man in the grocer's outfit is lifted straight into the air. He's wearing a harness that's hooked into a rope-and-pulley system, and a team of three men in T-shirts have all put their full weight on the other end of that rope. Once the grocer is about four feet off the ground, he takes hold of a loop of rope hanging from the ceiling and positions it around his neck. The pulley team wavers slightly, and our grocer calls out as the rope digs into his throat. They recover, pulling him a few inches higher.

"Three, two, one, *kaishi!*"

The man in the black suit and the two in blue uniforms take a few slow paces toward the hanging man, with the camera sliding forward on a track. The black-suited man speaks a few quiet lines to the grocer as his suspended body spins in a slow circle. A crackling walkie-talkie breaks the tension.

"Okay, cut, cut."

The grocer removes the rope from his throat and is lowered back to the ground.

"Let's try this," the walkie-talkie commands. "Before he goes up, let's put someone there to hold on to his feet so he doesn't go spinning so much."

"I'M READY FOR WHEN THAT MOMENT COMES"

After a couple more lifts and lowers of the grocer, the shot is in the bank. An employee from the Hengdian Group introduces me to the man in the black suit, Ruan Shengwen (pronounced roughly "Roo-ahn Shung-when"). He changes from his heavy costume into a gray T-shirt, and we settle into a pair of camping chairs in the next building. Tall and handsome, Ruan has soft features but a gaze that might land him more roles as an antihero than a heartthrob. For today's role he is sporting a curt black mustache.

Ruan originally trained as a professional dancer, a foundation that gave him a certain grace and presence on camera. A decade ago, Ruan pivoted into acting just as China's entertainment industries were taking off. Asked to describe his career since then, he uses four words: "High-high, low-low." He was offered a major role in a television series at his first audition but quickly felt that he was out of his depth in the new field. He took on smaller roles in movies and TV shows, trying to apply the same discipline he learned as a dancer to honing this craft. Ruan's major break came in 2015 when he played a bushy-eyebrowed villain in a popular historical fantasy series set in the tenth century.

The success of that series finally got Ruan to a place where he can exercise more artistic judgment in choosing roles. He's modeled for beer and car commercials, but in conversation it's clear that he is someone who takes film seriously as an art form. We discuss how the voracious demand at the box office has impacted his own work and the type of films that get made.

"This phase of making highly commercial films is inevitable," he tells me. "We all believe that it's part of a process, but the most important thing is that Chinese audiences can be more thoughtful in the way they appreciate films. If that happens then the value placed on art will go up, and we'll see the coming together of both commerce and art."

That phrase, "a process," comes up repeatedly in our conversation. He uses it to describe the widening cultural horizons of China's middle class, the role that the censors play in policing content, and the evolution of Chinese film in relation to Hollywood.

"I'm not afraid to say that I study Hollywood, or even that I imitate parts of it. This is part of a process: every master of a craft goes through this phase."

Sitting in the chairs, I listen as Ruan and a producer describe the genesis of the current project. Ruan was working on another film outside of Beijing when the producers sent him the script for *Shadows and Echoes*. After giving it a read, he told them that he thought it could work, and that afternoon the director and a producer drove out to meet him on set.

"We didn't talk too much about the script," he recalls. "We talked more about what it is we wanted to do for the film industry, and the effort we're willing to spend doing it."

He says that a shared desire to move Chinese film forward is what unites this production team as it is putting in long hours in the Hengdian heat.

Duties on set have pulled the producer away, and I don't want to take up all of Ruan's downtime. But before getting up to leave, I ask him: After ten years of ups and downs in the industry, do you still have a dream that you're chasing?

"My dream is that the Chinese market can be more thoughtful in the way it looks at art, and I believe this time is just around the corner. Right now I'm just trying to prepare myself, to make sure I'm ready for when that moment comes."

———

I'm happy to be back in an air-conditioned car after ten hours shuttling between sets. The driver is an executive from the Hengdian Group, and as he chauffeurs me from one ancient palace to the next, we talk about the relationship between Hollywood and Hengdian. I've been pressing him on the questions that are front-of-mind for most American visitors to this town: Won't audiences get bored if all your movies take place in the same buildings? Doesn't censorship make it hard to produce good stories? And why not invest more in technology rather than physical sets? He looks at me quizzically before answering in the kind of slow, simple sentences one uses to explain things to a child.

"To make movies you need all these visual things going on in the background. In Hollywood they use all these computers and special effects to create them. But why would you spend all that money to do it on a computer, when we could just build the real thing from scratch?"

That rhetorical question has me stumped. It's an approach that would make no sense to the kings of global culture in Hollywood. But it has a certain logic in a place like Hengdian, where cheap labor is abundant but the more abstract aspects of visual storytelling are in short supply. And it's kind of been working.

THE WOLF OF OUR STREET

I get my first glimpse of a new breed of Chinese blockbuster on my first night in Hengdian. I've seen a few headlines about *Wolf Warrior 2*—articles calling it "the Chinese Rambo" or deriding it as jingoistic CCP propaganda—but I've intentionally avoided reading reviews or analyses. I want to first experience the movie in a Chinese theater with a Chinese audience. I book a ticket on my phone and hop on a shared bike that I pedal across Hengdian.

One fact about the film that I haven't been able to overlook is its unprecedented box office showing: over the course of 2017, *Wolf Warrior 2* will set a new all-time record of $857 million at the Chinese box office.[17] That's the second most that any film has ever made in a single market, just behind the $936 million haul for *Star Wars: Episode VII* in the North American market. The difference between these two movies is that while *Wolf Warrior 2* will take in around $4 million outside of China, *Star Wars* earned over $1 *billion* outside of North America. The Chinese box office may soon grow larger than any other single market, but Chinese films still aren't getting much traction with international audiences.

I arrive at the theater a couple minutes late, and the movie is already in the midst of its first action sequence when I enter. Clambering over families on the way to my seat, I issue a running apology for the disturbance. It turns out the mea culpa was entirely unnecessary. The crowd here is boisterous and talkative, with audience members freely sharing their commentary with those around them and much of their WeChat contact list. The WeChat app limits videos users post to a maximum of ten seconds, but that hasn't deterred some of my fellow film patrons, who appear determined to capture the entire 121-minute film in ten-second increments that they can send to their friends.

What they are capturing is a relentlessly paced and slickly produced action flick about a soldier kicking ass and taking names in an unnamed African country torn by war and disease. It's a familiar plot for most American viewers, except in this case the soldier is Chinese, and the asses he is kicking are American. I had come into the theater hoping to check my citizenship at the door, but that simple reversal of roles is jarring enough to get my American testosterone pumping.

Just as surprising is the fact that the film *looks good*. There are exceptions—tanks and explosions that resemble old PlayStation 2 graphics—but for the most part the action sequences are in the same visual ballpark as their Hollywood equivalents. That's due in part to the fact that the producers hired the Russo brothers—the Marvel action gurus behind the *Captain America* franchise—to consult on the project. It's also due to a decent budget and the steady improvement in the technical chops of Chinese filmmakers.

My surprise at what I see on screen is an immediate reminder of just how bad many Chinese films—especially action films—tend to look on a purely visual level. Even to an untrained eye like my own, the special effects often look shoddy, and there's just something *off* in the color palette. But *Wolf Warrior 2* is a leveling up in this category. It won't win any Oscars for cinematography, but it does pull off the Hollywood trick of appearing both highly stylized and hyperrealistic.

The film's plot is predictably predictable, a mash-up of movies like *Black Hawk Down, Rambo: First Blood Part II*, and any of the dozens of others in the genre of "badass Americans stranded in foreign war zones." It comes replete with the standard glorification of violence and plenty of condescension toward the local people our protagonist is supposedly there to save. ("It doesn't matter if it's war, disease, or poverty—once they're around the bonfire, all their cares go away.") Wu Jing, the director/writer/star behind both *Wolf Warrior* movies, has a genuine machismo and swagger that you don't find in many other Chinese stars. He looks good, fights hard, and gets the girl too.

Chest-thumping patriotism—and not-so-subtle political symbolism— puts the cherry on top for this audience. In the climactic fight scene, the cold-blooded American mercenary, "Big Daddy," holds a blade to Wu Jing's neck and taunts him: "People like you will always be inferior to people like me. Get used to it. Get fucking used to it." Blinded with rage and righteous patriotism, Wu reverses the move, flips Big Daddy on his back, and beats him to death using a bullet lodged in his fist. Leaning over the dead American, Wu delivers the clincher: "That's fucking history."

A line that sends a shiver up the spine of this American sends a raucous cheer through the audience around me in Hengdian. This is the movie they've been waiting for, and China's adolescent film industry finally made it happen for them.

As the credits roll, I can't help feeling that I've just caught a glimpse of the future of Chinese film. In terms of the visual product, *Wolf Warrior 2* feels a lot more Hollywood than Hengdian, and its leveling up of production values poses a threat to both the latter and the former. Hengdian will continue to churn out many of the imperial dramas and low-budget war movies that populate Chinese screens, but the golden era for that brand of filmmaking may be passing. In the weeks that follow, serious local filmmakers will tell me that watching *Wolf Warrior 2* had a deep impact on them, raising the bar for Chinese movies and inspiring them to push themselves harder.

From an international perspective, the movie serves as an early warning that Hollywood no longer has a total monopoly on the kind of slick action or fictional war-mongering that drives popcorn sales. Language barriers and cultural inertia will keep many of these Chinese blockbusters bottled up in their home market, for now at least. But if *Wolf Warrior 2* is a sign of things to come, then Hollywood might face some more competition for growing markets in Southeast Asia, Africa, and elsewhere.

The Hollywood–China story has plenty more twists and turns in store for us, and the greatest stockpiles of international soft power are still found on the American shores of the Pacific Ocean. But bouncing between Los Angeles, Shanghai, and Hengdian, there's a sense that the story of global culture is evolving quickly, and not necessarily toward the Hollywood ending many Americans would have expected or hoped for.

It's a lot to take in, and my brain is too fried to explore it all from the vantage point of this movie theater. So with images of exploding tanks and martial arts warriors rattling around my head, I walk out into the Hengdian night, searching for a taxi that will take me home.

5

THE MAYOR WHO
LOVED CHINA

Rex Parris would make an outstanding Chinese mayor. He has the ambition, the bombast, and the disdain for dissent. He has the personal fortune, the business instincts, and the soft spot for social engineering. He runs a tight ship and focuses far more on results than elections.

But Rex Parris isn't the mayor of a major Chinese metropolis. He is the mayor of Lancaster, California, a desert town on the fringe of Los Angeles County, a place best known for neo-Nazis and meth labs. Crowned the "worst city in L.A. County" and "the most stressful city in California," Lancaster has a serious PR problem.[1]

The drive from downtown Los Angeles to Lancaster is an hour and a half without traffic, but that can double during rush hour. Highway 14 weaves its way northeast through the arid San Gabriel Mountains, finally flattening out as you settle down into the Mojave Basin. It's on this stretch of highway that you first catch sight of Raymond "Rex" Parris, his face looming large over the highway on billboard ads for his personal injury law firm. Sporting a full white beard and an almost mischievous smile—a look that has been compared to country singer Kenny Rogers—

Rex's watchful gaze blankets much of the city. Even when you're reading rants against him in the comments of local news sites, banner ads for his practice loom above the text: "R. Rex Parris Law Firm: Restoring Lives Since 1985."

Described by the *Los Angeles Times* as "more Old West sheriff than diplomat," Rex does everything big, and a little bit off-balance. He flies an "eye-in-the-sky" police drone over his city and made it his personal goal to wipe out the city's pit bulls. He piped bird sounds into the main boulevard to "lower cortisol levels" and launched a campaign against neckties after learning they reduce blood flow to the brain by 7.5 percent. He's tried to bar the San Bernardino shooters from being buried in a nearby cemetery and passed an ordinance requiring all new homes in Lancaster be built with enough solar panels for net-zero energy consumption.

And here in Lancaster, Mayor Parris is also putting his energy and eccentricities toward turning his town into an unlikely oasis for Chinese investment in green technology.

"We're just this small to midsize city here. The only thing we were known for was crime, and we're changing the world," Parris tells me confidently while leaning back in his City Hall office in March 2014. "Our view is we're going to do that with China—that is, if the State Department would get out of our way; if the federal government would get out of our way."

"THE DAY OF AMERICA RULING THE WORLD IS OVER"

Lancaster and China make for an odd pair, but the world around Rex Parris is full of these off-kilter juxtapositions: a climate-obsessed Republican mayor working hand in hand with the world's biggest polluter; China's richest man betting on a down-and-out American town; and a city built on the American aerospace industry turning into the launchpad for Chinese electric vehicles.

"The day of America ruling the world is over, just over," Parris tells me. "If we're going to compete we'll have to start treating other countries respectfully, and we really haven't, especially Asian countries. They're doing us a favor. We're not doing them the favor. We're the ones who need the jobs."

Treating China as a respected partner is a tough sell in today's political environment. The Trump administration has shown itself to be more interested in trade wars than cross-border investment, and more excited about bringing back coal than striking climate deals. At the national level, the relationship between the world's two superpowers is increasingly characterized by deepening mistrust and bare-knuckle competition.

But while Washington and Beijing played geopolitical tug-of-war, local leaders in California and China were trying to work out the nuts and bolts of a new economic and environmental relationship, one built on cross-border investment and cooperation in combating climate change.

Between 2010 and 2016, annual Chinese direct investment in the U.S. skyrocketed from just $6.6 billion to $55.8 billion.[2] After decades spent churning out cheap exports for global markets, Chinese companies were now looking across the Pacific for technology, talent, and prestige. Hollywood studios, IBM processors, and Virginia hog farms were all on the auction block, with Chinese firms paying record sums for U.S. brands and bringing more than 100,000 American jobs onto their payrolls in the process.[3] Motives for these investments vary widely. Some investors want to acquire U.S. talent or intellectual property. Some want to boost their brand value in the Chinese market by stamping "Made in U.S.A." on their products. Some politically precarious billionaires—such as Wanda's Chairman Wang—might just be looking to squirrel away some cash offshore in case of trouble at home.

California has been at the forefront of that investment explosion, taking in the largest and most diverse swath of Chinese money. Between 2000 and the first half of 2018, California led all other states with 598 investments worth over $30 billion.[4] The state's attraction to Chinese investors is part nature and part nurture. California's status as a global mecca for both tech and entertainment make it a natural magnet for Chinese investors looking to climb their way up the global value chain. Chairman Wang's billion-dollar buying spree in Hollywood, BAT's strategic investments in Silicon Valley, and hundreds of other deals that never made the headlines all signaled attempts by Chinese entities to purchase from California what they struggled to create in China.

But California's leaders have also nurtured Chinese investment through proactive outreach to Chinese businesses and government leaders. Mayors like Rex Parris have been at the front lines of this cross-border investment boom. Part pitchmen and part policy makers, mayors have the incentives and the flexibility to court Chinese investors. In a small town, every new storefront counts, and mayors have been less paralyzed by the weight of geopolitical machinations. They generally don't lose sleep over disputes in the South China Sea or worry too much about the impact of a local factory on national economic competitiveness. Their careers ride on getting things done in their jurisdiction: creating jobs and housing, safe streets and good schools.

"Entrepreneurial governors and mayors are an important driver of more positive relations with China to produce economic benefits for their localities," Paul Gewirtz, director of Yale Law School's China Center and leader of a U.S.–China Track II Dialogue, told me in 2016. "They're pushing ahead projects in their own region while things are increasingly gridlocked at the national level."

Mayor Parris has placed his chips on China. He believes grassroots ties with the country will reinvigorate Lancaster, bringing in good jobs and emissions-reducing technology. Parris is an evangelist on the dangers of climate change, and he's doing the legwork to make Lancaster a laboratory for on-the-ground solutions.

"It's a problem of gigantic proportions that the world is just now waking up to. But I also don't think it's going to be solved by nations; it's going to be solved by cities. We're attempting to create the template," Parris told me in 2014. "Obama doesn't issue building permits. I do."

That legwork paid off when BYD, the Warren Buffett–backed Chinese electric vehicle company, chose Lancaster for its first factory on U.S. soil. Since opening in 2013, that factory has brought hundreds of new jobs, injecting income into a city that saw its manufacturing base hollowed out in the 1990s.

But BYD's arrival also brought major blowback. The company's triumphant entrance to California—trumpeted by the state's own Governator, Arnold Schwarzenegger—quickly turned into a case study of the good, the bad, and the ugly of the Transpacific Experiment. BYD was picketed by activists, attacked in the media, and investigated by the state of California. The company has been accused of everything from making unsafe buses to importing $1.50-an-hour Chinese laborers at jobs it promised the city would go to low-income Los Angeles residents. BYD fought back against these allegations—and won—but the stumbles cost it key contracts and public goodwill. Now, eight years after entering the U.S., BYD is back on its feet and beginning to look like a success story: a Chinese company that brought much-needed jobs and green technology to a town that could use both.

Mayor Parris's open-armed embrace of China met similar backlash in Lancaster. Attack ads and political cartoons depicted the Chinese Red Army marching into the city. Critics accused him of mirroring the politics of the People's Republic, running Lancaster like an authoritarian state.

"The hardest problem was getting people to relax," Parris tells me. "The Chinese hordes were not coming to take them over."

Tracing the story of Rex Parris and BYD reveals lessons for players on both sides of the Pacific. With national leaders abandoning high-level climate commitments, how can cities take the lead on concrete actions to reduce carbon emissions? How can U.S. cities bring in Chinese investment that will generate good jobs and sustainable growth? How can Chinese companies avoid being branded as foreign invaders, clueless about local laws or how to deal with democratic institutions like a free press? Are Americans ready to answer to Chinese foremen, and are Chinese companies ready to answer to U.S. judges?

A GOLDEN COMPANY IN THE GOLDEN STATE

Those thorny questions likely weren't on the minds of California's political royalty when they gathered at Los Angeles City Hall on April 30, 2010. That day, Governor Arnold Schwarzenegger stood alongside two generations of Los Angeles mayors to celebrate BYD's decision to locate its North American headquarters in the City of Angels. The announcement came just fifteen days after *Bloomberg Businessweek* named BYD—a cell phone battery maker turned electric-car golden child—the eighth most innovative company in the world.

"I welcome BYD with open arms and look forward to growing California's relationship with China to mutually benefit the environment and economy," said Schwarzenegger, gesturing toward BYD founder Wang Chuanfu.

Attendees gushed over BYD's battery-powered cars and California's trailblazing emissions-reduction policies. Politicians predicted the imminent arrival of thousands of new "green collar" jobs in the city.

The imagery—a forward-thinking Chinese electric car company arriving on U.S. soil—was particularly potent given the timing. Beijing's dazzling opening ceremony for the 2008 summer Olympics had felt like a coming out party for a twenty-first-century superpower. Five weeks later, the collapse of Lehman Brothers had the feel of a funeral for American hegemony. In BYD, California politicians saw a chance to flip the script on decades of job losses to China, to get in on the ground floor of the next big thing.

Los Angeles policy makers pulled out all the stops to woo the company. They reduced tariffs at the port and promised to install home charging stations for anyone who purchased an electric car. They promised to display BYD products at the Los Angeles Airport and arranged a $1.6 million grant to refurbish BYD's headquarters—money obtained through President Obama's stimulus package.[5] City leaders even promised to get a celebrity to drive a BYD car to the Oscars party.

BYD's founder described those incentives as "hard to resist." In return for the grant, BYD signed a contract promising to create fifty-eight full-time jobs by August 2015, with half of those jobs going to low-income workers and Los Angeles residents. In its own publicly released "Employment Action Plan," BYD predicted hiring 102 full-time workers by the fall of 2013.[6]

L.A.'s optimism was understandable given the hype surrounding BYD at the time. The company was founded in 1995 by Wang Chuanfu, the child of poor farmers in one of China's poorest regions. Both of his parents passed away before he reached high school, and Wang was cared for by older siblings. An undergraduate and master's degree in chemistry led him toward an interest in rechargeable batteries, a path that would eventually turn him into China's richest man.

Wang founded BYD in 1995 as an upstart challenger in the market for cell phone batteries. The company quickly conquered those markets and then pivoted away from them. In 2003, Wang bought up a struggling state-owned automaker in central China and set his sights on China's booming market for personal cars. BYD developed a ruthlessly efficient process for reverse engineering popular foreign models and producing them at cheaper prices. The company's F3 was such a close clone of the Toyota Corolla that some BYD dealers reportedly offered new buyers a chance to instantly swap out the BYD logo for the more prestigious Toyota badge for a small fee.[7] After five years of cranking out cheap gasoline-powered vehicles, in 2008 Wang Chuanfu announced that he'd be synergizing his two businesses, combining his batteries and his cars to make electric vehicles.

That move attracted the attention of the world's most famous capitalist and communists. Few institutions have the power to move markets like Warren Buffett or the Chinese Communist Party, and just as the global financial crisis unfolded, the two both made moves that would launch BYD into the international spotlight.

In the fall of 2008, a subsidiary of Buffett's Berkshire Hathaway bought up a 10 percent stake in BYD for $230 million.[8] Buffett's right-hand man, Charlie Munger, was gushing in his praise of BYD's founder: "a combination of Thomas Edison and Jack Welch—something like Edison in solving technical problems, and something like Welch in getting done what he needs to do. I have never seen anything like it." That endorsement turned heads internationally, garnering glowing praise for BYD from analysts and the press.

Just months after the Buffett investment, the Chinese government entered the picture. As the global financial crisis wiped out demand for cheap Chinese exports, the government poured stimulus money into infrastructure investment and renewable energy technology. In spring 2009, the government announced its goal of ramping up hybrid and electric car production from 2,100 vehicles in 2008 to an astonishing 500,000 in 2011.[9]

China appeared ready for an electric car revolution, and BYD was in the driver's seat. The company's stock price surged by 600 percent, making Wang Chuanfu the richest man in China in 2009.[10] That excitement soon bubbled over into plans for a U.S. headquarters that would serve as a beachhead to enter American auto markets. The timing couldn't have been better. With financial markets in free fall, U.S. companies were recoiling into a defensive crouch. BYD—whose initials stood for "Build Your Dreams"—was springing onto the global stage.

"I don't have any doubt that they're going to be as big as Toyota," Rex Parris told me in early 2014. "They're the most innovative, and that's who usually wins."

DOWN AND OUT IN THE ANTELOPE VALLEY

Lancaster could use a company like Toyota in town. During the 1980s Lancaster and its neighbors in the Antelope Valley flourished, churning out bombers and fighter jets for the nearby Edwards Air Force Base. High school grads could raise a family "bucking rivets" for Lockheed, and engineers could pull in good salaries working for NASA.

But when the Cold War ended, the aerospace jobs that buoyed Lancaster's middle class abruptly disappeared. Between 1990 and 1992, unemployment doubled to over 10 percent.[11] In 1995, USA Today crowned the neighboring city of Palmdale "the foreclosure capital of California." Methamphetamine use spiked alongside gang violence.

Local high schoolers now looked ahead to an adulthood of grim job prospects and a social contract torn to shreds. In a 1997 New Yorker article titled "The Unwanted," reporter William Finnegan documented a year's worth of clashes between youth neo-Nazi gangs and rival antiracist skinheads in the Antelope Valley. Methamphetamines, absent parents, and knife fights defined the teenage years for these kids. Finnegan's article was a bombshell, one that shaped the town's reputation for years to come, and that locals still reference today.

Lancaster never fully recovered from the industrial evacuation, and when the 2008 financial crisis struck, the city's unemployment rate soared to 17.2 percent.[12] But as Lancaster was sinking into the abyss, Rex Parris was rising.

Rex grew up poor and ostracized. His mother waited tables and his father disappeared, leaving the family to rely on welfare at times. As a teenager, he suffered from social anxiety so crushing that he couldn't bring himself to walk through a school cafeteria.

"I'm different," he told me. "When you're rich, you can be different—it's called eccentric. When you're poor and different you're weird and shunned."

He dropped out of high school but found his way from a community college to University of California Santa Barbara and then a local law school. Parris returned to Lancaster with his wife and founded his personal injury practice, all while navigating life as a "full-blown cocaine addict." He eventually kicked his addiction and turned multimillion-dollar personal injury verdicts into a source of tremendous wealth: a private plane, large philanthropic ventures that got a high school named after him, and a family mansion with private tennis and basketball courts.

During that period, he also became a powerful behind-the-scenes force in Antelope Valley politics. For thirty years, he and a close-knit group of prominent Republicans pulled the strings and made the donations to keep city politics leaning in their direction. But Parris eventually grew impatient with what he deemed weak local leadership, and in 2008 he ran for mayor. He poured $400,000 of his own money into the campaign and won by just 352 votes.

Rex Parris came into office guns blazing. In his first term, Parris managed to outrage the ACLU and make enemies with motorcycle gangs. Playing to a deeply religious base, Parris declared Lancaster to be "a Christian city" and insisted on opening city council meetings with a prayer. Those prayers led to a warning from the ACLU and a three-year lawsuit against the city, in which Lancaster eventually prevailed.

Then Parris took on gangs.

"I want gangs out of Lancaster," Parris told the *Los Angeles Times* in 2009. "I want to make it uncomfortable for them to be here. Anything they like, I want to take it away from them. I want to deliberately harass them."

He first launched campaigns to neuter or euthanize pit bulls, animals he claimed gang members wielded for intimidation. (Other locals characterized the campaign differently: a thinly veiled move against young black men in Lancaster who often raised pit bulls.) When the Mongols Motorcycle Club, a violent biker gang allegedly involved in meth distribution, booked a Lancaster hotel for their annual gathering, Parris demanded the hotel cancel the reservation. When the hotel refused to do that, Parris ordered police to put a chain around the hotel, forcing it to shut down under the pretext of unpaid taxes.

"I may have gone too far," Parris acknowledged, "but it also gave me a lot of credibility."

According to local crime statistics, violent crimes fell roughly 33 percent in Parris's first five years in office.[13]

Fascinated by psychology research, Parris treats Lancaster like a macro-level social psychology laboratory. He wants sidewalks built with gentle wavelike curves because it allegedly calms the mind of those walking them. He cites high levels of cortisol—the "stress hormone"—as a root cause of gang violence and poor school performance.

"We raise these children in a culture of cortisol," Parris told me. "What I had to do was to lower the cortisol levels, to lower the fear."

To that end, he tried piping recorded birdsong into schoolyards and the city's main boulevard. Tweaking local demographics is another pet project in Parris's quest to make Lancaster great again.

"Good things happen when you're able to increase your Asian population to a certain threshold: crime rates go down, education levels go up,"

Parris told me at his City Hall office in 2014. "Interestingly, the same thing happens with the gays. That's why I put the new performing arts center right downtown."

But no number of gently curving sidewalks or gay-friendly hangouts could solve Lancaster's fundamental problem: there just weren't enough good jobs in the city. Parris saw part of the solution to that problem in one thing Lancaster had in abundance: sunlight. Ever since becoming mayor, he relentlessly promoted Lancaster as the solar capital "of the universe." That ambition dovetails perfectly with the mayor's other passion: local solutions to global warming. Parris talks about climate change with the passion of a born-again Christian, framing the dangers in apocalyptic terminology.

"We're in a struggle for survival here, survival of this planet," Parris said to me. "We don't have time to fuck around anymore."

In 2011, the Lancaster city council passed a measure setting the goal of Lancaster becoming the first net-zero energy city in the world. To that end, the city dramatically streamlined permitting for installing solar panels and mandated all new homes come with them, tripling installations in eighteen months.[14] Lancaster is working to buy back streetlights for LED retrofits and forging partnerships between solar panel companies, homebuilders, and municipal utilities.

"There becomes a synergy to such relationships, and they develop more and more technologies," Parris told *Forbes*. "It's fascinating what happens when you start telling people: 'We want innovation now. We want you to help save the planet with us.'"

That frantic pursuit of climate solutions is what excited Parris about BYD, a cutting-edge energy company that saw a future for itself on U.S. soil.

CHINESE INVESTMENTS AND CLIMATE COMMITMENTS

BYD wasn't the only Chinese company with ambitions in America at that time. The financial crisis marked the takeoff point for Chinese foreign direct investment (FDI) in the United States. FDI refers to a foreign company either acquiring a large stake in a U.S. firm or setting up its own operation on American soil. Those corporate and physical structures make FDI more stable than portfolio investments, which can be liquidated at the first sign of trouble. FDI generates a concrete footprint in the recipient country and often requires a stable operating relationship for years to come. Investments by Chinese firms have been diverse: construction of a new copper tube factory in one of the poorest parts of Alabama, acquisition of an LED manufacturer in Oregon, and the $2 billion purchase of the Waldorf Astoria hotel in New York.

FDI can be broken down into two categories: acquisitions and greenfield investments. In an acquisition, a Chinese company purchases a U.S. entity outright, while a greenfield investment involves the Chinese firm building up its own operations—factories or front offices—from scratch on U.S. soil. These two investment formats have different benefits and drawbacks for the U.S. side. Acquisitions are often larger and can serve as the ultimate payoff for American entrepreneurs who built something great. But they can also be an avenue for Chinese entities to buy intellectual property, helping China leapfrog hard-won American advantage in key industries. Greenfield investments create new jobs on American soil, kick-starting growth by bringing Chinese capital into long-neglected places like Lancaster. But the face-to-face interactions inherent in a greenfield investment also raise the stakes, creating frictions between Chinese bosses and American employees and increasing the likelihood of a local backlash against the new arrivals. Nationally, acquisitions have made up over 90 percent of the dollar value of Chinese investment in the U.S., but from the perspective of an ambitious mayor, a large greenfield project is the Holy Grail.[15] It presents opportunities for job creation, photo ops, and new sources of tax revenue.

And in the case of BYD, that investment also dovetailed perfectly with the second major strand of transpacific politics: climate cooperation. For years, the United States and China—the world's two largest emitters of carbon—had been at loggerheads on climate change. The U.S. side refused to sign any deal that didn't include substantial Chinese commitments to emissions reductions, and China argued back that countries that had gotten rich on decades of pollution couldn't suddenly take away the punch bowl when developing countries began to catch up. That stalemate made any meaningful international agreement on averting a climate disaster appear impossible.

But in that vacuum, California began its own climate outreach to China. Driving that process was an enterprising group of California politicians, bureaucrats, academics, businesspeople, and scientists, all looking for ways to move the ball forward locally while things remained stuck nationally. In that process, they could take inspiration from an oft-repeated Chinese proverb about local politics: "Heaven is high, and the emperor is far away." Translation: forget what goes down in the capital; local politicians do what they want.

Governor Schwarzenegger had kicked off California's own emissions-reductions actions with the passage of the Global Warming Solutions Act of 2006. Succeeding Schwarzenegger was Jerry Brown, the unconventional septuagenarian politician who was serving his third term as California governor. Brown had previously served two terms beginning in 1975 and had spent the intervening three decades running for president of the United States, studying Zen Buddhism in Japan, running for president again, and then serving as the mayor of Oakland and attorney general of California. When he returned to the governor's office in 2011 after twenty-eight years away, he became the oldest governor the state has ever had.

Brown has long been vocal on environmental issues, and he shares Rex Parris's enthusiasm for weaving together Chinese investments and partnerships on climate change. During a 2013 investment-promotion trip to China, he launched a campaign of state-to-state climate diplomacy that would help lay the groundwork for future national agreements. Brown signed a series of memorandums of understanding (MOUs) with Chinese provinces and government ministries, pledging to work together on climate in any form they could. These partnerships included sending delegations of Chinese regulators to visit the California Air Resources Board, knowledge exchanges on creating carbon markets, and broader commitments to "enhanced cooperation" on clean energy and climate solutions.

In many ways, Governor Brown's state-level initiatives and Mayor Parris's moves in Lancaster complemented each other well. While Brown's MOUs were strongest on public signaling and symbolism—opening new channels for dialogue and keeping hope alive for broader China–U.S. agreements—it could be hard to tell where that symbolism converted into concrete cuts in emissions. And Parris's courtships of clean energy businesses weren't going to directly produce an international climate treaty, but they would churn out the electric vehicles that reduced actual emissions in cities around the world.

Those twin forces had a moment of synergy at the end of Brown's China trip in April 2013. While touring the BYD headquarters in Shenzhen, Brown announced that the electric vehicle company would be setting up its first U.S. factory in Lancaster. Riding one of the company's electric buses after the announcement, the seventy-five-year-old Brown did a couple of pull-ups on the bus's handrails.

"We're not waiting for Washington," Governor Brown would later say at the opening ceremony for that factory in Lancaster. "We're building a very powerful partnership right here on the edge of the Pacific."

COURTING CHINA: FACE AND FUNCTION

That factory in Lancaster was the long-run payoff for a 2009 dinner hosted by L.A. County Supervisor Michael Antonovich. Antonovich's Chinese-born wife, Christine, had worked as a successful actress on the mainland, and she maintained connections there that she put into play when the couple invited Rex Parris to dinner with Wang Chuanfu.

"I had no preparation. I show up at this dinner and meet the richest man in China," Parris recounted to me. "But I knew a lot about solar and transmission at that point, so I just started talking. And Christine Antonovich, who is from China, kept kicking me under the table and saying, 'Keep talking! Keep talking!'"

Following the dinner, Parris believed Lancaster had a chance at landing BYD's U.S. corporate headquarters, a notion that, in hindsight, he considers "arrogant." But that arrogance was the spur to action that Lancaster needed to win the factory that BYD would soon be obligated to build.

After the 2010 ceremony in which Governor Schwarzenegger celebrated BYD's decision to locate in California, the company's business had quickly lost steam. Electric cars were not ready for mass market, either in the U.S. or China, and the much-hyped Chinese government goal of 500,000 hybrid and electric vehicles by 2011 fell completely flat: only 8,159 vehicles were sold that year.[16] BYD's stocks and profits fell by 80 percent in 2010 and 2011 as sales of their traditional gas-powered vehicles—which still made up the majority of their fleet—slumped.[17] In response, the company decided to pivot its American operations toward electric buses, a vertical that only required winning over cost-conscious fleet managers, as opposed to fickle American consumers. The catch was that many American municipal bus contracts, especially those using federal stimulus money for procurement, came with a "Buy America" provision that required the buses be built on U.S. soil. And so BYD went on the hunt for a city to build itself a factory.

Parris already saw China as a pseudo-savior for his city—a gargantuan source of both capital and green technology—and he threw himself into a full-court press campaign to lure BYD out to the Mojave. That campaign took on two key dimensions: face and function. The "face" dimension involved flattering Chinese executives and officials with public shows of respect. The "function" dimension meant brushing aside the bureaucratic obstacles to BYD setting up shop in Lancaster.

In Chinese culture, the concept of "face" is the water on which most social interactions—especially those between men—float. Amorphous as it can be, "face" roughly equates to one's public status, the amount of deference others treat you with. It can be "given" through public shows of deference to others, or "lost" if someone fails or feels disrespected in a public setting. If the right amount of face is given by the right people at the right time, an interaction floats along smoothly. If one side feels publicly slighted—especially the more senior party—things quickly sink.

Government officials and business executives in China are painfully conscious of face when interacting with foreigners. Deep-rooted insecurities about China's place in the world form an unspoken undercurrent to otherwise straightforward exchanges: Do these foreigners respect China and Chinese culture? Do they truly see us as equals? In this context, giving a little face goes a long way.

Rex Parris proved to be a master at bestowing face on Chinese visitors. When Chinese officials visited the city, he had motorcycle police meet their car at the city limits and escort them into town. He made a well-received pilgrimage to BYD's headquarters in Shenzhen, part of a delegation led by Supervisor Antonovich. He printed bilingual business cards for city employees—one side English, the other side Mandarin—and hired a Mandarin tutor for his staff. No one on staff learned functional Mandarin, but like Zuckerberg's own mission to learn Mandarin, making the effort to pick up even a couple phrases earned brownie points with Chinese interlocutors.

Even more fundamental has been Mayor Parris's own attitude. Those gestures of respect aren't just cynical ploys to ingratiate oneself with dumb money. In conversation, it's clear that Parris takes China seriously—as a country and culture that America can learn something from. He cites Chinese leader Deng Xiaoping as his personal hero and rails against American arrogance in dealing with non-Western countries.

"I really like Asians," Parris told me. "I have a different view of their culture. It's thousands of years old. They have so much to offer that we just can't. . . . It is shocking to me what really goes on in America," he said. "This inflated view of ourselves, how the rest of the world is corrupt and we're pristine, is just so untrue."

But it takes more than a well-timed toast or a well-received compliment to successfully court Chinese executives. Business schools are littered with case studies of American companies that believed the key to making things happen in China was mastering the intricacies of Chinese business etiquette. When tens of millions of dollars are on the line, it's not just about how you hold your chopsticks. Chinese executives need to know this is a place where they can do business.

That's where "function" comes in. Parris's key insight for the courtship involved guiding Chinese companies through the American bureaucratic web. Where other cities tend to throw money at companies, Parris focused far more on hand-holding.

"When I first visited BYD I knew they were ahead of the curve, but they were also bogged down in an inability to shift to American culture in some things," he told me. "You have this huge company with almost no contacts in the U.S."

Chinese companies looking to invest in the U.S. are rarely short on cash; their international ambitions are often the spoils of conquering their home market. What they lack is the ability to navigate America's dense thicket of legal, labor, and environmental regulations. In China, it's often better to ask for forgiveness than permission. The country's regulatory and legal environment is just a few decades old and constantly evolving, meaning many Chinese businesses learn the limits by testing the gray areas. American society's stable legal code and enduring love affair with lawsuits has instilled a greater degree of caution in most traditional U.S. businesses, with armies of corporate lawyers and lobbyists dotting i's and crossing t's to mitigate risk.

So Parris sought to simplify the process, creating a one-stop shop for permitting and approvals. Each time a potential project arises, Mayor Parris calls the heads of various city agencies—everything from sanitation to air quality—together for a work lunch on the top floor of a local hotel.

"Everyone that has any say in the development of the project is at the table the very first time we actually get serious about it," Parris told me. "That's a huge thing. When we build something of significant size in L.A. County, it's two to three years just to start, just to put sticks in the ground. Companies don't like the uncertainty; they like to be able to predict."

That no-nonsense approach impressed Stella Li, BYD's senior vice president and head of its U.S. operations.

"They ask what you need, and they do it," she told the *Los Angeles Times*.

As part of the hand-holding process, Parris's team introduced BYD to the owner of a local RV factory that had fallen on hard times during the financial crisis. The shuttered factory could be easily retrofitted to produce buses, and BYD even agreed to hire the owner of the RV factory to stay on as general manager of the new plant. Dangling one final carrot for the company, Lancaster pledged that if BYD hired 200 workers in its first three years, the city would gift it thirteen acres of surrounding land to build a second factory.

With that, the deal was done. On May 1, 2013, the first-ever overseas factory for BYD opened its doors in little old Lancaster, California. At the factory's opening ceremony—attended by Governor Brown and Supervisor Antonovich—Parris was triumphant.

"[This project] is about creating a place that is actually going to solve global warming, and I honestly believe that it will happen here in Lancaster," he told the assembled dignitaries. "When you take China and put it together with the U.S., something different happens. Something emerges."

That optimism on climate cooperation was bubbling up from small towns to the California state house, and finally the White House. Within a year of Governor Brown's climate MOUs with Chinese partners, the Obama administration began its own outreach campaign across the Pacific, hoping to strike a bilateral deal that could set the table for the 2015 negotiations in Paris on an international treaty. The Obama team brought on veterans of the China–California climate partnerships to guide those negotiations, and the push paid off. In November of 2014, Presidents Obama and Xi in Beijing announced the first national-level climate agreement between the countries. The U.S. pledged to double its pace of emissions reductions, while China agreed for the first time to peak its emissions by or before 2030 and move to 20 percent renewable energy by that point.[18] The following year, those twin pledges became the foundation for the Paris Climate Agreement.

CONTRACTS AND CONTROVERSY

But just as things were finally looking better at the national level, the messy details of grassroots international relations were stirring up trouble in Lancaster. BYD's factory looked like the crowning achievement of Parris's China outreach, but his lofty ambitions quickly got bogged down in a muck of corporate miscues, American insecurities, and tone-deaf blunders.

Before BYD and Lancaster ever inked a contract, the seeds were sown for a public backlash that would derail BYD's early contracts and jeopardize Parris's vision of Lancaster as an oasis for Chinese investment in green technology. Soon after BYD opened the doors to its L.A. facility, the company came into the crosshairs of two powerful forces that rarely surface in China: a free press and vocal activists. BYD proved woefully unprepared for life in that kind of a civic fishbowl.

The trouble began with BYD's first major orders in early 2013: ten all-electric buses for Long Beach Transit, followed by a contract with L.A. Metro for up to twenty-five buses. But the bidding process for the Long Beach contract—which BYD won over American electric bus manufacturer Proterra—put an end to BYD's golden public image. The Long Beach Transit board was split on the decision, and media soon glommed on to the decision. Local journalists and bloggers called the decision to grant BYD the contract over Proterra "anti-American." They attacked the safety of Chinese-made buses—detailing each glitch as BYD buses went through durability testing—and called on L.A. Metro to reject the Chinese company's bids.

BYD was caught flat-footed. In typical fashion for a Chinese company, they clammed up and hoped the storm would pass. Instead of reaching out to local media, they tried to blacklist one particularly critical reporter.

But this was all prologue to the real PR nightmare ahead: accusations that BYD had violated minimum-wage laws, bringing in Chinese laborers and paying them $1.50 an hour. In October 2013, investigators for the California Labor Commissioner's Office acted on a tip when they conducted a surprise inspection of BYD's facilities in Los Angeles and Lancaster. The office quickly slapped nearly $100,000 worth of fines on BYD for a combination of minimum wage, pay stub, and rest break violations.[19]

Allegations that BYD underpaid its Chinese workers originated in a lawsuit filed by Sandra Itkoff, BYD America's former vice president of strategy. After being fired from BYD in 2012, Itkoff—who was the only non-Chinese employee in L.A. at the time—sued the company for wrongful termination and discrimination on the basis of national origin. In a written complaint filed one month before the commissioner's office's inspection, Itkoff claimed that she'd been excluded from all-Chinese staff meetings, that BYD buses were riddled with safety issues, and that BYD brought cheap labor from China to its Los Angeles headquarters, paying workers $5,000 to $8,000 per year.

Local activist Madeline Jannis seized on Itkoff's accusations, passing them along to the California labor commissioner. Jannis's union-affiliated organization, Jobs to Move America, first set its sights on BYD when it received the $1.6 million grant to refurbish its headquarters. That grant required BYD to hire fifty-eight full-time workers by 2015, with over half of those jobs going to low-income workers and Angelenos hired through career development groups. Jannis said that from the beginning BYD was uncooperative in working with those groups and that it spurned approaches by local unions.

After the labor commissioner's investigation went public, Jannis organized protests outside BYD headquarters, with signs reading THIS IS A SWEATSHOP PAID FOR WITH OUR TAX $$ and $1.50 PER HOUR BARELY PAYS FOR BUS FARE and WHERE ARE THE JOBS? A group called Asian Americans Advancing Justice attempted to hand out Chinese-language flyers to BYD workers informing them of their rights. *The New York Times* and *Los Angeles Times* both featured damning articles on the company. Worse than any fine from state inspectors was the narrative building from the incident: a Chinese company given local government money to create American jobs was flying in temporary Chinese laborers and paying them pennies.

To put out the raging PR wildfire, BYD brought in legendary Washington spinmeister Lanny Davis. Nominally a lawyer, Davis has spent the last two decades doing crisis management for the rich and powerful. He rose to prominence energetically defending Bill Clinton during the pre–Monica Lewinsky scandals and later sold his services to multinational corporations and foreign powers. Famously tireless in promoting—and unscrupulous in choosing—his clients, Davis lobbied on behalf of Honduran business interests supporting a 2009 coup and represented the notorious dictator of Equatorial Guinea. One of Davis's favorite selling points as a PR man is that he still enjoys attorney-client privilege—people can tell him exactly what it is they've done, and he can never be compelled to speak of it. With characteristic zeal, Davis launched into a full-throated defense of BYD. He worked the phones and the press, but calls kept mounting for Long Beach and L.A. to ditch BYD.

And then, just as the crisis reached fever pitch, the labor commissioner's office abruptly reversed course. After BYD submitted documents showing that temporary Chinese employees in L.A. had actually been paid twelve to sixteen dollars an hour in wages to their Chinese bank accounts, the state agreed to drop the minimum-wage charges. In the end, the Labor Commissioner's Office fined BYD $1,900 for paying temporary Chinese employees in Chinese currency rather than dollars, and an additional $30,000 for errors in the way they gave out wage stubs and divided rest breaks.

"When the labor raid came, they were expecting a sweatshop with a bunch of workers, and there weren't," said Micheal Austin of BYD America. "There were technicians working on equipment."

Rex Parris was convinced that local unions orchestrated the raids to pressure BYD into accepting union representation of its workers.

"BYD is going to be as big as General Motors, certainly as big as Toyota, and they are not kowtowing to unions. I suspect that's the reason."

Lanny Davis was predictably irate in his response to the final fines levied against BYD.

"This is not a *Saturday Night Live* satire of bad government; this is for real," he squawked to me over the phone. "Is it possible that a bureaucracy does such unnecessary things to a start-up company that is the reverse of the narrative that everybody complains about? . . . You would think that the state of California would say to the labor commissioner, 'Are you kidding? Nineteen hundred dollars because they paid in RMB rather than dollars? Aren't we trying to attract foreign investment?'"

"WE DON'T GET TO CALL THE SHOTS"

But the "satire" Davis described had one final act. BYD had managed to emerge from the minimum-wage debacle clinging to two key contracts: Long Beach Transit and L.A. Metro. But just when the road ahead looked clear, the Federal Transit Administration (FTA) stepped in and blocked Long Beach Transit from using a federal grant to purchase BYD buses, effectively forcing Long Beach to cancel the BYD order.

Why? Because at the time of bidding in early 2013, BYD had not yet submitted a Disadvantaged Business Enterprise (DBE) compliance plan. DBE requirements force bidders on federally funded contracts to set percentage goals for the amount of business they will likely conduct with companies owned by minorities and women. BYD had met its DBE requirements, but their plan had not been submitted until after the initial bidding process.

The FTA informed Long Beach Transit that if they wished to use federal funds they would need to reopen the bidding, giving Proterra another shot at the contract. Two months after that decision, former secretary of transportation Ray LaHood joined the board of Proterra, BYD's main rival in the bid process. As President Obama's secretary of transportation, LaHood had overseen the FTA until July 2013. During his tenure, he wrote glowingly of Proterra after a visit to their factories.

"In 2009, Proterra did not have the financial resources or customer orders to commercialize its fast charge battery bus," LaHood wrote on the *White House Blog*. "But with help from Department of Transportation grants to transit agencies across the country, Proterra has been able to make that leap."

Rex Parris was incensed.

"The BYD bus is twice the bus that Proterra is. But you're putting every obstacle you can in front of it, and at the same time we're bitching about China's obstacles," Parris told me. "If we want to bring those jobs back, we have to recognize that we don't get to call all the shots, that it has to be fair both ways. We don't get to get even because they were copying. There's this attitude that the rules don't apply when you're dealing with China, and that is going to bite us in the ass eventually."

RED SCARE IN LANCASTER

That bite in the ass came, but the ass in question belonged to Rex Parris himself. Just as the BYD saga began brewing in Los Angeles, Parris was facing major pushback in Lancaster.

When Parris first traveled to China to court BYD, there were already rumblings of discontent in his caucus. Lancaster is a patriotic place, a city whose history is inseparable from the United States military and its decades-long standoff with the Soviet Union. The Soviet Union had now given way to China as the new challenger for global dominance, and not everyone in the Antelope Valley was pleased with Parris's courtship of Chinese enterprises.

During Parris's first reelection campaign in 2010, a political opponent harkened back to the Soviet "red scare" with anti-Chinese television advertisements. One ad featured footage from a Chinese military parade in Tiananmen Square juxtaposed next to a television interview with Parris about investment promotion efforts.

"You know, you have to be Chinese-friendly," says Parris in the ad, as the Chinese flag is unfurled by the People's Liberation Army. "That's why we're getting the staff to learn Mandarin. We're doing everything we can to send the message out that you're going to like it here, and we're going to like you."

Pasted over the footage was text: "Stop Rex Parris Before He Brings 200 Chinese Communists to Live in Lancaster!"

Debuting on local cable television shortly before the election, the ads caused an uproar. Mayor Parris called the ads "the most racist commercial I've seen in twenty years. . . . This is saying anyone from China is a Communist, and that's racism." Parris's opponent in the mayoral race denied any involvement with the commercials. But the ad's creator, former Democratic Party candidate Robert Davenport, went on the offensive in local media.

"Here is a news flash for Mayor Parris and all other China appeasers out there: According to the current version of the Central Intelligence Agency's *The World Factbook*, the government in China is a 'Communist state,'" Davenport told a local paper.

"If Mayor Parris and the Communists he pals around with and wants to have as business partners thought everyone here was going to welcome them with open arms and blank minds into a region of America that plays a vital role in our national defense, they were absolutely wrong. I believe most Americans are like me: Proud, hardworking capitalists that are strongly anti-Communist."

MAFIA TOWN

As strong as those anti-Communist sentiments may have been, they weren't enough to swing the imminent election. Parris won reelection with 67 percent of the vote.[20] But that kind of electoral landslide wasn't just the result of organic local enthusiasm for what Parris accomplished in office. Instead, it was partly the result of far darker political currents pulsing through Lancaster. Political rivals, local activists, and ordinary citizens say that Parris has fostered a political culture that mirrors the worst aspects of some of his international interlocutors: cutthroat, autocratic, and corrupt.

"The way [Lancaster] is run is like a mafia," said Johnathon Ervin, a former member of Parris's planning commission and a fierce critic of the mayor. "Basically, he rules by fear and money."

Ervin and others describe a city in which Parris and a handful of partners have seized control of the levers of local power. Lancaster's elections are held in April, when the lack of other contests on the ballot guarantees anemic voter turnout. They say Parris then panders to local megachurches and employs racial dog whistles to galvanize a deeply conservative Christian base. When it comes to his agenda, Parris brooks no dissent.

Ervin left Parris's planning commission after breaking with him over a proposed Walmart, and Ervin then ran for city council. Parris responded by distributing a flyer calling Ervin, who is African American, the "gang candidate" for attending a protest against police brutality. The flyer warned that Ervin would pass sensitive information about police activity to "his friends." It was a totally transparent act of race-baiting in a city with an ugly history of violence.

Ervin lost the election to Parris's chosen candidates by 749 votes.

For his part, Ervin viewed the incident as an example of the mayor's Machiavellian tendencies, a willingness to do anything to advance his own personal legacy.

"Does he make racist statements? Yes, of course he does. He makes unabashedly racist statements," Ervin told me. "But there's a means to an end when he does that. It's to instill fear and manipulate the populace that's going to vote for him."

Other local activists see Parris as a deeply problematic and complex figure. Xavier Flores, a spokesperson for the local League of United Latin American Citizens, called Parris's dog whistling "cynical to its core." He cited one of Rex's most outlandish pledges: a $1,000 "bounty" for information generating convictions of members of the Bloods or Crips gangs. But Flores supported Parris in a voting-rights lawsuit against the neighboring city of Palmdale, and he commends the mayor's outreach to China.

"Just because he's done these things that we're absolutely against . . . that's not going to stop us from working with him on solutions that we believe are correct," Flores told me.

Parris, for his part, acknowledges accusations of authoritarian tendencies and says he understands why many felt the "gang candidate" flyer was race-baiting. But he brushes off the incident and others like it, arguing these are the eggs that need breaking for the omelet he's cooking up in Lancaster. It's the kind of rationalization you'd expect from Parris's personal hero, Deng Xiaoping, the Chinese leader who both dragged China out of Maoist poverty and ordered the tanks toward Tiananmen Square.

"I walked into a city that was on the edge of the abyss . . . and you don't pull it out and make it thrive by the normal way decisions are made in times of calm," Parris told me. "Am I autocratic in how I do it? Yeah, I am. Are they eventually going to vote me out because of it? Yeah, they will. But what gets left behind, they're not going to be able to undo."

BIRTH HOTEL CALIFORNIA

But Parris overplayed his hand when he launched his most out-there China initiative: bringing in Chinese birth tourists to fund a cash-strapped community hospital. The Fourteenth Amendment to the U.S. Constitution guarantees citizenship to every person born on American soil, a fact that has long drawn foreigners to the United States to give birth. Congressional Republicans still rail against poor Mexican immigrants and "anchor babies," but in recent years it has been rich Chinese families that have been making use of U.S. birthright citizenship.

There is nothing inherently illegal about Chinese women coming to the U.S. to give birth. As long as prospective mothers don't lie in their visa interviews or overstay their visas, they are legally in the clear. But the practice rankles both build-the-wall Trump supporters and pro-immigration activists alike. Somehow, wealthy families from Shanghai and Beijing don't seem to fit well into either the nativist or the nation-of-immigrants narratives that dominate American political culture today. It's yet another way in which China's growing footprint forces some to think harder about dearly held California values: Is openness to immigration predicated on the premise that the immigrants are poor? Or particularly hardworking? Or from a certain part of the world?

Looked at from a strictly *financial* perspective, birth tourism can make a lot of sense. Hospitals—especially those with Chinese-speaking staff—can reap a financial windfall from expectant Chinese mothers. That cash flow can help make up financial ground lost by treating uninsured patients or those unable to cover their copays. Lancaster's Antelope Valley Hospital could use the help. It had been limping along financially, suffering from declining government support and huge numbers of patients unable to pay their bills. In June of 2013, Moody's credit rating service put the hospital under review for a possible downgrade to "junk bond" status.

To solve those problems, Parris dreamed of transforming the hospital into a destination for birth tourism, possibly building an entire wing dedicated to serving China's rich. He took the idea to Dr. Abdallah Farrukh, a Lebanese-born neurosurgeon who chaired the hospital's board of directors.

"I was going to revitalize the hospital with it," Parris told me in 2016. "We were going to buy one of the hotels. We were well into the process when all of a sudden it blew up like this was a crime."

At the same time the California labor commissioner was preparing to raid the BYD factory, nurses from the hospital publicly confronted Dr. Farrukh during a board meeting. They demanded to know what was going on and why the decision had been made behind closed doors. Farrukh tried to dance around the issue by citing "trade secrets" but eventually gave a simple explanation: we need the money. Farrukh claimed that 40 percent of the hospital's patients were uninsured residents getting free service and that the hospital needed a new revenue stream from birth tourism to stabilize cash flow.

"It's a welcome business," he told a local reporter. "It's phenomenal. They pay up front, and they pay double what Medicare pays."

The cat was out of the bag, and Lancaster was not happy. A poll in the *Antelope Valley Press* showed 95 percent opposition to the plan. A cartoon in *The Antelope Valley Times* showed an endless stream of Chinese women in military fatigues marching out of the hospital, a baby cradled in one arm and Mao's *Little Red Book* in the other. The cartoon's caption: "Coming Soon: Birthing tourism citizenship included. Made in COMMUNIST CHINA. Delivered in Lancaster, USA."

Parris was blindsided by the uproar.

"To me it made perfect sense," Parris told me. "You have affluent Chinese coming over here, and their children become U.S. citizens. We don't want that? I thought the State Department was in on it because they were giving them visas! . . . What we should be doing is saying, 'If you have a PhD in money, we'll pay you to come.' Seriously!"

Farrukh appeared similarly baffled at the backlash.

"We have been doing this for free for years, mostly for the Hispanic population," Farrukh told a local reporter. "These people from China, they come here and they pay. People say it is unethical to deliver for the Chinese woman for money. . . . Why is this unethical? I am having a hard time comprehending that."

Parris and Farrukh's bafflement notwithstanding, the plan just wasn't going to fly. Bringing Chinese mothers to the Mojave Desert to pop out American citizens for a small fee touched too many raw spots: immigration, the decline of middle America, and the rise of "Communist China." Parris backed down, quietly shelving the plan and bitterly absorbing the first public defeat in his quest to partner with China.

"I think there are a lot of racist people in this city who are really opposed to us doing business with people in China for no other reason than that they are Chinese."

JAPANOPHOBIA REDUX

Backlash against foreign investment in the U.S. isn't new. The last time a rising economic power was buying up hotels and opening up factories on U.S. soil, America found itself swept up in "Japanophobia"—widespread fear that the Japanese were economically infiltrating and conquering America through their exports and investments.[21] A glance back at Japan's own global investment wave and American reactions offers perspective on the promise and pitfalls that a rising Asian power faces when setting up shop in the United States.

Economically, Japan was the China of the 1970s and '80s. Roaring back from its World War II defeat, Japan turned itself into an export powerhouse and embarked on a three-decade "economic miracle," one that foreshadowed the rise of the manufacturing-driven economies in South Korea, Taiwan, and then mainland China. Japanese firms, benefiting from strategic government interventions, initially conquered their home markets and then pushed their products around the globe. First came the textiles, cheap electronics, and cars, but by the mid-1980s Japan's most eye-catching export was capital.

Brash Japanese investors threw down huge stockpiles of cash for trophy acquisitions across the U.S.: Pebble Beach golf course, the Rockefeller Center, Columbia Pictures. At the same time, trade tensions led to a large increase in Japanese greenfield investment in the U.S. With cheaper and more fuel-efficient Japanese cars decimating market share for American brands like General Motors, U.S. trade negotiators pushed their Japanese counterparts to accept "voluntary export restraints" on the number of cars produced in Japan and shipped to the U.S. To get around those restraints and keep their market share increasing, Japanese companies like Toyota responded by simply moving those factories to the U.S. That compromise created new jobs in the U.S. but also brought American workers face-to-face with Japanese bosses for the first time. In the eyes of many Americans, Japan appeared primed to establish a global economic empire, and these investors and foremen were its emissaries.

Americans looked at Japan with a mix of admiration and fear. College students poured into Japanese language classes. Airport bookstores stocked their shelves with paperbacks on the secrets to Japanese business success. Blockbusters like *Blade Runner* and *Back to the Future Part II* depicted Japan as surpassing America as an economic and cultural force. The media fanned those fears with inflammatory and sometimes xenophobic depictions of Japan as an alien conqueror. When Japanese conglomerate Sony Corporation bought Columbia Pictures for $3.4 billion in cash, *Newsweek*'s cover depicted the Statue of Liberty draped in a kimono next to the headline JAPAN INVADES HOLLYWOOD. Even respected journalists fed the narrative with attacks on "voracious" and "canny" Japanese tycoons using their investments as a Trojan horse for subjugating American society.

Anti-Japanese attacks did damage. By the late 1980s, Americans were telling pollsters that Japanese economic dominance posed a greater threat to the U.S. than the dangers emanating from the Soviet Union.

Apart from that overblown rhetoric, many sober analysts did present substantial reasons for monitoring and potentially curbing Japanese investment. Those reasons largely fell into two buckets: national security and fairness. As Silicon Valley played a larger role in both consumer and military equipment, the lines between these industries blurred, making the acquisition of certain technology firms suspect. Concerns around fairness centered on the way the Japanese government protected and promoted its own companies. Japan's own restrictions on import and investments kept American companies out of Japan's home market, while currency policy and liberal bank loans strengthened the balance sheets of Japanese firms.

Those twin fears hit political prime time in 1987, when Japanese IT juggernaut Fujitsu attempted to buy Fairchild Semiconductors, a computer chip manufacturer and frequent military contractor. Reagan's secretary of commerce and secretary of defense publicly objected to the deal on national security grounds, claiming the U.S. military couldn't be dependent on foreign powers for crucial communications technology. *The New York Times* quoted a senior official as saying, "This is a test case. If Japan can come in and buy this company, it can come in and buy them all over the place. We don't want to see the semiconductor industry under Japanese control." Japan also stood accused of hindering market access for American-made supercomputers and of skirting recent agreements on semiconductor exports. Disrupting the Fairchild agreement was widely seen as payback for Japan's protectionist policies. With public anger and political pressure mounting, Fujitsu withdrew its bid, citing "rising political controversy in the U.S." The following year, Congress passed the Exon-Florio amendment, which further empowered the president to block such mergers or acquisitions of domestic firms by foreign companies if they harm national security. After the Fairchild debacle, scrutiny from CFIUS and the executive branch—or even the possibility of one—led other Japanese firms to abandon acquisitions of American companies in industries such as precision machine tools.

On the factory floor, Japanese businesses faced different issues. When

Japanese firms began opening offices and factories in the American heartland, these places became petri dishes for international exchange and fertile ground for culture clashes. The biggest cultural blind spot for Japanese firms lay in discriminatory HR practices. Coming from a much more homogenous society, and one with deeply gendered workplace norms, Japanese managers learned about workplace discrimination the hard way: lawsuits. During the late 1980s, Honda, Nissan, and many other Japanese firms stood accused of racism and sexism in the way they treated African Americans and women. In an added twist, the early 1990s saw a spate of lawsuits for discrimination based on national origin—essentially a glass ceiling for all American workers. In 1990, an American marketing executive sued his former Japanese employer, claiming that he had been fired and replaced by a Japanese employee solely because of his nationality.

"They keep us long enough to learn what we know," the dismissed executive told *The New York Times*. "Americans are disposable commodities for them."

The Chinese investment wave of recent years has had an eerily back-to-the-future quality: the patterns, pitfalls, and politics all echo Japan's arrival a generation ago. Chinese investment had its Fairchild moment in 2016 and 2017, when heightened scrutiny led CFIUS, President Obama, and President Trump to nix a series of Chinese takeovers, including of financial services firm MoneyGram and Lattice Semiconductors. Chinese investment got its Exon-Florio when the DIUx report led to the Foreign Investment Risk Review and Modernization Act discussed in chapter 3. The "Buy America" provision that forced BYD to set up shop in the U.S. echoed the "voluntary export restraints" placed on Japan, and BYD's own legal problems stemmed from Sandra Itkoff's national origin discrimination lawsuit against the company.

Those melodramas are playing out against a geopolitical backdrop eerily similar to the 1980s: an America unsure of its place in the world, anxious about a rising Asian power, and uneasy with the foreign faces laying claim to pieces of the American landscape.

But twenty-five years after this wave of Japanophobia peaked, Japanese investment in the U.S. looks like a success story. Despite a dramatic drop in new investment following Japan's 1991 stock market collapse, existing Japanese investments continue to generate jobs, income, and even innovation. Its auto facilities in the U.S.—which produce primarily for American consumers—have continued to grow and eventually thrive. In 2015, Japanese auto firms alone employed close to half a million Americans in their factories, offices, and dealerships.[22] Three-quarters of Japanese-branded vehicles sold in the U.S. are now made in North America.

In the end, the biggest contributor to quieting fears of Japanese investment was the collapse of the Japanese economy itself. The implosion of Japan's asset bubble in the early nineties meant less foreign money chasing trophy properties on U.S. soil. The ensuing "lost decade" of anemic economic growth also put to rest fears of American subservience to Japanese overlords. Meanwhile, the Japanese-owned companies that had already set up shop here slowly wove themselves into the fabric of America. For many people growing up in the 1990s, brands like Sony Pictures feel as American as Columbia ever was.

RESURRECTION

By late 2013, BYD looked like anything but a beloved American company. Over the preceding months, the firm had been tagged with the most negative stereotypes about China. It stood accused of exploiting workers at a taxpayer-sponsored sweatshop, of manufacturing cheap and unsafe products, and of forming the vanguard in a communist invasion of the American heartland. It had been investigated by the state of California and saw its first major contract snatched from its hands. Four years after the governor welcomed the company to the state, BYD's California dream was slipping away.

And then, slowly, steadily, the company regained its footing. Despite the protests and calls for a boycott, L.A. Metro stuck with its original contract for five BYD buses. In December, the Antelope Valley Transit Authority, which covers Lancaster and adjoining cities, went in for a pair of forty-foot BYD buses. Funding for those buses came from a grant arranged by Supervisor Antonovich. And in April 2015, BYD once again entered the bidding process for the Long Beach contract that it had lost to FTA maneuvering. The Chinese firm won again, with Proterra finishing third behind the Canadian company New Flyer.

With those contracts under its belt, BYD finally hit its stride in late 2015. That September, BYD came out on top of bidding for the largest electric bus order in U.S. history. Washington State took bids on a fleet of 800 electric buses in twelve different categories, with BYD winning ten of the twelve categories.[23] A few months later, the Antelope Valley Transit Authority—now chaired by Rex Parris's vice mayor—pledged to become the nation's first 100 percent electric bus fleet, ordering eighty-five BYD buses. Those contracts quickly translated into jobs in Lancaster. By 2016, the company was up to 257 full-time equivalent jobs, and by mid-2018 that number had shot up to over 700.[24]

Encouraged by the progress on jobs and clean energy, Parris got back at it. He began courting China Power, the country's massive state-owned electricity producer, hoping the company would launch a hydrogen energy project and plug directly into Lancaster's grid.

"China Power is all over the world," Parris told me, referencing some of the company's international hydropower projects. "But they're not here in the U.S. because everybody is scared of them. Now, are they going to bring spies with them? Probably. That's the FBI's job."

That tension between local engagement and national retrenchment has become all the more striking in recent years, as the national-level U.S.–China relationship on investment and climate has deteriorated. Chinese capital controls of 2017 curtailed a series of billion-dollar acquisitions, including both Chairman Wang's adventures in Hollywood and high-profile purchases of technology companies. Meanwhile, U.S. expansions to CFIUS and the downward spiral of President Trump's trade war squeezed investments even further. After peaking at $55.8 billion in 2016, Chinese FDI in the U.S. plummeted to just $9.1 billion in 2017 and dropped even further in 2018.[25]

On the climate front, years of fragile progress was shattered when President Trump took office. Donald Trump has repeatedly called climate change a "hoax," one that was "invented by and for the Chinese in order to make U.S. manufacturing noncompetitive." In June of 2017 he made good on his campaign threats to unilaterally withdraw from the Paris treaty.

But amid that national backsliding, BYD and California's own climate efforts bucked the trend. As an established greenfield business that earns revenue in U.S. dollars, BYD has been able to sidestep the effects of both Chinese capital controls and U.S. investment restrictions. And on the same day that President Trump announced his withdrawal from the Paris Agreement, I sat down with Governor Brown in his office to discuss his upcoming trip to China, during which he'd announce a series of new agreements, including new university research partnerships and a joint clean energy fund.

"The problem is not survival today—it's survival tomorrow. Is there enough wisdom to take the action now to make survival possible? That's the open question," he told me. "So we have to get going. That's why I'm going to do everything I can to encourage China and work with them."

LESSONS LEARNED

Rex Parris's China dream and BYD's American dream serve as both a playbook and a cautionary tale for Chinese greenfield investment in the U.S., yielding lessons for both the American and Chinese sides.

The first lesson for mayors and investment promotion offices is to spend time—not money—when wooing Chinese investors. Years of canceled contracts, petty fines, and negative news coverage could have been avoided had Los Angeles never offered, or BYD never accepted, the $1.6 million grant to renovate its headquarters. That grant was pocket change to BYD—equal to just 0.01 percent of BYD's $14 billion valuation that year—but it set off a chain of events that would drag the company and its L.A. boosters through the mud for years to come.[26] A government handout to a big-name corporation—especially a *foreign* corporation—is like blood on the shark snout of American civil society. Journalists hungry for a scoop see red when politicians open public coffers to private companies.

Chinese companies arriving in the U.S. don't need handouts; they need hand-holding. These firms may strut confidently onto the world stage, but they can be somewhat clueless when it comes to local American laws, regulations, and business practices. They struggle under the strictures of U.S. employment rules, and they make major mistakes in dealing with confrontational journalists.

Rex Parris's approach to investment promotion worked because it was hands-on and multidimensional. He rolled out the red carpet and rolled up his sleeves on regulatory issues. He logged the hours needed to convince BYD that Lancaster was serious about making this relationship work. He went to bat for the company and pulled levers behind the scenes to help them secure legitimate business contracts. Yes, there was a financial incentive in the form of adjacent land gifted to BYD, but that incentive only kicked in *after* BYD had hired over 200 local employees. What won the day was Parris's ability to help the company navigate an alien environment.

That fish-out-of-water phenomenon reveals the central lesson for Chinese firms setting up shop in the U.S.: forget everything you think you know about government, business, and civil society. China's business environment is as complex and cutthroat as anywhere in the world—industrial espionage, corrupt tax collectors, and predatory pricing are all run of the mill. But Chinese executives can look hopelessly naive when confronted with the American equivalent: a free press and rabble-rousing activists.

A person working with the governor's office on BYD's recruitment told me that the company essentially transplanted their model for doing business in China. The first priority? *Gaoding yige shuji*—"lock down a Communist Party secretary"—in this case the governor or mayor. That's because in China good government relations can overcome almost anything. If a company has its political ducks in a row, liberal bank loans, glowing media coverage, and cooperative policing can all be secured. Entire businesses are built on the premise that one personal relationship with a key official—an uncle in the transportation bureau or an in-law with the police department—will guarantee profitability.

So when BYD got the red-carpet treatment from governors and mayors alike, they assumed they had it made. Pesky reporters and vocal activists were ignored, because pesky reporters and vocal activists are virtually non-existent in most Chinese industries. What could go wrong? The company failed to recognize that in America, a photo op with the mayor doesn't make you a winner; it makes you a target.

American reactions to Chinese investment are inextricably tangled up with feelings about our own place in the world. Unchallenged for decades as the preeminent world power, Americans look to China's global ambitions with a mix of awe and anxiety.

Meanwhile, China is going through superpower puberty: after a dramatic growth spurt, it's still getting comfortable in this new body. Chinese firms are stretching their legs and feeling out their limits on the global stage. They have plenty more ambition than experience, and that's showing in local frictions from Kenya to Lancaster.

In that sense, China and its leading companies are at a stage not unlike where the United States was at the turn of the twentieth century: confident in its destiny, but unsure of how to get there. When it comes to investment on American shores, Chinese firms could take advice from the man who pushed America onto the global stage during those first tentative decades. Speak softly, and carry a big stick.

CAREER DAY IN LANCASTER

When I return to Lancaster in May 2016, BYD is in the midst of a hiring spree. On a blazing-hot desert day, a local employment agency is hosting a BYD jobs fair at a community center in the corner of a city park. The midday sun has emptied the park, but the one-room community center is packed. BYD is looking to fill 74 positions this weekend—welders, painters, mechanics—and another 225 before the end of the year. The air-conditioning is on full blast as volunteers hand out Scantrons for a math and reading test.

Most of the applicants are people of color, many in their twenties and thirties. Some are fresh out of school, others trying to patch together contract jobs into a living. Few of the people that I spoke to knew that BYD was a Chinese company.

Adam, a thirtysomething white man with a big beard and a belly to match, tacks a "yes, ma'am" or "no, sir" on the end of all his sentences. He grew up in neighboring Palmdale and worked for a local RV company but had been laid off the day before his child was born. Since then, he's been doing pool construction jobs in Hollywood, building pools for actors like Charlie from the *Mighty Ducks* movies. He's now applying for a job as a welder. He figures the entry-level jobs will make about $15 per hour, but there is plenty of room to up that with experience. Asked about Mayor Parris, Adam talks about the renovated downtown and local schools bearing his name.

Next to Adam sits a young African American woman, filling out her own application. This month she is finishing up her accreditation as an aircraft mechanic and applying to both a bachelor's program and a range of jobs in the region. Talking through her prospects, she looks up from the forms with something between a grimace and a smile.

"Whoever gives me a job, that's where I'll go."

6

A PHOENIX RISING
FROM THE TOXINS

I t's eleven thirty p.m. on a cool Los Angeles summer night, and I'm standing at the foot of one of the largest construction sites in town. The dark
concrete tower in front of me is sandwiched on top and bottom by flood-
lights: they bathe the construction crews at ground level in white light, and
some fifteen stories up they illuminate yellow cranes emerging from the
highest levels built thus far. Jackhammers are rattling just a few feet in front
of me, but I'm leaning back and looking upward toward the cranes swiveling
back and forth across the night sky.

Growing up in the San Francisco Bay Area, I didn't have many chances
to watch our physical world take shape in steel and concrete. The Bay Area
is notorious for its not-in-my-backyard opposition to new construction, an
instinct rooted in aesthetic considerations but also a desire to keep one's
home value high by snuffing out any new housing supply. So after moving to
China in 2010, I found myself entranced when watching construction crews
at work. I would talk my way into unfinished subway tunnels and half-built
high-rises. The sheer grit of the workers demands respect, and the pace of
development will take your breath away. Skyscrapers seem to be conjured
out of thin air, and new subway systems expand like spider webs in time-

lapse videos. The scene in downtown L.A. isn't as sweeping as some I've seen in China, but the stark lighting imbues it all with a sense of hyperrealism and drama.

My spell of industrial voyeurism is broken when a woman in a neon vest and yellow construction helmet rushes toward me. She's shouting something that I can't quite hear over the jackhammers, but her arm gestures make the message clear: back up—right now. I shuffle backward across the narrow street to the opposite sidewalk. She jogs across with me and extends her hand toward mine.

"My name's Deborah," she says with a smile. "Cold hands, warm heart."

Deborah is a sturdy black woman in what looks to be her midthirties. She removes her hard hat to reveal a blue bandanna holding her hair in place. I ask her what's going on with the development in front of us, a megaproject that its owners have dubbed Metropolis. She tells me about the rotation of day and night shifts, how they've closed down a nearby highway exit after rush hour to ease the loading of materials. From there, she launches into a treatise on the surrounding buildings. L.A. is almost all sprawl, but here in the downtown sits a gaggle of high-rises, and Deborah has a nickname for each of them.

"You know that building over there?" she says, pointing northeast. "I call it the tower. By the Ernst and Young, just in front of that. Know why I call it the tower? Because it's always on the news. If you turn on the TV, it's always showing that building. Actually, I call it my castle."

I can't quite keep up with Deborah as she rattles off her nicknames for the surrounding buildings, but it's clear that she's in her element out here.

She's not alone in that feeling. Fresh off carrying out the largest construction boom in history in their home country, Chinese real estate developers have now landed down in this corner of Los Angeles and made themselves right at home. Deborah's ultimate boss on this project is Greenland USA, a thoroughly American-sounding name for a company. In fact, Greenland USA is the subsidiary of a Chinese state-owned firm based in Shanghai, a massive developer that one industry insider described to me as "basically a wing of the Shanghai city government." And this narrow strip of land in downtown Los Angeles is ground zero for the largest Chinese building boom in U.S. history. Within just a half-mile radius of Deborah's construction site, Chinese developers have undertaken five major projects: luxury hotels, thousands of high-end condos, and hundreds of thousands of square feet of new shops.

"When all these megaprojects are finished," one local real estate executive told the *Los Angeles Times*, "they're going to have to reshoot the postcard picture of downtown L.A."

SKYSCRAPERS, SUBURBS, AND SUBSIDIZED HOUSING

Over the past six years, a wave of Chinese money has poured into U.S. real estate. The trend is national, but as usual the center is here in California. The Golden State is the top location for new Chinese-funded developments, as well as individual home purchases by Chinese buyers. That money is redrawing urban skylines, driving up home prices in the suburbs, and financing the construction of tens of thousands of new condos and McMansions across the state.

Chinese money enters California real estate markets through three primary channels: new commercial projects funded by Chinese developers (such as Deborah's project), home purchases by individual Chinese families, and EB-5 funding. The federal EB-5 program grants green cards to foreign nationals and their families who invest $500,000 into a U.S. business project that creates ten jobs. The program was intended to be a win-win-win: local projects get cheap funding, American workers get jobs, and would-be immigrants get green cards. Over the past decade, Chinese investors have come to dominate the EB-5 program, winning 80 percent of the available green cards in the program and pouring billions of dollars into real estate projects. The EB-5 immigrants are passive investors—they don't control the project or get a condo in return—but the cheap financing they provide has kickstarted some of the most sweeping master-planned developments in the country.

None of these inflows are without controversy. Control over land, hous-ing, and citizenship strikes at core questions facing both California and America as a whole. As Chinese home buyers, developers, and immigrant investors set down roots on U.S. soil, they've met with backlash from neigh-bors, rival developers, and U.S. senators. All that activity has set the stage for local tensions with international dimensions.

EB-5 projects have presented some of the thorniest questions. In San Francisco, the program has been used to finance the city's largest real estate development in decades, a master-planned community on an abandoned naval shipyard that is set to add over 12,000 homes to a city starved for housing. The development, the San Francisco Shipyard, is unfolding in the Hunters Point–Bayview neighborhood, the poorest and last predominantly black neighborhood in the city. Local residents look toward the Shipyard with hope for construction jobs and affordable housing but also with fear of displacement via another wave of gentrification—this time funded by distant Chinese investors whose only hope for Hunters Point is that it gets them a green card.

Nationally, the EB-5 program has come under blistering attacks. Crit-ics contend that corporate developers have hijacked the program, turning American green cards into a subsidy for attracting low-interest loans from foreigners. Accusations of corruption found a focal point when Jared Kush-ner's family used the program—and their brother's position in the Trump White House—to raise money from Chinese investors for a luxury develop-ment in Jersey City.

But in the world of real estate financing, beggars can't be choosers, and when it comes to funding major developments in communities like Hunt-ers Point, even America's largest developers are often beggars. That reality has forced locals, businesses, and policy makers to confront uncomfortable questions. If American banks won't invest in our poorest communities, is it time to outsource that task to Chinese millionaires? When both anti-immigrant sentiment and working-class desperation are running high, are we okay trading green cards for construction jobs? Can money really make you an American?

Out in the suburbs, these questions have taken on a different tint. In my hometown of Palo Alto, a technology boom and great public schools have already turned this leafy suburb into a very expensive place to live. But beginning in 2012, a major influx of Chinese home purchases ratcheted up prices even further. That sparked a backlash from some Palo Altans who hated that newly purchased homes were left empty and who feared that foreigners were pricing them out of their own neighborhoods. The hyperliberal suburb prides itself on embracing diversity and "disruption," but some residents began venting their frustration over Chinese home buyers who they see as inflating home prices and imposing "Chinese values" on Palo Alto. Those outbursts were sparked by a role reversal that has turned the traditional immigrant narrative on its head. America built its identity around opening its doors to "your tired, your poor, your huddled masses," but what happens when the immigrants are richer than us?

THE PHOENIX

On a sunny June afternoon in 2013, San Francisco's political leadership gathered at a hilltop in Hunters Point–Bayview for a groundbreaking ceremony. Dressed in a dark suit, designer sunglasses, and a white fedora, former San Francisco mayor and legendary local power broker Willie Brown worked the crowd. Ed Lee, San Francisco's first Chinese American mayor, gave interviews and chatted with community members. The mood was boisterous, and for good reason. After more than two decades of planning, bidding, and decontamination, development was finally under way on the San Francisco Shipyard. Building on the site of the abandoned Hunters Point Naval Shipyard—700 acres of industrial land that went unused for decades—the project is slated to be one of the largest in San Francisco history. Developers envision 12,000 new homes, 3.5 million square feet of retail and office space, and 300 acres of parks covering Hunters Point and neighboring Candlestick Point.[1]

The project is unique in its scale and also its location, taking place in the most impoverished part of one of the wealthiest cities in America. After the closure of the Hunters Point Naval Shipyard in 1974, the area was drained of its economic lifeblood. For decades, Hunters Point grew increasingly economically and demographically isolated from the rest of the city, as both poverty and crime spiked. Chemical and radiological pollutants had burrowed into the area's dirt and made their way into the air, with locals pointing to these as the cause of abnormal cancer clusters in the neighborhood. That untreated contamination kept this land fenced off for decades, and it continues to haunt the project and the people who make their lives there.

Boosters for the Shipyard promise it will turn things around. The construction alone will bring thousands of new jobs to the area, and a benefits package negotiated with the developer promises to both subsidize community programs and set aside affordable housing for local residents. The development project, they hope, will infuse new life into San Francisco's last predominantly black community.

"For decades, the Hunters Point Shipyard was the economic engine for San Francisco and for the people—even my own family—who came from the South to work there. Its closure really hurt this community," local city supervisor Malia Cohen told one reporter. "It's going to take a lot of work and a lot of money to continue to move down the right path, but what we are seeing now is a renaissance. We are turning it around, like a phoenix rising up from the toxins."

What no one at the groundbreaking ceremony in 2013 mentioned was where exactly the money was coming from: China. The Shipyard project was decades and billions of dollars in the making, but at the critical juncture following the global financial crisis, financing froze up. Battered by bad loans and crumbling derivatives, banks stopped lending, especially to infrastructure-heavy projects like the Shipyard. Investments in basic infrastructure for master-planned communities—grading the slopes, laying down the roads, digging the sewer lines—can take decades to generate real returns. America's institutional lenders just didn't have the stomach for it.

With no one else willing to front the money for the project, the developer and the city of San Francisco turned to China. In 2012 the Shipyard's developer, Lennar Corporation, came close to a deal with China Develop-ment Bank for a massive $1.7 billion loan to finance both the Shipyard and a similarly huge development on Treasure Island, in the middle of the San Francisco Bay.[2] But when those talks fell apart over questions of control over the project, Lennar turned to the EB-5 program. It joined up with a politically connected San Francisco firm that raises EB-5 capital and began aggressively pitching the Shipyard to Chinese families looking for a short-cut to getting a U.S. green card. Over the next four years, Lennar would take on over $300 million in EB-5 financing from 600 foreign families, more than 80 percent of them Chinese.[3]

That money breathed new life into the Shipyard. Infrastructure was laid down, new houses went up, and a counterintuitive bond was forged between a group of Chinese millionaires and the residents of San Francisco's poorest neighborhood.

FROM SHRIMPERS TO NUCLEAR RADIATION

This wasn't the first time Chinese immigrants made their presence felt at Hunters Point. One hundred and forty-two years earlier, in 1871, Chinese fishermen set up a series of shrimping camps along the land's northern shoreline. Italian fishermen had pioneered the shrimping business in San Francisco just a few years earlier, but their nets used a relatively loose weave that brought in a modest haul. When the Chinese shrimpers arrived, they brought with them techniques used in their home province of Guangdong: nets with a tighter weave that brought in massive hauls of small shrimp and other fish. They soon dominated the business, selling some plump fresh shrimp locally and drying a large portion of their catch for export back to China.

But that dominance engendered resentment. White fisherman argued that the Chinese nets were sweeping up too many small fish, and beginning in 1901 they passed a series of laws limiting the shrimping season and ban-ning the export of dried shrimp. The Chinese shrimpers challenged these laws, and their case made it all the way up to the United States Supreme Court. But they ultimately lost the case, and in 1911 Chinese nets were banned outright.

By the 1930s, Chinese shrimpers had staged a brief comeback, and shrimping outfits with names like the Quong Duck Chong Company operated in and around Hunters Point. But once World War II began in Europe, Hunters Point was deemed too valuable of a dock for Chinese fishermen. They were evicted, and the shacks at their seaside encampments set on fire. A photo from 1938 shows men from the San Francisco Fire Department looking on with arms crossed while one building goes up in flames. It would be seventy-five years before Chinese enterprise would once again shape this shoreline.

During that time, the vast swath of the land on which the Shipyard sits has been either the engine driving the local economy or the millstone dragging it down. The construction of the Naval Shipyard during World War II displaced the local Chinese shrimping encampments but created tens of thousands of jobs building the warships that fought in the Pacific. Photos of the Naval Shipyard from that era show America's military-industrial behemoth firing on all cylinders: battleships the length of football fields stand upright in the shipyard's dry dock, cranes swap out gun turrets, and blocks of soldiers march in formation while longshoremen hustle on and off the ships. My own grandfather, Leo Sheehan, took part in this wartime shipbuilding boom, working as a night watchman at the Richmond Shipyards fifteen miles to the north of Hunters Point.

By the end of World War II, the Hunters Point Shipyard employed 18,000 workers, one-third of them African American.[4] Many of those black workers had arrived as part of the Great Migration of the mid-twentieth century, leaving the Jim Crow South in pursuit of industrial work in cities of the north and west. Some of those workers at the Hunters Point Shipyard helped load the fissile material for "Little Boy," the atomic bomb dropped on Hiroshima. But that explosion signaled the beginning of the end of the shipbuilding era and a transition to Hunters Point serving as a center for radioactive decontamination and experimentation. During the early Cold War years, the navy attempted to decontaminate the ships used in Pacific nuclear tests at the shipyards and headquartered a radiological experimentation facility that tested the effects of radiation exposure on goats, rats, and the Bay's tidal currents. The environmental fallout from those tests would poison the soil and leave the area unlivable for decades.

When the navy ceased all operations at the shipyards in 1974, the region's economy came undone. White workers could leverage federal policies encouraging home ownership to move out of the area, but black Americans were deliberately excluded from these programs and the emerging middle-class neighborhoods they built. Economic and social conditions around Hunters Point deteriorated, with guns, gangs, and police brutality all taking a toll. Pollution from nearby coal-fired power plants and hazardous waste dumps plagued the area. In 1989, the navy declared that the level of radiation contamination required the area be turned into a Superfund site, a designation for the nation's most expensive and drawn-out decontamination processes. The cleanup in Hunters Point would take multiple decades and cost hundreds of millions of dollars, and rumors continued to swirl that the navy was cutting corners and putting local residents in danger. But those residents were told not to worry: once the land was all cleaned up, it would set the table for a redevelopment project that would transform the area, and their lives, for the better.

THE RUG GETS PULLED

While the navy began mopping up its radiological mess, the city courted developers. Lennar Corporation, a Fortune 500 company with a specialty in rehabbing derelict military bases, won over the city with a unique proposal for shouldering costs and sharing profits. Lennar paid nothing for the land, instead promising to take on the costs of building basic infrastructure in the area. It also promised to share profits with the city after the company reaped a 25 percent return on investment.

But just as the project was gaining momentum, the national subprime mortgage boom came unraveled, dragging the global economy down with it. Institutional lenders with large bets on housing or land saw their valuations evaporate overnight. Those lenders retreated from markets to lick their wounds and slowly repair the damage to their balance sheets.

"The housing markets, the whole capital markets, collapsed, which certainly slowed down access to credit to begin any vertical construction," Kofi Bonner, regional vice president for Lennar Urban and head of the Shipyard project, told me in 2014. "We found that land development capital was very, very difficult to find in the U.S."

Bonner had been updating members of the Hunters Point Shipyard Citizens Advisory Committee (CAC) regularly on timelines for obtaining funding and starting construction. Many of the community benefits Lennar had promised—and the long-term hope for revitalizing the community—hinged on Lennar securing loans to kick-start the project. But as the financial crisis spread, CAC member Christine Johnson noticed a shift in Lennar's presentations.

"I remember that the conversations changed a lot about financing. In 2007, even into 2008 and somewhat into 2009, it was not a concern. We saw quarterly pro formas, and when you looked, it had sources and uses." But as the full depth of the crisis became clear, "you started to see some sources of funds fall away. And then at the end of 2009, I noticed that Kofi was in China all the time."

TRANSPACIFIC HOUSE HUNTERS

While Kofi Bonner was crossing the Pacific to court Chinese financing for Hunters Point, Chinese home buyers were flocking in the other direction. In the years following the global financial crisis, China's polluted air, stultifying education system, and precarious economic fundamentals spurred well over 100,000 Chinese families to buy homes in the United States.

Between 2011 and 2015, the value of residential real estate purchases by Chinese buyers more than quadrupled to $28.6 billion, turning China into the top source of foreign home purchases.[5] The average price paid for a home by Chinese buyers also shot up. According to data from the National Association of Realtors (NAR), in 2011 Chinese were paying just $370,902 on average for a home. In 2016, that average was approaching a million dollars, with around two-thirds of those purchases made with all cash.

Chinese home buyers dabbled in several major "gateway cities" throughout the country—Los Angeles, New York, Miami, and even Detroit—but California took in the lion's share of buyers. In 2013, NAR data showed that 53 percent of reported purchases by Chinese buyers were in the Golden State. That number slipped to 37 percent in 2016 as buyers began to diversify, but California still outstripped the next five states (Texas, Florida, Illinois, New Jersey, and Massachusetts) combined. Within California, Chinese home buyers had their favorite locations, and one of them turned out to be my hometown of Palo Alto.

In many ways, Palo Alto is a perfect storm of things Chinese parents are looking for: blue skies, good schools, and a strong Chinese community. Despite American fascination with the academic success fostered by Chinese "tiger mothers," many Chinese parents themselves are looking for an escape from the suffocating competitiveness and rote learning endemic in China's public schools. Palo Alto offered top-notch public schools combined with a more laid-back American pedagogy and also took on plenty of shine from the refracted glow of Silicon Valley. *Chuangxin*—"innovation"—was emerging as the national buzzword in China at exactly the same time these home buyers began heading overseas. For wealthy and status-conscious buyers, Palo Alto's connections to Stanford and companies like Google placed it in a class all its own. Steve Jobs—who's almost as worshipped in China as in the U.S.—made his home in the town. In the eyes of many Chinese parents, that was endorsement enough.

THE NEW SWISS BANK ACCOUNT

But the outbound real estate rush was about more than finding a healthy environment for raising kids. It also represented a safe haven for hard-earned (and ill-gotten) gains. The Chinese economy was undergoing a major transition, and real estate abroad became a way to stash cash far from China's precarious financial system and currency. For corrupt Chinese officials or businesspeople who earned that cash in less-than-scrupulous ways, overseas real estate became both a way to launder that dirty money and also a landing pad should they need to flee their own country. For China's millionaire class, American homes were becoming the new Swiss bank account.

China had powered through the global financial crisis largely unscathed, but it did so by flooding the country with spending on new highways, high-speed rail lines, and high-rises. In the three years spanning 2011 through 2013, the country used more cement than the United States did in the entire twentieth century.[6] But as the economic adrenaline rush of the stimulus faded, Chinese people and companies grew increasingly jittery about the fundamental stability of the country's property markets and financial system.

The country's stock markets remained immature and highly erratic, so Chinese households looking to preserve and grow their savings poured them into multiple home purchases. Chinese private housing markets had only existed since the 1990s, and prices had done nothing but rise since then. Even relatively low-income people—taxi drivers or fruit sellers—might own three or four apartments. But in the years following the global financial crisis, Chinese housing markets took on all the telltale signs of a bubble: prices totally detached from local salaries and massive tracts of uninhabited apartment towers on the edges of cities. The country's financial system was also showing strains. Shadow banking and complex "wealth management products" proliferated, while traditional banks issued new loans to help borrowers keep up with payments on old loans. Many analysts warned of the imminent implosion of a housing bubble, one that would make the U.S. subprime crisis look like child's play.

Adding to that anxiety was a major power struggle at the highest ranks of the Chinese Communist Party. In early 2012, China's most handsome and charismatic high-level official, Bo Xilai, came crashing down in a lurid corruption scandal. Bo had seemed destined for the politburo before his police chief fled to the American consulate and the public learned of sex scandals, mansions on the French Riviera, and his wife's poisoning of a British business associate. In the run-up to China's once-a-decade leadership transition that fall, the country was rife with rumors of political intrigue, coups, and even assassination attempts against China's new leader, Xi Jinping.

Suddenly, keeping all of one's wealth inside China didn't seem like such a safe bet. Many Chinese families began seeking a safe haven on foreign shores. Ironically, for that safe haven they chose the asset that just a few years earlier had set off the greatest financial crisis in over seven decades: U.S. real estate.

THE LUXURY BUYERS BUS

In the fall of 2013, I was back home in Palo Alto recovering from my broken ankle. I returned to a city caught up in a flurry of Chinese home purchases. A surge in Silicon Valley IPOs had already sent home prices through the roof, and Chinese buyers threw fuel on the fire. During 2012 and 2013, median Palo Alto home prices shot up by 50 percent to nearly $2 million.[7] During that period the pace of foreign buying accelerated rapidly, with some local realtors estimating that 15 to 25 percent of all home sales in town were going to Chinese buyers.[8] Those purchases tended to be high-end and done using all cash.

"I just sold a house yesterday where there were four people from China interested, and none of them had seen the house," one real estate broker told me at the time. "There has been an impact on market values because they're all coming with cash and they know that in order to beat the other four, you need to bid it up."

Locals were already feeling the impact, but nothing highlighted the phenomenon like the Chinese buyer bus tours. As the Chinese buying trend gathered steam, local real estate firm DeLeon Realty purchased a fourteen-seat Mercedes limo bus, painted DeLeon's logo on the side, and hired a Chinese driver. Americans—especially rich Americans—might chafe at the idea of being herded onto a bus with other buyers and shuttled from house to house. Wealthy Chinese people loved it. The tours tapped into a cultural fondness for buying in groups, and requests for spots on the bus poured in.

So on a crisp October morning, I join a group of Chinese families in the parking lot outside DeLeon Realty's offices on El Camino Real. Today's tour will include homes in both Palo Alto and Menlo Park, the neighboring town where Facebook has its headquarters. A couple of the buyers hail from Taiwan, but the majority are mainland Chinese. As we wait to depart, the men huddle in one corner of the parking lot, smoking cigarettes and complaining in Mandarin about their business woes back home. On the bus, a few women chat, and one mother tries to keep her young daughter from hoarding all the complimentary bottles of water. The bus has tinted windows, and the black exterior looks like it has recently donned a fresh coat of paint. Inside, the vehicle sports rows of crisp leather seats, with purple lights running the length of the ceiling. At ten a.m., the men stub out their cigarettes and we all clamber on board.

Kim Heng, DeLeon's China lead, stands in the center aisle, welcoming everyone and introducing DeLeon Realty. She speaks primarily in Mandarin, sprinkling in English words for neighborhoods and street names. As we roll through town, Kim rattles off statistics about schools, neighborhoods, and pricing trends. She hands out a brochure that goes into further detail on local school rankings, but it is one picture of the Great Wall of China that catches my eye. The photo shows the Great Wall snaking through the mist, but as you trace its brick spine down toward the bottom of the page, the wall blends seamlessly into a picture of Stanford campus, with the school's signature Hoover Tower becoming just another guard post on the Great Wall. Tracing the transpacific wall farther down the page, it links up with the spires and spans of the Golden Gate Bridge, turning the San Francisco landmark into an extension of China's ancient wall.

Our first stop is at a Palo Alto home just up the road, a petite two-bedroom with an asking price over $1.5 million. The property is perfectly fine, but it's the second home that really catches the buyers' attention. Just over the border into Menlo Park, we step off the bus onto a wide lawn of thick green grass, looking up at a bona fide mansion. Entering the front door, we face a sweeping marble staircase climbing up to a second-floor balcony. Wandering through the house and then out to the backyard, there is a limestone patio, a water-spouting statue, and a glistening swimming pool. One of the Chinese men can't help but crack a joke.

"*Wo cao!*"—Fuck me!—"It's such a beautiful place. Why didn't Bo Xilai come here to buy his villa?"

The group has a good laugh at that one, but the question isn't totally off base. As home purchases shot up, so have revelations of corrupt Chinese officials laundering massive sums of wealth through California homes. Just two weeks before our tour, Chinese-language media broke the story of a businessman and official from Zhejiang Province who borrowed half a billion RMB before fleeing the country. The fugitive plowed a good chunk of that money into seven different mansions in Orange County.

None of the participants in today's tour are eager to talk to the American journalist on board. There's nothing particularly unusual about that—Chinese people, especially wealthy ones, tend to see no upside and plenty of downside in engaging with media. But from sprinkles of conversation on the bus I discern that a couple of the men work in the industries that drove China's economic boom: electronics exports, steel, and real estate. Once a home is secured, they hope to send their wives and children stateside with an EB-5 green card. In China, many male breadwinners choose to forego the green card and continue running their businesses back in China. Getting a green card would mean paying U.S. taxes on their global income, and no one wants that. Sometimes the mother and child will set up shop in Palo Alto while the father drops in for periodic visits. Other families will buy a home here and leave it empty except for summer and winter vacations.

That arrangement makes perfect financial (if not necessarily emotional) sense for these Chinese families. But it's also a source of friction with their neighbors. Even amid the deluge of tech money that has entered the city, longtime Palo Altans have worked to maintain a strong sense of community in these neighborhoods. Every weekend the city hosts multiple farmers' markets, and even high-flying tech executives still make time for block parties and their kids' soccer games. But many locals have begun to worry that this wave of foreign buyers represents a fundamentally different *kind* of money. We don't care where you're from, they say, but if you're going to buy these houses you should live in them and commit to our community. These folks don't want to see longtime neighbors replaced by absentee homeowners. They fret when they see untended lawns going yellow, or worry that unoccupied houses will turn into targets for burglars or squatters.

I've been hearing these whispers from neighbors and some of my own former professors in town, but no one on the bus today seems tuned in to this simmering resentment. To them, this corner of California remains a dream destination for their money and their children, if not themselves.

We stop in on a few more multimillion-dollar homes and a public garden, enjoying drinks and appetizers at the final house of the day. Returning to DeLeon's headquarters, we make our way off the bus and back into the cool Palo Alto sunshine.

THE HUNTERS POINT SHIPYARD CITIZENS ADVISORY COMMITTEE

Dr. Veronica Hunnicutt is holding court here in the basement of a local community center in Hunters Point. Wearing a long black dress, fur vest, and spectacles befitting a librarian, Dr. Hunnicutt calls the motions, hears the seconds, and registers the ayes (along with the occasional nay). She is flanked on both sides by other elderly black women from the community. With an air part grandmotherly and part professorial, she welcomes speakers up to the podium and banters with community members arrayed in folding chairs throughout the room.

The occasion is the January 2017 meeting of the Hunters Point Shipyard Citizens Advisory Committee, which Dr. Hunnicutt chairs. This CAC has been around for over twenty years and is tasked with providing local oversight and input for the Shipyard project. Essentially, its job is to make sure the community gets what it is owed when corporate developers, city politicians, and Chinese investors launch an $8 billion development project in the area.

Having worked as an educator in Hunters Point for decades, Dr. Hunnicutt has been witness to the rise, fall, and now promised "renaissance" of the area. She has made it her business to push the development forward and to make sure the benefits are shared. In this capacity, her grandmotherly disposition can be deceptive. In these meetings, she quickly pivots between chatting with her neighbors and directing pointed questions at city officials about the mechanics of a down-payment assistance program.

"The fact that this beautiful land out there has languished for so many years is too much for me to bear," she told me in 2014. "Given the potential opportunities for people in the neighborhood, as well as in the city of San Francisco, we just had to do what was needed to make this happen."

The process here is imperfect. Members of the CAC are not elected by residents, but instead appointed by San Francisco's mayor. As the organization's title suggests, they act in an "advisory" capacity, giving input to the local government but without actual veto power. And the CAC is just one of a cacophony of other local voices clamoring for a say in the project: the local Nation of Islam chapter, building contractors, a group called the Aboriginal Blackmen United, and unaffiliated local residents who just want a good job and an affordable place to live. The debate between these groups hasn't always conformed to the niceties of parliamentary debate.

"The first meeting I ever went to there was screaming; there was the Muslim Brotherhood blocking doorways; it was like four hours long," recalled former CAC member Christine Johnson in a 2017 podcast interview.[9] "I was wondering what I had gotten myself into."

But amid the mayhem, the CAC soldiered on. One of its core tasks was to negotiate a "Community Benefits Agreement" with Lennar. The agreement was essentially a package of financial and social benefits designed to make sure that the Shipyard uplifted local residents rather than displaced them. It included tens of millions of dollars in direct subsidies for youth workforce development, renovation of housing projects, new elderly service centers, and mortgage assistance. It also stipulated that 30 percent of the new homes in the development be priced at below-market rates. Dr. Hunnicutt was effusive in her praise for the agreement.

"It's a model program for the community, city, and really the nation," she told me.

PROTESTS, BENEFITS, AND EB-5

But when the financial crisis pulled the financial rug out from under the project, those benefits were suddenly in danger of disappearing. Kofi Bonner of Lennar thus began his trips to China, initially looking for a loan from China Development Bank, a massive policy-lending bank under direct control of the Chinese government. In December of 2012 local news reports signaled that a deal was near for a $1.7 billion loan that would fund both the Shipyard and a similar development on Treasure Island, but by April 2013 that deal had fallen apart.[10] In its place came the Shipyard's first dose of EB-5 financing.

The EB-5 program was created in 1990 to attract job-creating foreign investment into the United States, with a special incentive for investing in high-unemployment regions. If an EB-5 investor funds a project in a "targeted employment area," where unemployment levels are 50 percent higher than the national average, the required investment threshold is reduced to $500,000.

The initial legislation required that the investors create and manage the new business themselves. But in order to make the program more accessible for foreigners, the law was soon amended to allow for the pooling of EB-5 investments by a U.S. "regional center," essentially a financial institution that would collect a large number of $500,000 or $1 million individual investments and plow them into a large project that created the requisite number of jobs. These projects almost invariably turned out to be real estate developments, with the job creation of each investment determined by econometric analysis. Despite those changes to ease access, the EB-5 program largely sat idle for its first fifteen years. During that time, it never maxed out its annual allotment of 10,000 visas that served as the stepping-stone to green cards and U.S. permanent residency.

And then, Chinese millionaires discovered it. Beginning around 2010, wealthy Chinese began applying for the program in increasing numbers, going from 772 EB-5 visas in 2010 to over 6,000 by 2012. In 2014, the 9,128 visas issued to Chinese nationals made up over 85 percent of total EB-5 visas issued, with virtually all of the visas given for investments of $500,000 in targeted employment areas.[11]

That surge of Chinese EB-5 activity was the result of a perfect storm of push and pull factors. China's three decades of industrial development had produced a large crop of millionaires, but the choking air pollution that accompanied that development was also driving those millionaires to emigrate overseas. Moribund U.S. capital markets in the wake of the financial crisis had generated the demand for new forms of financing, with a new crop of EB-5 regional centers providing the bridge between these groups. For the developers, EB-5 financing required doing some extra paperwork, but it more than made up for that with its low interest rates. That's because the Chinese "investors" in these projects aren't really in it for the money. The U.S. green cards are the real return on investment they seek, and so developers can afford to pay out just a couple percentage points to their Chinese investors.

In 2011, Lennar began working with a politically connected regional center in San Francisco to raise EB-5 funds for the Shipyard. The megaloan from China Development Bank may have fallen through, but China's own millionaires were more than happy to make it up in small denominations. Lennar took on $77 million in EB-5 financing in 2013, allowing it to break ground on the first batch of eighty-eight homes in the Shipyard. The following year it took on nearly $100 million for more infrastructure work and the reconstruction of a housing project that abutted the development. Between 2013 and 2017, the development would take on over $300 million in EB-5 financing from around 600 Chinese families. According to economic models used by the U.S. Bureau of Labor Statistics, those investments created an estimated 12,121 jobs.[12]

Speaking to me in 2014, Dr. Hunnicutt described the EB-5 financing as crucial to moving the project forward.

"We're very grateful for the monetary support that our Chinese friends have lent to the city and county of San Francisco to make projects like the Shipyard happen," she told me.

The EB-5 program had forged an unlikely marriage between China's millionaire class and the poorest neighborhood in San Francisco. It was a partnership that spanned race, class, and nationality, but one that sometimes worked better at arm's length. Robert Xu, a San Francisco immigration lawyer, described the dangers of bringing potential investors to the site of the Shipyard itself.

"When I took a client to visit the site, suddenly ten police cars all swing by with their sirens on," Xu told me. "It was like a movie; we were afraid we were going to get shot."

Xu's client ended up investing in an EB-5-funded water park in Anaheim, California.

"He didn't go see it. He just looked at the map, saw that it's close to Disneyland, and figured it's good land."

GREEN LANDS AND WIDE OCEANS

It wasn't just Chinese families that were seeking both safety and prestige in U.S. real estate. Beginning around 2013, the country's most ambitious real estate developers—the architects of the largest construction boom in world history—began making their first ventures across the Pacific. Between 2010 and 2015, Chinese buyers forked over $4 billion to acquire U.S. land and planned to spend an additional $15 billion completing the projects.[13]

When Chinese developers build in the U.S., they tend to go big. They've acquired major plots to build statement pieces in premier destinations. That preference for large projects comes partly from habit; projects within China often unfold on an inhuman scale. But it's also a branding strategy. These first forays into America are meant to represent the growing global clout of these companies and China itself, a message written out in steel, glass, and concrete, on the soil of the world's most powerful country. That statement is directed at both Americans who have never heard of brands like Greenland or Oceanwide, and just as importantly at Chinese buyers back home, who make up the vast majority of these companies' consumer base. If Greenland Group is good enough for the glamorous people of New York and Los Angeles, the thinking goes, that shine should help sell the company's condos in Beijing and Shanghai.

Thus far, New York City has been the location of some of the most headline-grabbing Chinese acquisitions of U.S. commercial real estate, with nearly $10 billion in purchases of existing buildings just between 2010 and 2015.[14] President Obama notably broke with decades of presidential tradition by choosing to not stay at the city's legendary Waldorf Astoria hotel following its acquisition by the shadowy Chinese firm Anbang. The administration never stated whether the change was out of fear of Chinese eavesdropping or a subtle protest against the auctioning off of U.S. assets. Still, the snub sent a message.

But for all the hubbub over the Waldorf changing hands, the deal represented just that: a change in ownership that didn't mean much for the building itself or the people who worked there. High-profile acquisitions can be lucrative for a building's owner but don't impact cities and job markets in the same way as a brand-new development. For those, you have to look toward the West Coast.

————

Downtown Los Angeles and San Francisco have played host to the highest-density bursts of Chinese development activity, with L.A.'s building spree kicking off in 2013. That was when Oceanwide Holdings, a major property player from the southern Chinese manufacturing hub of Shenzhen, paid $200 million for a massive parking lot they hoped to turn into a luxury megaplex across the street from L.A.'s Staples Center, home of the Los Angeles Lakers.[15]

Just two months after Oceanwide's announcement, Shanghai's state-owned Greenland Group paid $150 million for a six-acre piece of land a few blocks north, promising to turn what had been just a parking lot into a "city within a city" called Metropolis. This is where Deborah would find work directing construction traffic and ushering curious reporters off the premises. Metropolis was slated to hold a hip boutique hotel called Hotel Indigo, approximately 70,000 square feet of shopping, and three towers of 1,500 condos priced between $500,000 and nearly $7 million each.[16]

For a city like Los Angeles, Metropolis is a major addition. For Chinese developers, it's a modestly sized project. One real estate insider told the *Los Angeles Times* that building on this scale was "child's play" for Chinese companies. For Greenland's chairman, Metropolis was reportedly the first time he didn't need a car to move around one of his building sites. In total, this corner of downtown L.A. saw five major Chinese developments break ground. Nine miles to the west, the Chinese developer Wanda also broke ground on a billion-dollar hotel and condo project in Beverly Hills.

Also beginning in 2013, downtown San Francisco saw the same surge in Chinese-funded towers. The City by the Bay may be best known for its rows of colorful Victorians, but in the city's downtown financial district, Chinese developers are leaving an indelible stamp on the city's skyline.

China's Vanke, the world's largest developer by volume, got things started in 2013 when it put $175 million into a joint venture to build Lumina, a pair of curvy green towers near the waterfront.[17] Developed with a U.S. partner, the towers hold 655 luxury condos, including the single most expensive penthouse in San Francisco history.

Lumina's groundbreaking occurred on June 26, 2013—the same day as the groundbreaking on the EB-5-funded Shipyard project—forcing Mayor Ed Lee to juggle multiple ceremonies for Chinese-funded mega-developments in one afternoon. Speaking against a backdrop of an open construction site and two massive excavators, Lee heralded Lumina as a sign that San Francisco development was back on track after the recession.

"[Lumina] is another great, solid foundation for confidence-building in our city," Lee said at the ceremony. "Especially in those years when the economy was very hard to deal with, bringing back investor confidence, international confidence in San Francisco . . . is truly remarkable."

Lumina signaled to China that San Francisco real estate was open for business, and soon a variety of Chinese developers began sniffing around the city for potential projects. Over the next four years, the four-by-six-block area around Lumina and the waterfront saw five different Chinese-funded or Chinese-built developments break ground. Those projects are slated to bring well over 1,000 new apartments and condos—many of them luxury units priced well above $1 million—onto the market.

"The majority of major projects over two hundred residential units in S.F. over the past 18 months have Chinese investment," Skip Whitney, executive vice president of commercial real estate firm Kidder Mathews, told me in the summer of 2017. "San Francisco residential real estate development has been propped up—the cycle has been extended—by Chinese investment. For whatever reason, the domestic capital sources have been unwilling or not prepared to step up and fund the projects."

Across the Bay, Oakland mayor Jean Quan helped connect Chinese conglomerate Zarsion with a local developer for a similarly splashy project: a sweeping redevelopment of abandoned piers on Oakland's industrial waterfront. Zarsion committed $1.5 billion to the venture that was supposed to construct 3,100 new homes and create over 10,000 new jobs, making it the single largest development in the East Bay.[18]

"Oakland has a lot of potential," Zarsion America president Arthur Wang told a local reporter. "Some people were a little bit worried about the city, but that's why we are here. We want to contribute to this community."

Chinese developers had taken California's premier cities by storm, with promises of glistening towers and thousands of construction jobs. But when it comes to real estate mega-developments, it's not what you announce that matters—it's what you end up building. Chinese money had given new life to land left fallow in the years after the U.S. financial crisis. But what would happen to that same land if China faced a crisis of its own?

"TO BECOME AMERICANS"

All was not well in paradise. Back in my hometown of Palo Alto—and other suburbs around the state where Chinese home buyers arrived in force—longtime residents began to chafe at the impact on prices and neighborhoods. Palo Alto is an ultraliberal tech hub, a place with plenty of lawn signs announcing that IMMIGRANTS ARE WELCOME HERE. But for some locals, these new arrivals didn't fit the "good immigrant" mold. In private conversations, many locals told me that Chinese money was threatening to destroy what made Palo Alto special.

The most common concern was absentee homeowners. Survey data from the National Association of Realtors showed that in 2017, just 39 percent of Chinese buyers of U.S. homes intended to live there full-time.[19] That didn't go over well with Palo Alto residents, who wanted neighbors they could chat with, or at least ones who made sure the lawn stayed green. Other locals took a harsher approach, one that danced on the thin line between reasonable concern for the neighborhood and xenophobic anger about what "those Chinese" were doing. Many Palo Altans are shy about airing these views publicly, but the anonymous comment sections of local news stories lit up with anger.

Beneath one 2016 story on Chinese buyers in the *Palo Alto Weekly*, residents lashed out at the "invasive tactics, arrogance, rudeness, entitlement, and racism" of Chinese people.[20] Complaints against the immigrants ranged from them stealing towels from local gyms to putting their elderly parents on Medicare while "displaying contempt for our system and society." Others saw the Chinese arrivals as bringing with them the worst aspects of contemporary Chinese society.

"The sheer scale of the capital flight from China means that these people bring their values with them," one commenter named Charlie wrote. "And they are not Californian liberal values about honesty at school, a prize being a prize for good work not plagiarism, and community building. And then if you dare to say these facts you are labelled a racist!"

As comments grew increasingly nasty and racialized, the website's moderators struggled to delete those that crossed the line, sometimes closing commenting entirely.

At a fundamental level, some locals view wealthy Chinese people's one-foot-in–one-foot-out approach to residency as an affront to America's immigrant heritage. This country's poor-huddled-masses mythology is built on the idea that immigrants go all-in on America. If we're going to open our country to you, the thinking goes, there should be no place you'd rather be. Many earlier waves of immigrants fit that mold: recklessly ambitious or just plain desperate people, mostly from poor countries, who came here and didn't look back. America wasn't a backup plan or a retirement home for these immigrants. It was fertile soil for them to work toward their yet-unrealized ambitions.

New Chinese buyers are turning that idea on its head. For them, a house in Palo Alto isn't the first step in an up-by-my-bootstraps immigrant narrative. It is instead the payoff for a wildly successful career back in China.

"That definitely changes the reasons and the footprint of this recent wave of immigration," Frank Shyong, a journalist who has covered the evolving Chinese American communities for the *Los Angeles Times*, told me. "They are here not because they love the American story and the American dream necessarily. They may love the entry rights of the American passport, or the prestige of an American education."

These homes in places like Palo Alto let them enjoy the things America has to offer them—clean air, a stable currency, good schools—but many new arrivals don't feel the need to invest in learning English or setting down more permanent roots here.

Some of the locals who took greatest offense at this were former immigrants or their children. In the comments on a news story about DeLeon's bus tours, Chris Zaharias, the Palo Alto–born son of Greek immigrants, laid into Chinese buyers who weren't ready to go all-in on America. Parts of his posts were removed by moderators, but the core message remained:

> When my parents moved here, they had the intention of raising a family here, speaking the language, learning the culture, being part of it, staying

here, dying here. Though it's not codified in any law, staying and assim-
ilating is the social contract whereby an immigrant becomes a local. . . .
The real Americans *ARE* the immigrants from *all* nations who come
here, not to invest or give their kids education [opportunities] they don't
have at home, but to *become Americans*.

KAREN

Wanting to put a face to these much-maligned immigrants, I arrange to
meet Karen, a recent home buyer from Shanghai, at a café in Palo Alto's
Midtown neighborhood. The café is just a few blocks south of my old middle school, and back in eighth grade I would sometimes come here with
friends after school to play board games. As I take a seat by the window and
wait for Karen, I can overhear three other conversations at nearby tables in
two different Chinese dialects, as well as a smattering of French and Spanish
spoken behind the counter.

Karen is in her forties, soft-spoken and a bit shy. She was born in Shanghai in the 1970s, living with her parents and sibling in a ten-square-meter
apartment provided by her mother's factory. She studied textile manufacturing in college and went on to work in sourcing for a German company and
then Adidas. Her husband works in equipment manufacturing. Karen first
came to California in 2014, bringing her two children to attend a summer
camp about traditional Chinese culture run by Taiwanese immigrants. The
kids loved it, and Karen and her husband decided it was time to get them
out of the Chinese school system.

"The most important factor was our kids' education," she tells me.
"We also didn't like the political climate in China, but then again, I never
thought that the political climate in the U.S. would get this bad."

They applied for the EB-5 program, putting $500,000 into the renova-
tion of an old San Francisco hotel, and by 2016 they had visas for Karen and
the children. The father remains in China for work, visiting every three to
four months. Karen and the kids initially stayed with a relative in a nearby

suburb, but Karen soon began searching for houses in Palo Alto. She made one offer on a house a few blocks from my own childhood home but eventually won a four-bedroom house in south Palo Alto for just over $4 million. They couldn't afford to pay all cash, instead taking out a mortgage.

She enrolled her daughter in a local middle school and her son as a freshman at my rival high school. The kids are learning English quickly and adapting well, she says. They like the lowered academic pressure but have found making friends to be a bit of a struggle. Karen says her Palo Alto neighbors have been really welcoming, offering to help with anything that can ease the transition for them. But national politics in the age of Trump has taken some of the shine off the country.

"I initially thought that America was such a tolerant and accepting place, but it really isn't," she laments. "Safety is also a big issue: every single day on the news I see another story about guns. There are places where you don't even dare leave your home at night."

Karen tells me she remains anxious that the Trump administration will find a way to revoke their green cards. For Karen herself, that wouldn't be such a tragedy—she finds life in Palo Alto a bit lonely and wants to return to Shanghai once the kids can live independently. But she hopes her children will remain in America long enough to fully adapt to the culture, while still maintaining their own heritage.

"I think they will always feel Chinese," she tells me as we finish our drinks. "Traditional white Americans even look at Asians who were born here and think they're not truly American. For those of us who came later in life it will be even harder."

TWO SIDES OF THE EB-5 COIN: HUNTERS POINT VERSUS TRUMP BAY STREET

While some down in Palo Alto griped about Chinese people buying up homes, in Hunters Point it was Chinese money that was getting new homes built. After the groundbreaking ceremony in 2013, a steady flow of EB-5 funding—almost $100 million per year for 2014–15—fueled the construction of the development's first homes. Around 150 homes were built and occupied by 2016, with that number doubling to 300 by early 2018. The developer planned to triple that to 950 by 2019. Most of these homes went for between $600,000 and $1.2 million, with average prices per square foot around one-third lower than the other new developments in the city.[21] Those new homes also meant construction jobs, with community organizations helping local youth enter the building trades and find work with Lennar's contractors.

But for all that on-the-ground progress at the Shipyard, the EB-5 program was turning into a magnet for scandals. Those issues ranged from local accusations of insider dealings all the way up to international scandals involving the president's own family. Locally, an analysis by the Center for Investigative Reporting turned up a tangled web of connections between the Shipyard's EB-5 fund-raiser and the San Francisco political establishment. Many of those links ran through Willie Brown, the former San Francisco mayor who was a principal in the firm raising EB-5 capital for the Shipyard. Meanwhile, Brown's political protégés at City Hall and elsewhere helped lobby the federal government on behalf of his firm and smoothed the way forward for the development itself.

None of these linkages amounted to anything criminal, and defenders of the development describe these ties between city officials and business leaders as crucial to advancing a project as massive and complex as the Shipyard. Given the hurdles the development has faced over the years, they may be right about that. What's more, these types of political entanglements would make perfect sense to many Chinese investors, who often credit political kickbacks for China's ability to pull off awe-inspiring public works at lightning speed. But the fact that Brown repeatedly publicly denied any ties to the EB-5 firm while publicly advocating for the Shipyard rubbed many observers the wrong way. Former Santa Clara mayor and government ethics scholar Judy Nadler said that a skeptic would likely describe the Shipyard's EB-5 fund-raising as an "inside deal."

Accusations of shady EB-5 deals went national in 2017, when Donald

Trump and Jared Kushner entered the White House. Even before marrying into the Trump family, Jared Kushner's family company operated a major real estate empire in New York. The Kushner Companies had even dipped into EB-5 funding back in 2015 for a luxury development called Trump Bay Street. But the Kushners' EB-5 connection became a national story in May of 2017, when Jared Kushner's sister, Nicole Meyer, journeyed to Beijing to raise $150 million in EB-5 capital for a planned pair of luxury towers called One Journal Square.

At the Ritz-Carlton Beijing, Meyer told a room full of wealthy Chinese investors that the project "means a lot to me and my entire family," describing how her brother recently left the company to serve in the Trump White House. A slide displayed during the event described President Trump as a "key decision maker" on the EB-5 program, and a separate advertisement for the project sold it with the tagline "Government Supports, Star Developer Builds." Correspondents from *The New York Times* and *Washington Post* attended the Beijing event (before getting kicked out), and their account of the event brought the entire EB-5 industry under intense scrutiny. Months later reports surfaced that the Kushner Companies were being subpoenaed by federal prosecutors over their EB-5 investments.

Most of the outrage focused on the Kushner empire's apparent attempt to parlay White House connections into Chinese investments, but the scandal also shone a spotlight on another issue with the program: real estate developers' manipulation of the program's "targeted employment area" (TEA) discount, turning a program that should be about job creation into an unneeded subsidy for corporations.

The TEA designation, which lowers the investment threshold to $500,000, is supposed to incentivize investment in economically distressed areas, measured by the level of unemployment in the project's census tract. If executed correctly, it should funnel money into job-creating projects in poor regions where developers may otherwise have trouble getting financing. But lax oversight at the federal level has made it so that real estate developers can gerrymander any project into being designated as a TEA simply by stringing together many census tracts until they hit the desired unemployment number.

The Kushner Companies' Trump Bay Street project, which took on $50 million in EB-5 financing in 2015, is a perfect example. The project is located in an affluent part of the New Jersey waterfront overlooking Manhattan, with the towers boasting 447 luxury apartments and a rooftop pool. The median household income in the census tract where the project is located is $164,488, and when the project applied for EB-5 status the unemployment rate was just 3.1 percent. And yet, by gerrymandering a narrow strip of sixteen census tracts extending southwest through Jersey City, the Kushners' EB-5 partners were able to hit the needed unemployment numbers and turn the ritzy neighborhood into a TEA, a poor area in need of federal assistance to encourage investment.[22]

It's a clear perversion of the program's intent, but it has been legal under regulations that let each state set its own restrictions on TEAs. Real estate financing scholars Gary Friedland and Jeanne Calderon say that the TEA designation has been rendered "meaningless" by a gerrymandering race-to-the-bottom among the states. The result is that most EB-5 money ends up flowing to luxury developments that would have been built with or without the program. Developers on these projects only use EB-5 money because Chinese investors demand a lower rate of return than other lenders—again, a green card is the real payoff here. Instead of creating jobs that otherwise wouldn't exist, these EB-5 investments end up padding the profits of developers themselves. Members of Congress have repeatedly introduced reform legislation aiming to curb these misuses of the EB-5 program, but as of spring 2019 each of these attempts at reform has been defeated or defused by developer lobbying.

This distortion of TEA status doesn't just help luxury developers. It also makes it harder for projects in genuinely high-unemployment areas, projects like the Shipyard, to raise money. The national EB-5 program maxes out at 10,000 visas per year, with special caps on countries that eat up a large portion of that allotment. By 2017 the program had become so overwhelmed by demand from

Chinese investors, many of them putting money into projects like Trump Bay Street, that new applicants were told they may have to wait eight to ten years before receiving their visas. Those multiyear waits and political uncertainty about the fate of the program began to turn Chinese investors off the program, leading to a major drop in applications.

The EB-5 program had begun as an attempt to leverage one of America's most coveted possessions (green cards) to create something it desperately needed (blue-collar jobs in poor neighborhoods). But after passing through the gauntlet of developer manipulations, campaign donations, and a dysfunctional legislative process, the program had managed to turn Chinese investments into just another subsidy for corporate America.

COMMUNIST CAPITAL CONTROLS

Those hurdles on the U.S. side were matched by even tighter restrictions coming from Chinese policy makers. In early 2017, the Chinese government implemented sweeping capital controls designed to halt the massive financial outflows of the previous years. After nearly five years of loose oversight, the government found that these outflows were rapidly depleting China's currency reserves and threatening to force a devaluation of the RMB. In response, Chinese policy makers slammed on the brakes. Many Chinese construction sites suddenly went dormant, and the tidal wave of home purchases began to recede.

The Chinese government had always limited its citizens' ability to move money out of China, allowing each person to convert just $50,000 into foreign currency each year. But for years savvy Chinese investors had found myriad ways around the controls. Some business owners would transfer money into a branch of their company in Hong Kong and then freely move it from there to the U.S. Others would use a technique known as "smurfing," a practice named for the communal sharing in the culture of the cartoon Smurfs. In smurfing, a would-be home buyer breaks up the cost of the house into $50,000 chunks, giving one chunk each to several trusted friends or family who use their allotted $50,000 in currency conversions to change it to dollars and transfer it to the U.S. separately. Once there, the money is then pooled back into the account of the original buyer and used to purchase a house. For years, imposing capital controls had been like a game of whack-a-mole between regulators and citizens, and the regulators were always a second too slow.

But this time was different. In early 2017, central government leaders forced banks to disclose the reason for each conversion of RMB into dollars and specifically banned these transactions from being used for real estate purchases. In July of that year, regulators further tightened the screws by limiting daily conversions to $7,000 and increasing the reporting requirements. Real estate agents in Palo Alto reported an immediate effect, with many all-cash offers drying up as Chinese couldn't move their money out of the country. Kim Heng of DeLeon Realty was more optimistic, finding that many Chinese buyers were now opting to take out mortgages but that the demand from Chinese buyers remained strong.

"Even with the restrictions, the money still flows," she told me. "It takes time, but they can find a way."

In commercial development projects, the effects were far more dramatic. After years of splashy billion-dollar deals, China's leading developers suddenly couldn't get money out of their home country to finish the projects. Cities that had staked their urban plans on massive Chinese developments suddenly saw the bulldozers go dormant. A fire sale ensued.

Dalian Wanda, the same conglomerate that made headlines by acquiring AMC Theaters and challenging Disney's dominance in China, began looking for a buyer on a $1.2 billion Beverly Hills luxury development that never progressed past a large hole in the ground. In Chicago, Wanda began trying to offload a $900 million half-built skyscraper that was slated for ninety-eight stories on the Lake Michigan waterfront. Zarsion, the developer that had pledged to put a billion dollars into revamping the Oakland waterfront, quietly retreated from those promises, leaving its American partner scrambling for new funding from EB-5 investors and American banks.

And in downtown Los Angeles, Greenland USA announced plans to sell off parts of the Metropolis development in chunks. Hotel Indigo, a hip boutique decorated with bowler hats and bicycle wheels that was one of the first structures completed, went on the market in early 2018 for $280 million.[23] Greenland reportedly hoped to use money from the sale to complete construction on the remaining towers. Just a few weeks later, real estate media reported that Greenland was looking for a buyer who could complete construction on tower three, the fifty-six-story structure where I had met Deborah eighteen months earlier.

Chinese real estate money had washed over America in the wake of the financial crisis, promising to breathe new life into land that had been abandoned by America's battered financial institutions. Five years later, policy reversals an ocean away had abruptly pulled the rug out from under those same projects. It was enough to give an observer whiplash. If Deborah was going to continue her work at the Metropolis site, she was going to need a new boss.

THROUGH THE LOOKING GLASS

Back at Hunters Point, San Francisco's most transformative urban development was also preparing to move away from Chinese funding. Ongoing congressional wrangling over EB-5 reforms created too much policy uncertainty, and Chinese capital controls were making it harder to raise money through the program. The Shipyard had also grown out of its need for the program. Chinese money had filled a gap at a crucial moment when American lenders weren't willing to do so, but as the project began to bear fruit, Lennar could finance it through ongoing home sales and traditional loans from American financial institutions. In 2017, Lennar raised its seventh and final round of EB-5 financing for the Shipyard. In total, over 600 Chinese families had received green cards in exchange for investing over $300 million in the project and creating an estimated 12,121 jobs.

In July of 2017, I decide to attend one more meeting of the Hunters Point Shipyard Citizens Advisory Committee. Dr. Veronica Hunnicutt is once again holding court, flanked by her fellow committee members and facing around fifteen members of the community sitting in folding chairs around the room. A series of presenters step up to the microphone to update the committee on various aspects of the project. A representative of Lennar's partner developer lays out the new "below-market-rate" homes that are now available for purchase. With the latest release of homes, residents with incomes 20 percent below the city average can now enter a lottery to purchase one-bedroom homes for just over $192,000, around one-quarter of the average price in the city.

Not all speakers bring good news. A few weeks earlier, a local environmental NGO brought forward a group of whistle-blowers who claimed that the navy's contractor for radiological testing and decontamination of the Shipyard had falsified the results of radiation tests on local soil. A speaker from the city government announces plans to bring in an outside radiation contamination expert, someone who can speak with any concerned residents about the contamination issue. But by early 2018, those whistle-blowers will force the navy to announce that widespread fraud by its contractor means it will have to redo all tests at the Shipyard. The discovery will outrage many locals, who for years had claimed that ongoing contamination was leading to cancer clusters in their neighborhoods. The retesting allegedly doesn't affect any of the houses already built, which lie outside of the original contamination zone, but it could lead to delays of many years in the next stages of the development. The Shipyard has already slogged its way through decades of Superfund cleanups, environmental reviews, development proposals, community outreach, financial troubles, and international outreach. Now, corner cutting and fraud by a private American contractor will set it back even further, or perhaps put an end to the project entirely.

After Dr. Hunnicutt declares the meeting adjourned, I make my way out the back door and up the stairs to ground level. Wanting to see the status of the development myself, I hop in my car and head downhill through the Bayview neighborhood and toward the waterfront. As I drive southeast on Innes Avenue, the road is flanked on the right by rocky slopes leading up to public housing developments where longtime community members still live. Approaching the Shipyard, the left side of the road opens up to spectacular views of the water and downtown San Francisco in the distance. Colorful billboards crop up with slogans for the new development: WELCOME, PIONEERS and A PROUD HERITAGE, A NEW BEGINNING.

Ahead of me, the first houses of the development come into view. They stand out from the surrounding homes: three stories tall, sharp geometric exteriors, tasteful wood paneling, and balconies rimmed with metal railings. The road climbs uphill toward a small playground, where two couples in their thirties are working out on a jungle gym. I park where the road dead-ends at the edge of the current development and get out of my car, heading toward a bluff that overlooks the vast swath of undeveloped land below.

Down to the right lie block after block of abandoned warehouses and factories, their structures unchanged since the 1940s except for the glass windows that have been smashed. Behind those buildings lie the empty docks, the Shipyard's iconic metal crane, and beyond that the frigid waters of the San Francisco Bay.

Just to my right stands a tourist telescope, the kind where you deposit a couple quarters to scan the horizon through a telescopic lens. The device doesn't have a slot for quarters, so I step up and put my eyes to the viewfinder. As I click a button atop the device, the viewfinder lights up with a gorgeous sunlit scene of these docks. Except it doesn't show the docks today; it is a full-color reproduction of the same view as it would have looked seventy-five years ago, at the height of World War II. Vintage cars are parked along the factory roads below, and in the dry dock sits a battleship. I scan the horizon, taking in the factories, the cranes, and the work crews, all of them frozen in time.

When I click the button atop the telescope again, a new scene emerges, this one an artist's rendering of what the area is supposed to look like upon the Shipyard's completion. The former factories are replaced by gleaming glass towers, the parking lots by open-air markets, and the rocky hillsides by grassy slopes dotted with families. The metal crane remains, but the warehouses are supplanted by chic research facilities and sprawling green open spaces. It is a stirring glimpse into an imagined future for this piece of land, something between a vision, a reality, and a mirage.

7

"CHINESE AMERICANS FOR TRUMP"

The atmosphere outside the San Jose Convention Center is electric, a potent current mixing excitement, anger, and dread. It is June 2016, and Donald Trump is scheduled to hold a rally for his supporters just days before the California primaries. Recent weeks have seen violence break out at several Trump rallies, with protesters and supporters bloodying each other. Tonight appears headed toward more of the same. As my dad and I maneuver through the crowds, the two sides get into close-range shouting matches that look to be just a few degrees shy of boiling over into fistfights. Obscene hand gestures accentuate the unprintable epithets hurled back and forth across the metal barriers that police are using to separate the two sides as we head toward the building.

After over five years living and working in China, I had moved back to the United States three months earlier, in March of 2016. It was a bizarre time to reengage with American politics. I had spent half a decade feverishly trying to build understanding between Chinese and American people but returned home to find my own country deeply fractured along geographic, racial, and political lines. Every week seemed to bring news of yet another police shooting of an unarmed black man or of violence at a political rally.

More than anything, I was astonished by the total inability of Americans on the two sides to even speak with one another. I decided I needed to see this new era in American politics up close. That desire led me to attend a Bernie Sanders rally in Palo Alto the day before, and my dad and me to become voyeurs at this Donald Trump rally in San Jose.

We enter the convention hall as candidate Trump is ripping into a standard set of political foes: "Crooked Hillary" and the "failing *New York Times*." But my eyes are on the crowd surrounding us. The crowd is predominantly white and older, but with a smattering of people who appear to be of Southeast Asian, Indian, and even Latino ancestry. Outside the rally, I had watched as one Indian American man taunted a group of Latino teenagers, claiming that he had waited years for a green card while they had just "jumped the fence." Watching how this segment of the crowd reacted to Trump's incendiary immigration rhetoric, it appeared that man wasn't alone in those feelings.

And then, down near the front, I spot something I never expected to see at a Donald Trump rally. A short woman stands with her arms extended above her head, holding up a white T-shirt with red Chinese characters printed across the back: "北美川普助选团." Literally: "North American Trump Election-Assistance Group."

I had been at a friend's apartment in Beijing when Trump announced his run for president in a now-infamous speech calling Mexicans "rapists" and blaming China for America's economic woes. I'd even written a piece about Chinese reactions to a video mashing up the hundreds of times Trump sneered "Chhyyynnnaa" in speeches and interviews. When talking about the People's Republic, candidate Trump displayed his uncanny knack for contradicting himself and yet appearing totally on message, alternately accusing China of "raping" America and following up by professing to "love China." I didn't know exactly what to make of it, but I felt sure of one thing: Chinese citizens—often hypersensitive about how their country is portrayed abroad—wouldn't like it.

Putting aside Chinese citizens, Trump's style and substance clashed with the politics of the Chinese Americans I'd known growing up. That group ranged from solid Democrats to more radical leftists, with many millennial Chinese Americans embracing causes like immigration reform and the Black Lives Matter movement. It wasn't a group receptive to nativist rhetoric or racial dog whistling.

And yet, there this woman stands. The fact that the shirt is written in simplified Chinese characters indicates that she is likely a relatively recent immigrant from mainland China (earlier waves of immigrants from Hong Kong and Taiwan still use the more complex traditional Chinese characters in writing). And she isn't alone; around her are several other Chinese folks with similar signs or T-shirts. I try to peer through the crowd to get a better look, but I can't make much out through the sea of red Make America Great Again hats.

When Trump's speech concludes, the crowd presses up against the front rail for autographs. I again try to maneuver toward the Chinese group and finally catch up with them outside the arena. The woman with the T-shirt appears to be in her thirties, and she is posing for photographs taken by curious passersby. I finally get to see the other side of her shirt: CHINESE AMERICANS ♥ TRUMP. It's signed by the man himself.

I approach to ask her what she likes about candidate Trump, but people are clamoring for more pictures of her, and the only answer she gives is to hold the T-shirt up for me to read. Police are hustling everyone down the walkway, and I'm quickly separated from the group.

There were just a handful of Chinese people at the San Jose rally, but over the coming months I would learn how new Chinese immigrants were mobilizing for Trump en masse. They were gathering in pro-Trump WeChat groups, knocking on doors across swing states, and renting space on billboards. In what became a signature move, they paid for planes to fly circles around American cities trailing a banner: the American flag and the words CHINESE AMERICANS FOR TRUMP.

As my dad and I move with the crowd onto the streets of San Jose, the tensions that had simmered before the rally boil over. Fights break out in the middle of intersections. My dad and I watch as a group of men chase one Trump supporter through an intersection, eventually tackling him on a piece of grass and roughing him up. Another woman is surrounded and pelted in the face with a tomato and eggs. Cell-phone videos from the post-rally chaos show sucker punches and bloodied faces, some of the ugliest scenes of the campaign to date.

The violence that night put a knot in my stomach, but the brief encounter with the Chinese American group left me curious. Who were the people I saw at the rally? What was their relationship to the staunch Chinese American Democrats I'd known growing up? And why did they support a man who seemed so fervently against both China and their fellow immigrants to America?

THE FOUR WAVES OF CHINESE IMMIGRATION

Understanding the shift under way requires first breaking down the myth of a monolithic Chinese America. In (white) America's popular imagination, most Chinese Americans are cast as direct descendants of a long-lost railroad worker who immigrated in the 1800s. But what to outsiders appears to be a homogenous ethnic identity is better understood as the cobbling together of four major waves of immigration. The people who made up those four waves are often separated by place of origin (Hong Kong, Taiwan, or mainland China), place of arrival in the U.S. (Chinatown versus suburbs), language (Cantonese versus Mandarin), and income (blue- versus white-collar). Taken together, these distinctions gave the members of each wave dramatically different entry points into the American narrative.

The first wave arrived in the three decades following the Gold Rush of 1849, when over 100,000 laborers came to U.S. shores in search of work harvesting gold or building the transcontinental railroad.[1] Members of this first wave were almost entirely men, and they came from a small collection of counties in the southern province of Guangdong (known then as Canton), meaning they mostly spoke Toishanese, a dialect closer to Cantonese than Mandarin. This group was leaving a war-torn and famine-racked country and bore the brunt of xenophobic violence against

Chinese immigrants. Many of them returned home after a few years of work, but those who stayed would form the kernel of Chinatowns in San Francisco, Oakland, Los Angeles, and New York that last to this day.

Following the Chinese Exclusion Act of 1882, new immigration came to a virtual halt. Over the ensuing decades, some men from the first wave were able to bring over spouses, and "paper sons" continued to pass through the Angel Island Immigration Station. But the total Chinese population in America declined during the sixty years of Chinese exclusion.[2]

The second wave began following the repeal of that act in 1943, a move designed to symbolize unity between Chinese and Americans in the face of Japanese aggression. The repeal set a minuscule quota of just 105 Chinese immigrants each year ("not even enough of you to make up a full set of mahjong tiles," one Chinese American columnist noted[3]), but exceptions for war brides, political refugees after the CCP seized power in 1949, and trained professionals led to far greater numbers of new arrivals. During the 1950s, the Chinese American population doubled to over 200,000.[4]

These new arrivals stood apart from the first wave in that they were often far better educated, were from more diverse regions of China (often by way of Taiwan), and primarily spoke Mandarin rather than Cantonese. Some settled in urban Chinatowns, but others began branching out into the suburbs. As they took up positions as scientists, doctors, and engineers, they helped lay the groundwork for the idea that Chinese Americans formed a "model minority": nonwhite citizens whose economic success could be used as an example of American meritocracy in action and as a way to justify the plight of African Americans.[5]

A third wave got under way following the Immigration and Nationality Act of 1965, which ended the long-standing preference for immigrants from northern European countries and opened new immigration options for relatives of American citizens. That shift unlocked large-scale immigration by relatives of Chinese Americans: working-class residents of Hong Kong gravitated toward Chinatowns, and white-collar Taiwanese immigrants often went directly to the suburbs. Immigrants from mainland China remained scarce, as the country was largely sealed off from emigration under Mao's maniacal rule. Between 1960 and 1980, the population of Chinese Americans more than tripled to over 800,000.[6]

Mainland Chinese immigrants reentered the picture during the fourth wave. This wave began in the mid-1980s and saw large numbers of mainland Chinese (and Mandarin-speaking Taiwanese) enter the United States as graduate students or technology professionals. Working-class, Cantonese-speaking immigrants continued to stream into the Chinatowns of New York and San Francisco, but this new crop of educational elites lived in a different world entirely.

They spoke Mandarin, often earned engineering PhDs from top universities, and settled into comfortable middle-class lives in the suburbs of California and college towns across the country. After 2008, this group received a new infusion of wealthy EB-5 investors, Silicon Valley programmers, and college students, but as of today it remains unclear whether these post-2008 groups constitute a new wave of immigrants or a rotating cast of visitors who will largely end up back in China.

It wasn't just that these distinct waves didn't share a common background. They often wanted little to do with one another. Frank Shyong, a Taiwanese American journalist who has written extensively on Chinese life in L.A. for the *Los Angeles Times*, found many fourth-wave immigrants wanted to distance themselves from their predecessors.

"I would ask them about Chinatown and kind of get scoffs," he told me. "They thought it was maybe historically interesting, but as something that represented Chinese people, they found it insufficient."

Some recent arrivals put an even finer point on it. Darlene Chiu Bryant came over from Hong Kong as a baby during the second wave, and her parents ran a series of successful businesses in San Francisco Chinatown. Working as the executive director of ChinaSF, a public-private partnership tasked with bringing Chinese investment to the city, Darlene has often tried to connect fourth-wave mainland investors with the city's historic Chinese community.

"Whenever I say, 'Hey, do you want to do something with Chinatown?' they say, 'No, I don't want to be associated with Chinatown. That's old-school China. I'm the new China. We're more sophisticated, and if I'm going to invest in a Chinatown, I'm going to start a new Chinatown.'"

"CONFUCIAN MISSIONARIES" TO "YELLOW POWER"

These divergent immigration journeys shaped different political beliefs, ideas that were manifested through decades of activism and political engagement. Early historical accounts—predominantly written by white historians—tended to portray Chinese immigrants as politically passive, "silent sojourners" who accepted their subordinate social status with quiet resignation. But more recent histories—many of them written by Chinese Americans themselves—have shone a light on over a century of Chinese American political engagement and activism.

First-wave immigrants found a champion in the flamboyant and razor-tongued Wong Chin Foo, a man often credited with coining the term "Chinese American." Born in China in 1847 and taken in by missionaries at the age of fourteen, Wong gained a mastery of English that he put to use in searing rhetorical broadsides against the anti-Chinese lobby in America. He became a naturalized American citizen in 1874 and toured the country, giving speeches as the first "Confucian missionary" and penning essays with titles such as "Why I Am a Heathen."[7]

Wong founded civil rights organizations to oppose the Chinese Exclusion Act and even challenged the anti-Chinese Irish agitator Denis Kearney to a duel, offering Kearney a choice of weapons: chopsticks, Irish potatoes, or Krupp guns. Wong would later outwit Kearney in a one-on-one debate before the press, but his career and life ended in tragedy. On a return trip to China, he saw his American passport revoked, and he died of a heart attack soon after in his home province of Shandong.

Even during the exclusion era (1882–1943), Chinese Americans continued to shape American politics, often through litigation in U.S. courts. The 1898 U.S. Supreme Court case of *United States v. Wong Kim Ark* enshrined the principle of "birthright citizenship," and a lawsuit by a Chinese laundry operator in San Francisco set an early precedent against de facto discrimination. The Chinese shrimpers at Hunters Point similarly filed suit against local regulations on Chinese-style nets but lost at the U.S. Supreme Court. During the early years of World War II, Chinese Americans agitated for U.S. aid to Japanese-occupied China, as well as an end to the Chinese Exclusion Act. These early forms of political activism were largely defensive in nature: they sought to protect vulnerable Chinese Americans (or, in the case of World War II, China) against aggression.

But during the second and third waves of immigration, Chinese Americans began to engage with American politics in a new way: as members of progressive, panracial coalitions. The American civil rights movement and the Vietnam War had inspired a new generation of activists, many of whom were radicalized on U.S. college campuses. This group often clashed with the conservative Chinatown business establishment on community issues and advocated for racial justice nationally and anticolonialism internationally. Coalitions of Japanese, Chinese, and Filipino activists cast off the stereotype of Asian immigrants as "perpetual foreigners" and came together to replace the term "Oriental" with "Asian American." Campuses such as San Francisco State University even played host to a "Yellow Power" movement that contributed to the creation of the first ethnic studies department at a U.S. university.

Some of that radicalism mellowed in the 1970s and 1980s, and Chinese Americans began to enter government. In the Bay Area, future Chinese American mayors such as Ed Lee and Jean Quan took up positions on public commissions and school boards. And in the Los Angeles suburb of Monterey Park, a social worker named Lily Lee Chen entered the political arena.

"WE AMERICANS"

Lily Lee Chen remembers the moment she began to feel like an American. The year was 1963, and she was studying for a master's degree in social work at the University of Washington. It was late November, and Lily was eating in the student cafeteria when a news bulletin came on: Walter Cronkite informed the nation that President John F. Kennedy had been assassinated.

She was devastated. She had arrived in America just a few years earlier and had fallen in love with the president and his vision for the country. To have that snatched away without warning felt like a punch in the stomach. Lily's husband, Paul, was waiting in a car outside, and she struggled to explain her smudged makeup to him through almost uncontrollable sobs.

"That was too much for me to bear—it was too much," Lily told me over lunch in her Monterey Park home. "I felt, my gosh, this beautiful dream is going to be broken. He's gone, he's gone."

Over the coming weeks, she grieved with the nation. She also began to notice subtle differences in the letters she wrote to her father in Taiwan. Where before she had referred to America as "their country," she now started to refer to it as "our country." When she wrote the Chinese word for "we," she now used it to mean "we Americans."

Lily had been born in the northern Chinese city of Tianjin in 1936. Her family suffered under the Japanese occupation of World War II due to her father's membership in Chiang Kai-shek's Nationalist Party. That same party affiliation forced them to flee mainland China following the Chinese Communist Party's victory in 1949, catching the last boat to leave Tianjin for the Nationalist holdout of Taiwan. There, Lily excelled at school, winning a national speech competition and accepting the award from Madame Chiang Kai-shek herself. Three years later, twenty-year-old Lily was chosen by the U.S. State Department to participate in an international youth leadership program that would bring her to the United States for six months.

During that time, she stayed with two different American host families: the Phillipses, an African American family in Grand Rapids, Michigan, and the Martins, a white family in Syracuse, New York. It was a crash course in the diversity of the American people, and Lily loved it. She went to backyard barbecues and relished the chance to share tidbits of her culture with Americans who had never met a Chinese person.

Following the State Department program, Lily returned to the United States in 1958 to study communications at San Francisco State University.

During a dinner with friends, she began talking to a fellow Chinese student named Paul. A few minutes into the conversation, they discovered that they had both sailed from Tianjin to Taiwan on the same boat. Within a few years, Lily and Paul were married. They spent a couple years in Seattle while Lily got her master's in social work and Paul worked for Boeing. It was there that the Kennedy assassination shook her, and that Lyndon Johnson's package of social programs known as the Great Society inspired her. Recalling the sense of possibility of that era, the excitement still shows on Lily's face fifty-three years later.

"How lucky can I be? I mean, it was made for me. I wanted to do social work, and the Great Society is very much a dream of America and of Johnson, but it's just as much Chinese."

Explaining that cultural connection, she cites one of her favorite quotations from the ancient Chinese philosopher Mencius: "Honor old people as we do our own aged parents, and care for others' children as we do our own."

The couple moved to Los Angeles, where Lily began work as a medical case worker at El Cerritos County Hospital. But the Huntington Beach community where they lived was almost entirely white, and Lily feared her two young children would grow up without experiencing diversity or any connection to their own Chinese identity. She decided to move the family to Monterey Park, a middle-class suburb with a precisely balanced population: one-third white, one-third Latino, one-third Asian.

"THE CHINESE BEVERLY HILLS"

That ethnic breakdown was made possible by Johnson's Immigration and Nationality Act of 1965, the bill that opened the gates to the third wave of Chinese immigration. During the 1960s and 1970s, "family unification" visas brought hundreds of thousands of new arrivals from Hong Kong and Taiwan. The Hong Kong immigrants, many of them blue-collar workers with a family connection to first-wave immigrants, gravitated toward Cantonese-speaking Chinatowns. But the new immigrants from Taiwan were instead more likely to be linked to second-wave immigrants of the 1940s and '50s, people like Lily and Paul whose college degrees and good jobs landed them in the suburbs.

Of all the American suburbs these immigrants could land in, one of them exhibited a magnetic draw: Monterey Park. A quiet suburb wedged between three Los Angeles freeways, Monterey Park once boasted a "Norman Rockwell flavor." But an ever-mounting influx of third-wave immigrants rapidly turned it into the "first suburban Chinatown," and eventually the first American city with a majority Asian population.

Johnson's legislation may have opened the door for these immigrants, but it was an enterprising realtor named Frederic Hsieh who ushered them toward Monterey Park. Unbeknownst to the city's residents, Hsieh began publishing advertisements for Monterey Park real estate in newspapers throughout Hong Kong and Taiwan. In the ads, he gave the city a new brand: "the Chinese Beverly Hills." During the 1970s, Monterey Park's Chinese population nearly quadrupled.

Lily's career as a social worker rose alongside the arrival of third-wave Chinese and other Asian immigrants. As more Asian immigrants entered Los Angeles—including a large influx of Vietnamese refugees after 1975—language barriers and geographic isolation cut them off from social services. Lily spent the 1970s serving those communities, moving from a frontline case worker to the head of a new outreach program for Asian communities across Los Angeles County. There she hired bilingual staff and established outposts at the natural hubs of these communities: the Japanese Pioneer Center, the Chinese Consolidated Benevolent Association building, and a Korean church. She also successfully pushed to have the county recognize Asian and Pacific Islander as the fourth officially acknowledged minority group alongside African Americans, Hispanics, and Native Americans. That move gave Asian Americans access to more public resources, as well as the benefits of affirmative action in some college applications and government jobs.

Lily's work also meant building coalitions that went beyond "Asian." Lily had been inspired by activists like Martin Luther King Jr. and Cesar Chavez, and as she made her way up through social services in Los Angeles County, she worked hand in hand with black and Latino community groups: the United Way, United Farm Workers, and local Baptist and Catholic churches. That meant forging compromises on allocation of public money and acting as a mediator when these groups butted heads. It was work that brought her to the attention of presidents Ford and Carter, who appointed her to national commissions on women's rights and adult education.

But when Lily entered politics herself, it was at the local level: as a member of the Monterey Park City Council. She had lost her first campaign in 1981 by twenty-eight votes, and so she and Paul responded by doubling down on voter registration efforts, setting up booths outside Chinese supermarkets and enrolling Chinese Americans who had never before participated in American elections.[8] In the following year's election she won the largest vote tally in city history, earning a spot on the council and the first rotation among council members to serve as mayor of Monterey Park. When she took the oath of office in November 1983, she became the first Chinese American woman to serve as mayor of an American city. *The Washington Post*, Reuters, and China's *People's Daily* all covered the milestone.

Following in Lily's footsteps, Chinese American politicians during the 1980s and 1990s chalked up a series of "firsts": U.S. senator, cabinet secretary, governor. The frequency of those firsts would eventually dial down the coverage dedicated to each one. But as the symbolism became subtler, it also sometimes became more poignant.

In 2013, the Bay Area saw the completion of a new segment of the Bay Bridge linking the cities of San Francisco and Oakland. At the time, the two cities were led by a pair of Chinese American mayors and longtime friends, Ed Lee and Jean Quan. Both were descendants of working-class Chinese immigrants, and both had entered politics as activists on labor and community housing issues. When it came time for a photo op to mark the bridge opening, the two mayors couldn't help but think of a similar photo op 144 years earlier.

That was when railroad tycoons and ordinary workers gathered for a photograph commemorating the hammering down of the "golden spike" that completed the transcontinental railroad. In the iconic image, engineers from the railroad companies stand at the center, flanked by white railroad workers on both sides. The Chinese workers who had taken on the most grueling and dangerous work are conspicuously absent. Not a single Chinese face appears in the photo. At the new Bay Bridge opening, another massive construction endeavor that linked up two cities, Quan and Lee weren't going to let that positioning happen again.

"It was sort of a joke between us," Mayor Quan later recalled. "This time the Chinese were in the middle."

AFFIRMATIVE ACTION AND MANDARIN RADIO

Looking back, that September 2013 photo of the activists turned mayors may have been a high-water mark for unity in Chinese American politics. That's because within months, an issue would emerge that awakened a new generation of Chinese American activists: fourth-wave immigrants with an agenda that would fracture the community.

I got my first taste of this divide in February of 2014. My journalist visa for China was still in limbo, and I was desperate to keep my Mandarin up while living at home. So I began turning on local Chinese-language AM radio stations whenever I was out driving, taking an odd comfort in listening to call-in shows about local real estate and test-prep classes. And then, seemingly overnight, the hosts of the shows found a new obsession: affirmative action.

Every time I turned on the radio, the hosts would be discussing the mechanics of affirmative action, Supreme Court precedents on the topic, and anti-Asian bias in college admissions. They brought on guests, including one black conservative scholar that I heard multiple times, who would lay into affirmative action as unjust and un-American. The hosts would interview him in English, immediately translating their questions and his answers into Mandarin.

All throughout the programs, the hosts kept repeating one English phrase: SCA-5. That was the name of a bill in the California legislature for amending the state constitution. If passed, SCA-5 would have overturned a 1996 ban on affirmative action in the state, effectively reintroducing race as one consideration in admissions to California public universities.

The bill had been introduced by Democratic state senator Edward Hernandez. After passing the state senate with the required supermajority, it was on track to move through the state assembly, and then would likely win final approval from California voters. After nearly twenty years of "color-blind" admissions, the country's most liberal state appeared ready to bring some form of affirmative action back.

Affirmative action has been a touchy subject in the Asian American community for decades. When the policy was introduced in the early 1960s, it helped many Asian immigrant families by bolstering representation in schools, the workplace, and government. Lily's work to get official recognition for "Asian and Pacific Islander" was about expanding access to resources reserved for minority groups. But by the 1980s, Asian Americans came to be "overrepresented" at many American colleges relative to their percentage of the population. They no longer received a boost from affirmative action in college admissions, and some Asian parents began to suspect that the policy was working against their children.

Conservative groups opposed to affirmative action started to hold up Asian Americans as the "real victims" when race is considered in admissions. They argued that while Asian students may be *overrepresented* relative to the population, they were *underrepresented* relative to their academic qualifications.

In making those arguments, they often cited a 2009 Princeton study showing that Asian applicants needed to score 140 points higher on the SAT than their white peers to have the same chance of admission. Lawsuits forcing universities to disclose application decisions found that Asian American applicants were consistently rated lower on "personality" scores. Reviews of actual applications uncovered plenty of comments from admission counselors seeming to indicate that Asian American students were "all the same."

Anti–affirmative action groups compared discrimination against Asian students to the quotas that many Ivy League schools put on Jewish students in the 1920s and 1930s.

But for the most part, progressive Asian American advocacy groups remained strong supporters of affirmative action. Many second- and third-wave Chinese immigrants who led these groups had participated directly in the civil rights movement, and they saw affirmative action as part of a centuries-long struggle for racial equality in America. They valued coalitions with black and Latino groups and weren't about to switch sides on this issue just because Asian Americans no longer directly benefited. And prior to 2014, these groups had largely held sway, serving as the leading voice of the Asian American community in U.S. politics.

But that was before SCA-5 triggered a tidal wave of political mobilization by fourth-wave Chinese immigrants. This group—highly educated, Mandarin-speaking, and suburb-dwelling—saw the bill as a direct assault on their children's education prospects. Coalescing and coordinating in WeChat groups, they mobilized a series of protests that shocked progressive advocacy groups and elected politicians. Chinese American politics was in for a major change.

ALEX'S POLITICAL AWAKENING

One of the activists leading the charge was Alex Chen. Alex had been born in central China in 1978, right at the dawn of Deng Xiaoping's economic reforms. Years of intense study yielded an outstanding performance on the *gaokao*—China's daunting college entrance exam—earning him a spot at prestigious Tsinghua University. He graduated with a master's in electrical engineering, and he was soon recruited by a Silicon Valley firm that wanted his help designing microchips in California.

Alex and his wife came over on an H-1B visa in 2006, unsure if they would make a home in America or return to China. But after having their first son in California and weathering the financial crisis, Alex felt sure they were here to stay. One of his coworkers taught him how to fish, and he spent his free time on the water or hiking and skiing with his family. Many of his Chinese friends gathered online in forums organized around shared interests, and he became the administrator of the forum on fishing.

It was that all-American activity that first pushed Alex into activism. When fourth-wave immigrants first became aware of SCA-5, they had no existing organizations through which to mobilize. One of Alex's friends suggested to him that given his position as administrator of the fishing forum, he should take charge in organizing others to oppose the bill. He thought it over for a couple days and finally decided to form a new group: the Silicon Valley Chinese Association (SVCA). In the group's mission statement, it pledged to improve the image and status of Chinese people, to support politicians who fought for their interests, and to "take action on critical issues."

In the long term, that could mean a lot of things. In the short term, it meant defeating SCA-5. Alex had never taken civics classes or had much idea about how the California state government worked, but he and his friends dove into the mechanics of state constitutional amendments and the local legislative process.

"We're engineers, right?" he says. "The good part is we can learn very fast."

Alex and I had been introduced over WeChat, where his profile picture is him standing in front of the U.S. Capitol building. He agreed to an interview, and we met at a Starbucks in San Jose, not far from where he works. Speaking in accented but fluent English, he described the history of the legislation and the movement he helped lead to oppose it.

Sitting across the table from him, I couldn't help but shake my head at the incongruousness of the situation. The year that Alex arrived in the U.S., I was beginning my undergrad degree in political science. Along with my classes, I had interned at my congresswoman's office in Palo Alto and Washington, D.C., and worked as a precinct captain for Barack Obama's presidential campaign. But when it came to the actual functioning of California's state and local governments, Alex had to give me a proper civics lesson. He explained the workings of California's two legislative bodies, the history of affirmative action legislation in California, and the different ways you can amend the California state constitution.

When he began his research, Alex had quickly realized that the best shot at killing SCA-5 would be in the California State Assembly, where it required a two-thirds supermajority to pass. Based on the party affiliations and public statements, they would likely need to flip two votes to stop the measure.

"SKIN COLOR ACT 5"

Alex's organization looked up the seven or eight local assembly members who might be pressured into changing their stance and organized visits to their offices. They asked for meetings with the lawmakers, and if they were refused, they would protest outside. At one town hall meeting in the Silicon Valley city of Cupertino, a rambunctious crowd chanted, "SCA-5: No! No! No! SCA-5: Bad! Bad! Bad!" They held up signs: DREAM MY KIDS NOT JUDGED BY RACE BUT BY MERIT! and SAY NO TO SKIN COLOR ACT 5!

Feeding the intensity of that reaction was one widely disseminated piece of misinformation: that SCA-5 would create a hard cap on enrollment for each ethnicity, with the cap equivalent to that ethnicity's percentage of the state population. If such a policy were actually implemented, it would mean cutting the percentage of Asian American undergrads at a school like UC Berkeley from the current 40 percent to the 15 percent that matched the state's population breakdown.

"This statement was very, very powerful," Steven Chen (no relation to Alex), a fourth-wave immigrant who supported SCA-5, told me. "It scared people to death."

Steven tried to explain to fellow immigrants that SCA-5 did not mean quotas or caps on Asian enrollment. The U.S. Supreme Court has specifically banned the implementation of "racial quotas," while affirming the legality of what SCA-5 would actually do: allow race to be considered as one of many factors. But Steven's explanation didn't gain traction, and some outraged activists continued to promote the rumor of hard quotas. Alex said he viewed SCA-5 as creating "implicit quotas" on Asian students.

"There's a famous saying," he said to me outside the Starbucks, "if you walk like a duck and quack like a duck, you are a duck, right?"

During the protests, Alex was devoting all his free time and a decent part of his workday to organizing events, an obsessive focus that got him in trouble with both his boss and his pregnant wife. Along with the protests, the group launched online petitions, flooded assembly offices with mail opposing the bill, and encouraged members to donate to candidates who opposed the bill. It showed results: of the seven assembly people that the group targeted, they successfully flipped one vote.

Down in Los Angeles County, similar groups of fourth-wave Chinese immigrants were mobilizing in parallel. In Monterey Park, one of Lily Chen's political protégés, Assemblyman Ed Chau, faced an aggressive band of protesters holding up a banner denouncing the "Skin Color Act." The group demanded Chau promise a "no" vote. Chau, a Democrat who was born in Hong Kong and grew up in Los Angeles, appeared hesitant to disavow the legislation entirely but pledged to not vote for the bill in its current form.

With multiple new state assembly members now pledging "no" votes, the bill was dead in the water. Less than a month after the mobilization began, State Senator Hernandez asked that the bill be withdrawn due to lack of support. It was a stunning turn of events, an almost instant victory for the newly minted activists. Alex and his group celebrated at a local park with a barbecue.

CONFIDENCE AND ENTITLEMENT

While Alex and crew celebrated, their predecessors mourned. Activists and scholars from earlier waves of immigration recoiled at the protests, with groups like Asian Americans Advancing Justice calling them an attempt to "pit Asian Americans against other people of color." They argued that true justice could only be achieved when Asian Americans united with other black, Latino, Native American, and LGBT groups in pursuit of a shared agenda of social justice. But that narrative—forged in the fires of the civil rights movement—had little purchase on newly arrived Chinese immigrants, a group that didn't necessarily identify with "Asian Americans," much less the other groups.

The divisions went much deeper than politics. Regional, linguistic, educational, and class divides exacerbated tensions. Gordon H. Chang, a leading scholar of Chinese American history at Stanford, sees Chinese regional rivalries playing out on U.S. soil in the way that recent immigrants, many of them from the north of China, view their predecessors from the south.

"They have a prejudice against the southerners," he told me in his Stanford office, where he was finishing up an extensive research project on Chinese railroad workers. "They think the southerners were coolies, restaurant workers, laundry people: obsequious. 'They got kicked around, they were victims, and we're sorry for them. But they didn't stand up for themselves.'"

It's a tendency that clearly irritates Chang, who has spent decades documenting the struggles and activism of Chinese and Asian Americans.

"They're much more elitist, and they don't know anything about the history of Chinese in the United States, let alone the history of African Americans or history of the United States at all," he told me. "So they come in with a certain confidence and entitlement."

Accusations of condescension and discrimination go both ways. Multiple immigrants from northern China who grew up in Cantonese-dominated Chinatowns told me their parents told them never to speak Mandarin outside the house for fear of discrimination by Cantonese immigrants from the south. More recent immigrants who settled in the suburbs claim discrimination is now about a certain kind of social acceptability. They say that longtime Asian Americans see new immigrants as crude and ignorant because they don't subscribe to a certain set of political beliefs.

Alex Chen takes great care to emphasize that he respects earlier immigrants as "pioneers," and he has worked to open up dialogues with long-standing Asian American activist groups. But not all recent immigrants have been as thoughtful. David Wang, the flamboyant and controversial founder of Chinese Americans for Trump—the group behind the T-shirts I saw at the Trump rally—displays a sneering contempt for earlier immigrants. He has said that earlier working-class immigrants are valuable for serving up good Chinese food, but he clearly sees his highly educated peers in the fourth wave as an improvement.

"The new immigrants' superior social and economic position fills them with confidence," he told one Chinese-language publication. "They're not like the old Chinese immigrants: afraid of white people."[9]

"THE LAST AMERICAN LEAVING MONTEREY PARK"

Serving as mayor of Monterey Park, Lily Lee Chen certainly was not afraid of white people. When she took office in 1983, a backlash against new Asian immigrants was brewing in parts of the city's white community. Between 1970 and 1985, Monterey Park's Asian population had leaped from 15 percent to 40 percent, and many white locals complained about feeling like "strangers in our own land."[10] Lily may have ridden into office with a record-breaking vote tally, but tensions continued to simmer below the surface.

Those tensions found expression in a handwritten sign left at an abandoned Monterey Park gas station. The station's owner had sold it and left town, and shortly after it shut down, a large handwritten sign appeared in the window: WILL THE LAST AMERICAN LEAVING MONTEREY PARK PLEASE TAKE DOWN THE AMERICAN FLAG?

Lily was incensed, and in her capacity as mayor she fired off a letter to the owner, calling the sign "very distasteful, un-American, and racist." The station's owner launched a $2 million libel lawsuit, claiming that he had not posted the sign and that Lily's letter had subjected him to "hatred, contempt, ridicule and obloquy."[11]

The suit was dismissed, but anti-immigrant sentiments found a new outlet in a campaign to make English the "official language" of Monterey

Park. Leaders of the campaign described it as pushback against wealthy immigrants who wanted to "buy our city, buy our economy, and force their language down our throats." Lily and fellow members of the city council pushed back, and tensions boiled over during city council meetings. The leader of the campaign questioned the citizenship of Asian American elected officials. During one particularly heated exchange, he threw a copy of the U.S. Constitution in Lily's face.

Symbolic issues like the gas station sign and the English campaign dominated the headlines while Lily was in office. But much of her career—as a social worker, activist, and politician—was spent on more nuts-and-bolts issues of community life. Politically, this fell somewhere in between the somewhat abstract pan-ethnic coalition politics of some on the left, and the more narrowly self-interested advocacy of new immigrant activism. Instead, it focused on the mundane tasks of running a diverse and fast-growing American town.

Curious to hear more about this side of her career, I interrupt an interview at Lily's home with a proposition: How about we take a drive around town and you can tell me about Monterey Park?

Lily is still pretty mobile for an eighty-two-year-old, and she's excited to get out of the house for a bit. While she grabs a sweater, I pull my car up to her front door. We back out of her driveway and head west on Barranca Drive. If you flattened out the formidable hills that sculpt this neighborhood, it could be mistaken for hundreds of different California suburbs: wide streets flanked by subdued foliage and one-story yellow ranch houses.

Moving fluidly between English and Mandarin, Lily explains the demographic history of Monterey Park: how Japanese people were the first Asian immigrants to show up, and how second- and third-generation Chinatown residents began moving out here as their incomes rose and their children became more integrated into American life. She has me turn onto a side road running behind a park and the local elementary school.

"My first mission, my major participation in Monterey Park, was the building of this auditorium," she tells me as we roll past the school. "I worked hard. We were baking cupcakes—go straight—and trying to raise money."

The project started when she arrived in Monterey Park and joined the PTA, but it didn't come to fruition until after she became mayor and "did my politicking" up in Sacramento.

From there, we head out toward the city limits, and Lily tells me to make an illegal U-turn so that we can pass by the Monterey Park sign. I drive uphill, turning into a corporate office park that Lily worked to create. Perched on top of a hill overlooking L.A., this is the same parking lot where State Assemblyman Ed Chau—"a very good assemblyman," Lily tells me—met with SCA-5 protesters and pledged not to support the bill.

"Go to the end," she instructs me. "I'll show you where my husband's dialysis center is."

But first Lily has me pull up behind a nondescript office building. She wants to stop by a grocery store on our way home, and this is a good spot to grab some discarded cardboard boxes for carrying the cabbage and tofu. I load as many empty cardboard boxes as I can into the trunk, and we start back down the hill. Along the way, little landmarks keep reminding her of old campaigns and stories she wants to share: that free senior shuttle system that she got funding for, or the time she and other PTA moms defeated a plan by Chinese developers to open a gambling parlor.

Those campaigns were rarely easy, but they felt uncomplicated morally. Newer conflicts around SCA-5 have proven much thornier. It's been hard to watch the coalitions she worked so hard to build coming apart at the seams, but Lily doesn't rush to condemn either side.

"We had to fight hard for the inclusion as a minority, but the situations do change," she tells me back in her kitchen at home. "They're looking after their own interests, but they don't recognize the past struggles. They think: forget about your guys' past struggles, we just want equal treatment."

PROTESTS, SCAPEGOATS, AND THE VIRTUAL CHINATOWN

By 2015, new-wave Chinese activists had both broadened their base and shifted their focus. The new target of their energies caught many people off guard, and it once again put them at odds with progressive Asian American groups.

On November 20, 2014, rookie NYPD officer Peter Liang was patrolling a dark stairwell in a Brooklyn housing project. Liang had his gun drawn, and when he was startled by a noise he accidentally pulled the trigger, firing a bullet that would ricochet off a wall and strike twenty-eight-year-old Akai Gurley in the stairwell one floor below. Gurley died of those wounds, the latest in a series of unarmed black men to die at the hands of police officers across the country.

What separated this police shooting from so many others was that Liang was actually charged with a crime: second-degree manslaughter, with a maximum sentence of fifteen years in prison. Just four days after Liang shot Gurley, a Ferguson grand jury decided not to charge the officer who had shot and killed Michael Brown. Nine days later, a New York grand jury chose not to charge the NYPD officer who was caught on film choking Eric Garner to death while Garner repeatedly pleaded, "I can't breathe."

When Liang was finally charged, many progressive Asian American groups saw it as a rare instance of justice and accountability. Racial justice, they argued, was not about giving Asian Americans the same immunity and privilege as white cops who kill innocent people. But the new Chinese American activists had a different narrative: Peter Liang was being used as a scapegoat, a sacrificial Chinese lamb to appease public anger at the white establishment.

On March 8, 2015, over 3,000 Chinese Americans took to the streets of New York to protest the indictment.[12] When Liang was convicted of manslaughter a year later—the first NYPD officer convicted for a shooting in over a decade—over 10,000 protesters took to the streets in Brooklyn. San Francisco, Los Angeles, Philadelphia, and Grand Rapids all saw similar pro-Liang rallies. Protesters held up signs in English and Chinese reading ONE TRAGEDY, TWO VICTIMS and quoting Martin Luther King Jr.: INJUSTICE ANYWHERE IS A THREAT TO JUSTICE EVERYWHERE.

Driving those protests was the new secret weapon of Chinese American political mobilization: WeChat. The Chinese superapp had by this point spread to new immigrants living overseas, and it served as the central catalyst for the Peter Liang protests. Fourth-wave Chinese immigrants dispersed across the country were suddenly linked together in ever-buzzing group chats. The fact that the social network of choice for these activists was chat-based rather than web-page-based was crucial: it encouraged constant conversation between people and catalyzed connections between local groups in different parts of the country.

But WeChat had another advantage for organizing: the users and their political opinions are largely homogenous, creating a "virtual Chinatown." WeChat's American user base wasn't just entirely Chinese; it was almost entirely dominated by fourth-wave Chinese immigrants, people who downloaded the app to stay in touch with friends back in China. Earlier waves of immigrants saw little use for the app, and the American-born children of fourth-wave immigrants were busy on Snapchat. The result was a digital echo chamber far more insular than anything seen on Facebook or Twitter.

Steven Chen, the fourth-wave immigrant who tried to fight misinformation about racial quotas in SCA-5, watched with growing despair as "fake news" and outright lies abounded in political WeChat groups. People shared articles making bizarre claims about other ethnic groups—that Muslims use their own hands instead of toilet paper—but no representatives from these other groups were there to combat them. Steven and a few like-minded friends tried to push back, but he told me they felt like "lonely soldiers" fighting against an army. Hoping for reinforcements, Steven began writing articles in English and Chinese explaining the role of WeChat in the new Chinese American mobilization.

"The established American organizations, no matter which party they support, they need to reach out to this group," he told me. "This group cannot be left alone. They will cause much more harm if they are left alone."

"MOM, DAD, UNCLE, AUNTIE"

Christina Xu felt the same way. Born in China, raised in Ohio, and living in New York, Christina is an ethnographer and active supporter of the Black

Lives Matter movement. She was disheartened by the Chinese American rallies for Peter Liang—"the first time I saw Chinese Americans coming out for anything"—and taken aback when her parents called to tell her they were joining the protests.

"In their minds, they were like, 'Oh, you're into protests, you're going to be excited that we're doing this,'" Christina told me. "My reaction, of course, was the exact opposite."

The conversation did not go well, and Christina and her dad spent the next few weeks "sending angry infographics back and forth." They left things there for a while, but later that year, a misunderstanding around another police shooting spurred Christina to action.

On July 6, 2016, a Minnesota police officer shot and killed Philando Castile during a traffic stop, while Castile reached for his driver's license. In a wrenching Facebook live stream from the car, Castile's girlfriend mourned him and described the shooting: "It was a Chinese police officer that shot him. He's Chinese, about five five, five six and a half, heavyset guy." It would later come to light that the officer who shot Castile was Latino, not Chinese, but those initial reports made Christina worry that there would be another Peter Liang–esque backlash among Chinese Americans. Out of that fear, an idea was born.

Christina opened a Google Doc and began drafting a letter to her parents explaining why she supported the Black Lives Matter movement. She tweeted out a link to the Google Doc, encouraging other Asian Americans to help craft the letter and then translate it into their parents' native languages. She didn't expect more than a few people to join her. Within four hours, there were a hundred people in the Google Doc, all simultaneously writing and editing a letter that gave voice to their collective fear for their black friends and the hope that the Asian American community of their parents would support them.

"When a policeman shoots a Black person, you might think it's the victim's fault because you see so many images of them in the media as thugs and criminals," went the letter. "After all, you might say, we managed to come to America with nothing and build good lives for ourselves despite discrimination, so why can't they?"

It went on to outline the unique dangers that black people face in America, and the need for coalitions in fighting for racial justice. In collectively shaping the letter, paragraphs were written and rewritten hundreds of times by hundreds of different people. But the one piece of the final letter that Christina insisted on keeping intact was the way it was addressed: "Mom, Dad, Uncle, Auntie, Grandfather, Grandmother." She didn't want it to turn into an "open letter," a document that's more about the sender than the recipient. She wanted the letter to be personal and to come from a place of love and empathy.

"Throughout the process, whenever there was a conflict about what words to use, what topics to bring up, so on and so forth, I always just tried to bring it back to: If you were standing in front of your actual family member, what would you want them to know? What would you want to say? And how would you say it?"

Within twelve hours the letter was finished, and over the coming weeks it would be translated into dozens of languages: Mandarin, Vietnamese, Hmong, Tagalog, Farsi, etc. It garnered media attention, including an NPR interview with Christina. That necessitated an awkward phone call between Christina and her parents, one in which she explained that what had begun as a simple letter to them had quickly turned into a national news story about race in America. The letter also generated a virulent backlash in the world of right-wing WeChat groups. Christina was attacked in various articles posted on WeChat, including some posts promoting a distinctly Chinese conspiracy theory: she only created the letter because it would help her get into a good college.

Ironically, that WeChat backlash ended up bringing Christina and her parents closer together. They had initially been upset with her for stirring this thing up, but the bizarre intensity of the reaction on WeChat convinced them that these people were not to be trusted.

"In the process, my dad went from being kind of a political moderate to, if not a liberal, then at least an ardent anti-Trump person," Christina said. "So that actually set them up well for the election and everything that happened afterward."

ELECTION SEASON

While the letter was helping Chinese American parents to empathize with their own children, Alex Chen was learning to empathize with middle America. After founding the Silicon Valley Chinese Association and helping beat back SCA-5, Alex had put his energy into helping elect California officials who pledged to oppose race-based affirmative action. Entering the 2016 election, his main goal was to elect a Republican who would appoint a conservative, anti–affirmative action Supreme Court justice. Alex stayed neutral during the primaries, but once Trump was the nominee he dove in.

Like many Chinese Trump supporters, Alex was a green card holder but not a U.S. citizen (he would become eligible for citizenship in 2018). If anything, the fact that he couldn't vote increased his efforts for the campaign. He was at the San Jose Trump rally that I attended, handing out flyers. He organized phone banking events, bringing together over one hundred Chinese American volunteers, the vast majority of whom had never made calls for a candidate.

Alex himself hit the phones twice a week, calling Florida, Pennsylvania, Wisconsin, and Ohio. He estimates that over the course of the campaign, he made around 2,000 calls to voters. Many of those calls ended in obscenities and a dial tone, but Alex says it was that process of speaking to voters around the country that finally made him feel like an American.

"Before that, everything is about California," he told me. "But during the presidential campaign I began to think it's not just California, it's the U.S.: so many states, so many different people. We know New York and California are very rich, but in the Rust Belt states there are a lot of poor guys and we also need to care about them. I think it's time for me to move forward, to move further."

Speaking to me outside the Starbucks, Alex sounds quite moderate. He would be all right with affirmative action based on income but not race. He supports a path to citizenship for undocumented immigrants but thinks they should have to wait at least as long as legal immigrants like himself. He doesn't think Trump has a good personality but also doesn't think that's very important in a president. If you slightly tweaked which issues he prioritizes, Alex would be almost indistinguishable from your standard-issue white Republican voter.

That doesn't hold true for many other Chinese American Trump supporters. In other corners of the Chinese-Americans-for-Trump world, a more abrasive tone prevailed. This group was embodied by the brash founder of Chinese Americans for Trump: David Wang. Wang had come to the U.S. as a teenager in the 1990s and was a leader in the Southern California SCA-5 protests. Irreverent and media savvy, Wang was the man who called earlier generations of Chinese Americans "afraid of white people." He once told me that his teams of female Chinese volunteers were ten times more effective than I would be at knocking on doors, because I "look like a Mormon."

Wang is controversial even among conservative Chinese activists ("He just wants attention," Alex Chen told me). In our conversation, Wang told me he absolutely would not discuss his family background, and he ducked any questions relating to his work by saying he does "a lot of things." But as one of the earliest and most high-profile Chinese Trump supporters, he gained influence. According to Wang, his group paid for 174 hours of flight time in thirty-two cities by planes towing pro-Trump banners. They rented out billboards in swing states and knocked on thousands of doors in Pennsylvania and elsewhere.

On June 3, less than twenty-four hours after the San Jose rally, Wang and a group of his chapter presidents had a chance to meet Trump face-to-face during an event in Beverly Hills. Photos from the event show Trump and David Wang standing in the center of a group of around twenty Chinese supporters, Wang giving a thumbs-up and Trump holding up the same CHINESE AMERICANS ♥ TRUMP T-shirt I had first seen at the rally. The group was ecstatic.

"We have turned a regular political agenda into worship, into a religious matter," Wang told me. "People worshipped him as a god. Not a god-god, but I could even tell Jesus, 'I'm sorry, you know, I might have started idol worshipping.'"

RACISM, MAOISM, AND TRUMP'S AMERICA

The sources of that "idol worship" were complex but often disturbingly familiar to those acquainted with modern China's political history. Kaiser Kuo, a longtime Beijing resident and host of the *Sinica Podcast*, returned to the U.S. in 2016 and settled in Chapel Hill, North Carolina. Once there, his Chinese wife, Fanfan, got plugged into local WeChat groups for recent immigrants and Chinese moms with school-age kids. Kaiser and Fanfan quickly discovered just how popular Trump was among this group (winning three to one over Hillary Clinton by Fanfan's estimate), and why.

Affirmative action (just called "AA" in WeChat groups) was a constant topic of discussion, as was support for the North Carolina "bathroom bill" that barred transgender people from using the bathroom that corresponds to their gender identity. But laced throughout those WeChat conversations was the kind of casual racism that has alarmed liberal Chinese Americans. In an essay analyzing local Chinese support for Trump, Kaiser described what he was seeing in the WeChat groups:

> Many Americans would be shocked were they privy to conversations about race taking place in Chinese when participants think no one else is listening. The conflation of blackness with criminality among immigrant Chinese in America is appallingly commonplace. Anyone who pushes back on those assumptions is seen as simply denying the obvious, and is barraged by statistics on violent crime rates . . . devoid, of course, of any context. . . . [When it comes to institutional racism], there is this belief that it's an American problem and that their only interest is to ensure the short-term safety of their own families.[13]

Other Chinese American observers pointed to a deeper resonance between the strongman persona of Donald Trump and an authoritarian tradition in Chinese politics. In an essay for *The New Yorker* titled "The Maoism of Donald Trump," Jiayang Fan drew parallels between Mao's Cultural Revolution mobilizations for "class struggle" and Trump whipping up working-class hatred for his rogues' gallery of enemies: the mainstream media, the "swamp," and "Crooked Hillary." In the piece, she quoted a Chinese immigrant posting on a pro-Trump forum.

"It's too bad I won't be getting my US citizenship until December 1st," they wrote. "America is in real danger and he's the only one who'll do something about it. Trump would certainly have my vote."

With or without that soon-to-be-citizen's vote, on November 8, 2016, Donald Trump cruised to victory in perhaps the biggest upset in U.S. presidential history. David Wang celebrated at the Trump National Golf Club in Los Angeles by parading through the lobby with a giant American flag.

Exit polls would show Asian Americans going for Hillary Clinton by wide margins, but those polls didn't capture the impact of the pro-Trump Chinese Americans, a large portion of whom are still waiting for their citizenship. What had begun with outrage over an obscure California bill had gone national, alienating established Asian American groups, bumping up against the Black Lives Matter movement, and putting its energy behind President-Elect Donald Trump. The new immigrant activists had arrived.

"MAKE AMERICA DINNER AGAIN"

In the months following Trump's election, everyone dealt with the fallout in different ways. David Wang was appointed by Trump to an advisory committee on Asian American issues and began working closely with the Republican Party on election races around the country. His WeChat posts filled up with the pictures of a seasoned political operative: shaking hands with candidates for governor, accepting an award from the Republican National Committee, and attending receptions at the White House.

Lily Lee Chen was offered a spot on the same committee as David Wang, but she said she couldn't accept a position in Donald Trump's administration. She continues to support Chinese American elected officials in California and is working on an autobiography that she hopes will inspire young people thinking about a life in public service.

Alex Chen attended Trump's inauguration and helped organize an Asian American Leadership Forum where he met some congressional leaders in D.C. But he's since taken a step back from political activities. Trump's presidency has been a bit of a mixed bag. He was happy with Trump's appointment of Neil Gorsuch to the Supreme Court and felt that, on balance, the tax reform bill was a good thing. But Alex hasn't been a fan of Trump's trade war with China, arguing that it will end up dragging both countries down. He's got plans for a big trip across America where he hopes to see all fifty states, but thinks it might be another five years until he has the time to do it.

In early 2018, Alex received an invitation to an event hosted by a group called Make America Dinner Again (MADA). The organization seeks to promote civil discourse by hosting dinners that bring together people from across the political divide for good meals and real conversations. Founded by two Chinese American women, Justine Lee and Tria Chang, MADA doesn't specifically focus on Asian Americans, but in February 2018 it worked with BBC News to host a special Chinese New Year dinner in San Francisco. In attendance would be eight Chinese Americans from all over the political spectrum, including an educator in Oakland, a conservative Christian, a center-left millennial, and Alex Chen.

Justine and Tria had both grown up thinking of Chinese Americans as a relatively nonpolitical group. In recent years, they had noticed some of the rumbling against affirmative action, but the 2016 election had been a wake-up call.

"I had heard about a lot of Chinese immigrants who had voted for Trump," Tria told me. "To me, it was sort of like a mythological creature, and I was really curious to talk to them and learn more."

Justine and Tria held the dinner in a spacious San Francisco loft on the day after Chinese New Year. They wanted it to feel celebratory, so they stocked up on good wine, tasty Chinese dishes, and a roast duck from a Chinese supermarket. Still, both hosts felt some anxiety going in. Tria had plenty of experience with Chinese dinners in which people were "not polite or soft in the way they say things," and there was a fear that the conversation might not end up being a shining example of civil discourse.

But as the group gathered around the table, those worries quickly dissipated. The conversation was more animated than other dinners they had hosted but mostly in a good way. While the liberal members of the dinner tended to list immigration as their top issue, much of the conversation ended up centering on education. For a partner exercise, Alex was paired up with an activist and educator from Oakland, and they dug into several issues, particularly affirmative action.

"I'm nodding, but it doesn't mean I agree," Alex says in the BBC footage from the dinner. "It's just to be polite, you know?"

Everyone at the table has a laugh at that. There were some tense moments during the dinner, and the final segment—in which participants are supposed to state their takeaways from the night—dragged on as everyone tried to get the final word in the arguments. But as Justine and Tria began cleaning up, they were happy to see people exchanging contact information and lingering to chat in groups that didn't break down along party lines.

"I did feel very invigorated during and after the dinner," Justine told me. "I felt really proud to hear Chinese American voices speaking loudly and with conviction at the table."

One dinner wasn't going to paper over deep rifts in an increasingly diverse community, but you had to start somewhere.

"Everyone definitely left in higher spirits than when they arrived," Justine said. "I felt like I wanted to keep the conversation going."

Conclusion

BACKLASH OR NEW BEGINNING?

I n the ten years since I first went to China, and the six years since I started documenting the Transpacific Experiment, a lot has changed. China has gone from a distant developing country to the single largest international source of students, tourists, technologists, home buyers, and new immigrants on U.S. soil. The country has directly entered the lives of millions of Americans and stepped confidently out onto the world stage as a truly global superpower.

Though California remains home to the densest concentration of these ties, they've now spread out into every corner of the U.S. and around the globe, bringing with them the same thorny problems. Australian universities are struggling with new tensions as Chinese students assert their home country's values in foreign classrooms. Switzerland and Germany are debating whether to block Chinese acquisitions of chemical companies and robotics manufacturers. The continent of Africa remains a hot spot for frictions between Chinese foremen and local workers. And start-ups from Brazil to Indonesia are debating whether they should partner or do battle with China's tech juggernauts. All of these issues weave together the personal and the political, local business decisions and geopolitical strategy.

And while those ties often bring these countries and people into closer contact, they also sow the seeds of a looming backlash. In the United States, that backlash has long manifested itself at the local level and is now playing out at a national level.

In Washington, D.C., attitudes toward China have hardened dramatically. Policy makers and business leaders who had for decades supported a strategy of positive engagement with the rising power have reversed course. Many argue that China hasn't lived up to expectations for opening up its economy, its internet, or its political system. They now advocate for a more combative stance on everything from visas for Chinese students to Chinese investment in Silicon Valley.

President Donald Trump, whether out of conviction or just disposition, has taken that combative stance to the extreme. His administration has come out swinging, no longer feeling bound by the niceties of traditional diplomacy. Here, the one-dimensional language of a "trade war" has masked a much broader confrontation. The precise contours of this confrontation are still taking shape, but they already encompass many of the same issues found in the Transpacific Experiment: technological leadership, cultural influence, and the flow of people, money, and ideas between the two countries.

These conflicts are flowing up from the grassroots and feeding back down into them. Images of Chinese students as tools of their home government began on college campuses, but they have now been magnified and projected out from Washington, D.C. Backlash against Chinese influence in Silicon Valley and Hollywood has its roots in the decisions of film producers and start-up founders, but that backlash is now morphing into national policy that will restrict those same decisions. That two-way street is binding local and national issues together in a new way.

For the decade following the financial crisis, the Transpacific Experiment and the broader U.S.–China relationship were able to proceed on separate tracks. While the national relationship faltered, the grassroots ties that compose the Experiment continued to flourish. But as those national ties enter a new downward spiral, they are threatening to drag people-to-people contacts down with them. The threat of banning all Chinese students marks one of the more extreme scenarios, but even without such executive actions, the deepening negativity around the national relationship will likely discourage many potential students, home buyers, investors, and technologists from making the leap across the Pacific.

Exactly how much national politics impacts these personal decisions remains to be seen. Surveying the movers and shakers chronicled in this book, we see some stepping back from their transpacific ventures, while others forge ahead.

WHERE ARE THEY NOW?

Tim Lin continues to serve as CEO and editor in chief of College Daily, churning out the news, gossip, and dating advice that Chinese students want to read. In 2017, I briefly worked with one of his deputies to put out a Chinese-language video I'd made about Stanford's campus and culture. College Daily has also rebranded, changing its Chinese name from "North American Overseas Students Daily" to simply "Overseas Students Daily," a nod to the increasingly global reach of Chinese students and Tim's company.

Li Zhifei and Mobvoi are riding China's explosion of interest in artificial intelligence to raise their profile and expand their product offerings. Li was doing AI for a decade before it became the hot new thing, and Mobvoi is now embedding that technology into smart speakers, "TicPod" wireless headphones, and an AI-powered computer chip for voice recognition. Many of these products have a clear ancestor in the offerings of American companies like Apple and Amazon, but Mobvoi still stands at an enviable intersection of innovation, adaptation, and localization. In 2018, Mobvoi was chosen by research consultancy CB Insights for its list of the top hundred AI start-ups from around the globe. While the company continues to sell its hardware products overseas, no further direct cooperation with Google has been announced.

In the months following the revelation of Google's "Dragonfly" project, activist employees mounted an internal campaign against the censored search engine. They gathered over 740 signatures on an open letter demanding Google halt work on the project.

"Our opposition to Dragonfly is not about China: we object to technologies that aid the powerful in oppressing the vulnerable, wherever they may be," the letter read. "Many of us accepted employment at Google with the company's values in mind, including its previous position on Chinese censorship and surveillance, and an understanding that Google was a company willing to place its values above its profits."

A month after the letter's release—and further uproar from the Google privacy team that had been excluded from deliberations—the company "effectively ended" work on Dragonfly.

Chairman Wang—the billionaire real estate mogul who bought AMC Entertainment and brought Leonardo DiCaprio to China—has been forced to retreat from his ambition of dominating the global film industry. A crippling government campaign to rein in flashy overseas acquisitions and excessive debt forced his company, the Wanda Group, to sell off billions in assets. At one point, the company's stock price took a brief nosedive following rumors that Chairman Wang himself had been detained by Chinese authorities. Those rumors turned out to be untrue (for now), but Wang has been buffing up his patriotic credentials by pledging to quadruple the number of malls he operates in China, a move that some described as a "China first" strategy.

Janet Yang—the Hollywood producer who has been cross-pollinating the two film markets for decades—continues to keep an eye out for new China projects but is now enjoying the freedom to work only on those that really move her. In the fallout of the Harvey Weinstein scandal and several racially charged incidents in the industry, she has also become an outspoken advocate for both women and Asian Americans in Hollywood.

"China, for me, has become a source of just great intellectual curiosity," she told me while walking her Santa Monica neighborhood. "I don't think you can ever figure it out, but it presents so many wonderful examples of contrast or conundrum or contradiction. You're like, 'Wow, they're really doing it their own way.'"

Mayor Rex Parris was reelected in a landslide in 2016, meaning that he will have until at least 2020—twelve years in office total—to turn his vision for Lancaster into reality. But trouble may loom on the horizon: a new California law will soon force cities like Lancaster that hold off-cycle elections with low turnout to sync up with statewide elections. That combined with Rex's support for allowing medical marijuana cultivation—which he says alienated his religious base—may put an end to the reign of Rex. In the meantime, the mayor has stayed on the China grind. BYD has expanded to over 800 employees, and when I last spoke with Rex, he was in talks with Chinese investors to build a gleaming ten-story statue of the Buddha in Lancaster.

In Hunters Point, Dr. Veronica Hunnicutt continues to lead the Citizens Advisory Committee overseeing the redevelopment. But after years of progress, the discovery that an American contractor for the navy falsified results of radiation testing has thrown the project back into limbo. Whether or not new tests clear the way for new construction, Chinese EB-5 investors likely won't be the prime source of funding. A massive backlog of applications at the Department of Homeland Security, stringent Chinese capital controls, and continued congressional threats to end the program have dramatically reduced the supply of EB-5 capital for real estate projects.

Down in Monterey Park, Lily Lee Chen continues to work on her autobiography, as well as two film documentaries on her life, one in English and one in Chinese. Alex Chen has taken a step back from active political involvement, but his social media feeds serve up a steady diet of news about affirmative action and other conservative causes. Many of those posts highlight a lawsuit by a group called Students for Fair Admissions, which forced Harvard University to hand over admissions data showing that it consistently gave Asian Americans lower scores than white students on "personality." The lawsuit, spearheaded by a white investor who has mounted legal challenges to affirmative action and the Voting Rights Act, has a shot at making its way up to the Supreme Court.

A TRANSPACIFIC TAPESTRY

None of the individual people profiled here have been able to single-handedly change the course of the relationship between the two great powers of the twenty-first century. The countries and concepts involved are just too big and too unwieldy for that.

But all of these strands—the people, the start-ups, the protests, and the cultural mash-ups—are weaving together to form a tapestry that spans cultures and continents. No single narrative can sum up that tapestry, but in its complexity we catch glimpses of the tensions and synergies that are shaping our collective future.

How the United States and China relate to each other in the years to come will have profound consequences for people in every corner of the planet. Over the past decade, California has been the living laboratory for a massive real-world experiment in building that relationship from the ground up. It's allowed us to observe what happens when you mix together people and ideas from these vastly different countries and cultures. That's a potentially volatile experiment to run under any circumstances, and it's been made even more so by the high-stakes geopolitics looming overhead.

In tracing these stories and writing this book, I constantly wrestled with how to assess the outcome of that experiment. Is Chinese investment creating American jobs or just making off with American intellectual property? Is Chinese real estate activity funding affordable housing or just driving up prices for everyone? Are Chinese students laying the foundation for a friendlier era of U.S.–China relations, or will their arrival here end up driving these countries further apart? The transpacific stories in this book added new dimensions to my understanding of these questions, but rarely did they yield a clear answer.

The problem is not just that we can't pin down a precise cost-benefit calculation for these activities today. It's that we're only now witnessing the first-order effects of these phenomena. All of these interactions are like seeds being planted on both sides of the Pacific. We've watched as these seeds begin to sprout, but they won't finish bearing fruit for years or even decades to come.

THE FRONTIERSMAN'S HORSE

Grappling with this problem, I find my mind gravitating back to a Chinese idiom that I first learned in the summer of 2013, shortly before I broke my ankle: 塞翁失马，焉知非福. It's often translated into English as "a blessing in disguise," but that captures only a fraction of the meaning. Taken literally, it translates to: "The old frontiersman lost a horse, how to know it's not a blessing?" Like many Chinese idioms, the phrase is merely a capsule meant to convey an entire story that Chinese people know by heart. In this case, the story goes something like this:

During China's Warring States Period (475–221 B.C.), there was an old frontiersman who raised horses on the northern borderlands. One day, a horse of his wandered off into the lands of the hostile northern tribes and didn't return. But when neighbors came to comfort the old man, he appeared unperturbed by the loss. "How do I know it's not a blessing?" he asked rhetorically. The neighbors shook their heads, thinking that he just wanted to console himself.

A few days later, the old man's horse returned, this time accompanied by another horse that could be added to the herd. Again, the neighbors came to visit, this time to congratulate him. But the frontiersman remained impassive.

"How do I know this second horse is not a curse on my house?" he responded. Again, the villagers were puzzled, this time at his unwillingness to celebrate good fortune.

Several weeks later, the man's only son was riding the new horse when he lost control, falling off and breaking his leg. The break didn't heal well, leaving the son with a pronounced limp. The villagers returned to the man's house, this time knowing what to expect from him: "How do I know this is not a blessing?"

A year after the fall, the northern tribes were amassing for an invasion, and all the able-bodied men in the village were drafted into service. The old frontiersman's son was deemed unfit for service and remained with the family. The village soldiers held off the invaders, but virtually all of them perished, leaving their families without sons. Only the stoic frontiersman's son, unfit to go into battle, survived to carry on his family's line.

It's a distinctly Chinese tale. Far more than describing a "blessing in disguise," it's meant to convey a certain posture toward the unpredictable currents that push and pull our lives in different directions. During the early phases of my journey, the idiom became a personal mantra for me. I repeated it to myself constantly: after I broke my ankle, after that injury stranded me at home, after that delay led to a life-changing relationship and my dream job as a reporter in China, after a visa problem almost took that job away, and after all those twists and turns led me to stumble on the fascinating world of the Transpacific Experiment. During that whole process, the story of the frontiersman served as both consolation and inspiration.

Now, watching the ripples of the Transpacific Experiment make their way across the globe, I find the phrase once again floating through my head. We've witnessed high hopes turn to a harsh backlash, but the story is far from over. The uncertainty around these phenomena—the unintended consequences, and the unforeseeable blessings—shouldn't paralyze us from taking action or make us throw up our hands when things go wrong. The Transpacific Experiment is constantly being created, shaped, and reinvented by the actions of ordinary people like those I encountered over the past five years. If the story of the frontiersman teaches us anything, it's a kind of intellectual humility: a deep appreciation for what we don't yet know, and a real excitement to discover that same thing.

Acknowledgments

Creating this book has been a mammoth personal, professional, and intellectual project, one that would never have gotten to the finish line without the support and 加油's of dozens of people.

This project was born because a boy liked a girl and knew he had to make his way back to her side of the Pacific. Steph: you've given me the motivation, support, love, patience, and real talk needed to make this book a reality, and I can't thank you enough for that.

The Sheehan, Myatt, Vargas, and Zhang clans have been there for me and this project from day one. Patrick Sheehan has been a top-notch editor and tireless hype man, and he's turning into a hell of a good sociologist, writer, and little brother that I look up to. Daniel Sheehan has been a rock of steady support and a priceless intellectual interlocutor—I'm so lucky to have a brother and a brain like that around. Thanks to my dad, Thomas Sheehan, for instilling in us boys an endless intellectual curiosity and the preferential option for the poor. And thanks to my mom, Diana Sheehan, for teaching us the most important lesson: at the end of the day, it's the people in your life that matter.

Thanks to Mike and Staci for every Christmas, Thanksgiving, and all the in-between visits when you rolled into town and made the nuclear Sheehan family just a bit bigger. Big hugs to Zhangwen, Jeff, Ella, and my 干儿子 Louie for teaching me so much about family, friendship and China—you four are the pride of Hebei Province and the transpacific family that always puts a huge smile on my face.

Big ups to Matt Allen and Tina Tian for living that Chinafornia life-style from day one; to Kai哥 for being my inspiration from Xi'an to Poland; to Bobby Holley, Tessa Husseman, Max Rausch, and John Herring for these bedrock friendships since I've been back; to Mark Hoffberg and Patricia Lewis for taking me in on a broken ankle during the early days of this re-search; to Matjaž Tančič for being the best travel buddy and photographer I could hope for; to Sam Dreiman for bringing me in on his tireless transpa-cific hustling; to Nitai Deitel for adding grade A hype and hashtags to the journey; to Mao Baolong and his family for the friendship and noodles that fed me in Beijing; to Jeannette Lee for creating the beautiful Chinafornia logo, and the best illustration I could've imagined for my busted pants; to Leigh Bloomberg and Andrew Moffat for always offering up one free bed and two very different kinds of wisdom; to Beijing Big Brother ultimate for being my ride-or-DPH crew in the big city; to the friends from the West-ern Language Center and the Roujiamo Ultimate Frisbee team in Xi'an for showing me all the potential inside the young people of that city; and to the whole Chinafornia crew that keeps it 100 from 北 to Bay and back again.

Many of the stories in this book began when a broken ankle opened the door for my dream job as a China correspondent. Thanks to Peter Good-man for bringing me on board, to Nathan Gardels for empowering and entrusting me with such a momentous task and for allowing passages from my *WorldPost* articles to appear in this book, and to Katie Nelson for being the best editor an overseas journalist could ask for.

Behind the content and analysis of this book is the work of hundreds of China watchers and journalists. Major thanks go to Damien Ma, Evan Feigenbaum, and the whole MacroPolo team for bringing me on. They've all supported and shaped this work for years when most others were scratching their heads about it. Thanks to Bill Bishop for sharing a decade of China-watching wisdom via his Sinocism China Newsletter, and for making the introduction that kick-started my journalism career. Thanks to Kaiser Kuo for creating the gold standard of China podcasts in *Sinica*, and for all the wisdom, whiskey, stories, and support along the way. And special thanks to Laszlo Montgomery, whose *China History Podcast* has been a true gift to the world and to my own understanding of that country.

Thanks to Kai-Fu Lee of Sinovation Ventures, Connie Chan of Andreessen Horowitz, and Rui Ma and Ying-Ying Lu of the *TechBuzz China* podcast for expanding and deeply enriching my understanding of the technology ties between these countries. Thanks to Cecilia Miao for connecting me with Tim Lin, and for everything I learned from the excellent Channel C and lots of conversations about the Chinese student experience. Thanks to Darlene Chiu Bryant and Bing Wei for opening doors, sharing insights, and showing me what building these connections from the ground up looks like.

Thanks to all of the journalists I've quoted, cited, or learned from along the way. I hope readers will scan the (far from complete) list of sources in the end notes, and pay for the news subscriptions or buy the books of those folks. Special thanks to Frank Shyong for excavating dozens of transpacific storylines in Los Angeles and for generously sharing his insights as I researched and wrote this book. A major thanks is also due to the many readers of my Chinafornia Newsletter, who have given me feedback and shared their own invaluable stories and analysis along the way.

Thanks to Duncan Clark for all the on-the-ground knowledge you've contributed to this field and for the introduction to the Sandra Dijkstra Literary Agency. Thanks to Sandy for taking a chance on the book, and to Elise Capron for tirelessly advocating for me through all the ups, downs, delays, and sprints that made this book into a reality. Thanks to Dan Smetanka, Jennifer Alton, and the entire Counterpoint Press team for the guidance and impeccable edits that really elevated the writing.

Finally, I want to thank all the people profiled in this book—particularly Tim Lin, Li Zhifei, Janet Yang, Rex Parris, Alex Chen, and Lily Lee Chen. They all opened up and shared so much from their own lives and careers, and this book wouldn't exist without them.

Notes

Note: all links were accessed in January of 2019.

INTRODUCTION: WELCOME TO THE TRANSPACIFIC EXPERIMENT

1. Joshua Paddison, *American Heathens: Religion, Race, and Reconstruction in California* (Berkeley: University of California Press & Huntington Library Press, 2012), 178.
2. Mark Him Lai, Genny Lim, and Judy Yung, *Island: Poetry and History of Chinese Immigrants on Angel Island, 1910–1940*, Seattle, WA: University of Washington Press, 1991.
3. "Fall Enrollment at a Glance," University of California, www.universityofcalifornia.edu /infocenter/fall-enrollment-glance.
4. Matt Sheehan, "Can Chinese Millionaires Save San Francisco's Poorest Neighborhood?," *Huffington Post*, August 21, 2014, www.huffingtonpost.com/2014/08/21/eb-5-san-francisco -shipyards_n_5687158.html.

CHAPTER 1: FRESHMAN ORIENTATION

1. "2018 Fact Sheet: China," Institute for International Education, *2018 Open Doors Report*, www.iie.org/Research-and-Insights/Open-Doors/Fact-Sheets-and-Infographics/Leading -Places-of-Origin-Fact-Sheets.
2. "Data by State Fact Sheets," Institute for International Education, *2018 Open Doors Report*, www.iie.org/Research-and-Insights/Open-Doors/Fact-Sheets-and-Infographics/Data -by-State-Fact-Sheets.
3. "Places of Origin," Institute for International Education, *2018 Open Doors Report*, www .iie.org/Research-and-Insights/Open-Doors/Data/International-Students/Places-of-Origin.
4. The account of the Chinese Educational Mission draws primarily from the following book:

Liel Leibovitz and Matthew I. Miller, *Fortunate Sons: The 120 Chinese Boys Who Came to America, Went to School, and Revolutionized an Ancient Civilization* (New York: W. W. Norton, 2012), 159.

5. Liang Chenyu, "Class of '78: Studying in the US Post-Cultural Revolution," *Sixth Tone*, September 25, 2017, www.sixthtone.com/news/1000910/class-of-78-studying-in-the-us-post -cultural-revolution.

6. "GDP Per Capita (Current US$)," World Bank, data.worldbank.org/indicator/NY.GDP .PCAP.CD?end=2017&locations=CN-RW&start=1978.

7. "Higher Education in California: Institutional Costs," Public Policy Institute of California, November 2014, www.ppic.org/publication/higher-education-in-california-institutional-costs.

8. "Tuition and Fees, 1998-99 through 2017-18," *Chronicle of Higher Education*, November 28, 2017, www.chronicle.com/interactives/tuition-and-fees.

9. "Places of Origin."

10. Elizabeth Redden, "The University of China at Illinois," *Inside Higher Ed*, January 7, 2015, www.insidehighered.com/news/2015/01/07/u-illinois-growth-number-chinese-students -has-been-dramatic.

11. "Fall Enrollment at a Glance," University of California, www.universityofcalifornia.edu /infocenter/fall-enrollment-glance.

12. Frank Shyong, "Not Only China's Wealthy Want to Study in America," *Los Angeles Times*, December 28, 2015, www.latimes.com/local/california/la-me-chinese-students-20151228 -story.html.

13. "Fall Enrollment at a Glance."

14. Youyou Zhou, "More Chinese Students Are Returning Home after Studying Abroad," *Atlas*, www.theatlas.com/charts/rJ3L4kYVQ.

15. "Purdue Survey of Chinese Students in the United States: A General Report," Center on Religion and Chinese Society, November 15, 2016, www.purdue.edu/crcs/publications /survey-reports/.

16. "Fall Enrollment at a Glance."

17. "The University of California: Its Admissions and Financial Decisions Have Disadvantaged California Residents," California State Auditor, March 29, 2016, www.bsa.ca.gov /reports/2015-107/chapters.html.

18. "Fall Enrollment at a Glance."

19. "Fall Enrollment at a Glance."

20. "Black Cats on Skype: An Introductory Guide to Fraud in China Admissions and the Factors to Consider," Vericant, www.vericant.com/wp-content/uploads/2015/07/Black-Cats -On-Skype-%E2%80%93-An-Introductory-Guide-To-Fraud-In-China-Admissions-And -The-Factors-To-Consider-Vericant.pdf.

21. Associated Press, "World News Briefs; Dalai Lama Group Says It Got Money from C.I.A.," *New York Times*, October 2, 1998, www.ntimes.com/1998/10/02/world/world-news-briefs -dalai-lama-group-says-it-got-money-from-cia.html.

22. Teresa Watanabe, "UC Regents Approve First Limit on Out-of-State and International Student Enrollment," *Los Angeles Times*, May 18, 2017, www.latimes.com/local/education/la -essential-education-updates-southern-uc-regents-approve-first-ever-limit-on-1495123220 -htmlstory.html.

CHAPTER 2: SILICON VALLEY'S CHINA PARADOX

1. IDG News Service Staff, "China Celebrates 10 Years of Being Connected to the Internet," *PC World*, May 17, 2004, www.pcworld.idg.com.au/article/128099/china_celebrates_10_years_being_connected_internet.

2. Duncan Clark, "History of the Internet in China," *Sinica Podcast*, May 27, 2014, www.chinafile.com/library/sinica-podcast/history-internet-china.

3. David Barboza, "Yahoo to Pay $1 Billion for 40% Stake in Alibaba," *New York Times*, August 11, 2005, www.nytimes.com/2005/08/11/technology/yahoo-is-paying-1-billion-for-40-stake-in-alibaba.html.

4. Clive Thompson, "Google's China Problem (And China's Google Problem)," *New York Times Magazine*, April 23, 2006, www.nytimes.com/2006/04/23/magazine/23google.html.

5. The ad can be found at the following URL: www.youtube.com/watch?v=EPnmsFl__nU.

6. Loretta Chao, "Google Loses China Market Share," *Wall Street Journal*, April 27, 2010, www.wsj.com/articles/SB10001424052748703465204575207833281993688.

7. Evan Osnos, "Boss Rail," *New Yorker*, October 22, 2012, www.newyorker.com/magazine/2012/10/22/boss-rail.

8. Ethan Baron, "H-1B Use Skyrocketed among Bay Area Tech Giants," *Mercury News* (San Jose), August 14, 2018, www.mercurynews.com/2018/08/13/h-1b-use-skyrocketed-among-bay-area-tech-giants/.

9. Yaqiu Wang, "Read and Delete: How Weibo's Censors Tackle Dissent and Free Speech," Committee to Protect Journalists, March 3, 2016, cpj.org/blog/2016/03/read-and-delete-how-weibos-censors-tackle-dissent-.php.

CHAPTER 3: TOWARD THE NEW TECH LANDSCAPE

1. Ingrid Lunden, "Online Learning Startup Coursera Raises $64M at $800M Valuation," *TechCrunch*, June 7, 2017, techcrunch.com/2017/06/07/online-learning-startup-coursera-raises-64m-at-an-800m-valuation.

2. "US Startup Investments by China's Internet Giants Slow in 2016," CB Insights, November 10, 2016, www.cbinsights.com/research/china-us-startup-investments.

3. Liyan Chen, "Why China Just Spent $2.3 Billion on America's Hottest Startups," *Forbes*, May 27, 2015, www.forbes.com/sites/liyanchen/2015/05/27/why-china-just-spent-2-3-billion-on-americas-hottest-startups/#5257494e41af.

4. "The Rise of Chinese Investment in U.S. Tech Companies," CB Insights, December 2, 2016, www.cbinsights.com/research/china-investment-us-tech-startups.

5. "The Rise of Chinese Investment in U.S. Tech Companies."

6. This account of the conference is drawn from a description given by Rogier Creemers on the following podcast: "Rogier Creemers on Cyber Leninism and the Political Culture of the Chinese Internet," *Sinica Podcast*, April 8, 2015, supchina.com/podcast/rogier-creemers-cyber-leninism-political-culture-chinese-internet.

7. "中国互联网络发展状况统计报告: 2018年1月," China Internet Network Information Center, January 2018, www.cac.gov.cn/2018-01/31/c_1122347026.htm.

8. "Google Invests in Chinese Search-and-Smartwatch Startup," *Wall Street Journal*, October 20, 2015, www.wsj.com/articles/google-invests-in-chinese-search-and-smartwatch-startup-1445339005.

9. Cade Metz, "Google Unleashes AlphaGo in China—But Good Luck Watching It There," *Wired*, May 23, 2017, www.wired.com/2017/05/google-unleashes-alphago-china-good-luck-watching.

10. James Vincent, "China Overtakes US in AI Startup Funding with a Focus on Facial Recognition and Chips," *Verge*, February 22, 2018, www.theverge.com/2018/2/22/17039696/china-us-ai-funding-startup-comparison.

11. "Up to One Million Detained in China's Mass 'Re-education' Drive," Amnesty International, September 2018, www.amnesty.org/en/latest/news/2018/09/china-up-to-one-million-detained.

12. Darren Byler, "China's Government Has Ordered a Million Citizens to Occupy Uighur Homes. Here's What They Think They're Doing," *ChinaFile*, October 24, 2018, www.chinafile.com/reporting-opinion/postcard/million-citizens-occupy-uighur-homes-xinjiang.

13. Paul Mozur, "One Month, 500,000 Face Scans: How China Is Using A.I. to Profile a Minority," *New York Times*, April 14, 2019, www.nytimes.com/2019/04/14/technology/china-surveillance-artificial-intelligence-racial-profiling.html.

14. "ChinAI: The Talent," *MacroPolo*, macropolo.org/chinai/the-talent.

15. Toby Walsh, "Expert and Non-Expert Opinions about Technological Unemployment," *International Journal of Automation and Computing* 15, no. 5 (2018): 637–42, arxiv.org/abs/1706.06906; Katja Grace, John Salvatier, Allan Dafoe, Baobao Zhang, and Owain Evans, "When Will AI Exceed Human Performance? Evidence from AI Experts," May 24, 2017, last revised May 3, 2018, arxiv.org/abs/1705.08807.

16. Jon Russell, "Volkswagen Doubles Down on China with $180M Investment in Smart Tech for Cars," *TechCrunch*, April 6, 2017, techcrunch.com/2017/04/06/volkswagen-mobvoi-china.

CHAPTER 4: IS MICKEY MOUSE AN AMERICAN?

1. David Barboza, "How Disney Won the Keys to China," *New York Times*, June 14, 2016, www.nytimes.com/2016/06/15/business/international/china-disney.html.

2. Bai Shi, "Hollywood Takes a Hit," *Beijing Review*, February 6, 2014, english.entgroup.cn/news_detail.aspx?id=2194; Rebecca Davis, "China Box Office Growth Slows to 9% in 2018, Hits $8.9 Billion," *Variety*, January 2, 2019, variety.com/2019/film/news/china-box-office-2018-annual-1203097545.

3. "The 60th Academy Awards: 1988," Academy of Motion Picture Arts and Sciences, www.oscars.org/oscars/ceremonies/1988.

4. Stanley Rosen, "The Chinese Dream in Popular Culture: China as Producer and Consumer of Films at Home and Abroad," in *China's Global Engagement: Cooperation, Competition, and Influence in the 21st Century*, ed. Jacques deLisle and Avery Goldstein (Washington, D.C.: Brookings Institute Press, 2017), 366.

5. "Hollywood Takes a Hit."

6. Michelle Kung and Aaron Beck, "Chinese Conglomerate Buys AMC Movie Chain in U.S.," *Wall Street Journal*, May 21, 2012, www.wsj.com/articles/SB10001424052702303610504577417073912636152.

7. Lily Kuo, "Three Out of Five of Chinese Multi-millionaires Want to Be Able to Emigrate," *Quartz*, May 7, 2013, qz.com/82284/three-out-of-five-of-chinese-multi-millionaires-want-to-emigrate-out-of-china.

8. Patrick Frater, "Chinese BO Exceeds 17 Billion RMB," *Film Business Asia*, January 10, 2013, web.archive.org/web/20130115052657/http://www.filmbiz.asia/news/china-bo-exceeds -rmb17-billion.

9. A reference to the 1988 film *A Fish Called Wanda*, this pun first appeared in a September 23, 2013, expert conversation on the website ChinaFile: "A Shark Called Wanda— Will Hollywood Swallow the Chinese Dream Whole?" www.chinafile.com/conversation /shark-called-wanda-will-hollywood-swallow-chinese-dream-whole.

10. Associated Press, "Tycoon Plans $8 Billion Chinese Hollywood," *Mercury News*, September 23, 2013, www.mercurynews.com/2013/09/23/tycoon-plans-8-billion-chinese-hollywood.

11. Patrick Brzeski and Scott Roxborough, "After 'The Great Wall,' Can China-Hollywood Co-productions Be Saved?," *Hollywood Reporter*, May 18, 2017, www.hollywoodreporter .com/news/great-wall-can-china-hollywood-productions-be-saved-1005240.

12. "Iron Man 3: Foreign, by Country," Box Office Mojo, www.boxofficemojo.com/movies /?page=intl&id=ironman3.htm.

13. "Pixels: Foreign, by Country," Box Office Mojo, www.boxofficemojo.com/movies/?page =intl&id=pixels.htm.

14. Meg James, "Redstone Family Reaffirms Opposition to Paramount deal," *Los Angeles Times*, July 15, 2016, www.latimes.com/entertainment/envelope/cotown/la-et-ct-redstone-opposes -viacom-paramount-sale-20160715-snap-story.html.

15. Pamela McClintock and Stephen Galloway, "Matt Damon's 'The Great Wall' to Lose $75 Million; Future U.S.-China Productions in Doubt," *Hollywood Reporter*, March 2, 2017, www .hollywoodreporter.com/news/what-great-walls-box-office-flop-will-cost-studios-981602.

16. Aynne Kokas, *Hollywood Made in China* (Oakland: University of California Press, 2017), 43.

17. "Wolf Warrior 2: Foreign, by Country," Box Office Mojo, www.boxofficemojo.com/movies /?page=intl&id=wolfwarrior2.htm.

CHAPTER 5: THE MAYOR WHO LOVED CHINA

1. Cassy Perrera, "Study: Most Stressful Cities in California," CreditDonkey, www.creditdonkey .com/stress-california.html.

2. "The China Footprint: FDI," *MacroPolo*, macropolo.org/china-footprint/fdi/.

3. "Know the Numbers: Chinese Investments in America," *MacroPolo*, macropolo.org /know-the-numbers/.

4. "China Investment Monitor," Rhodium Group, cim.rhg.com/.

5. Matt Sheehan, "How China's Electric Car Dreams Became a PR Nightmare in America," *Huffington Post*, April 1, 2014, www.huffingtonpost.com/2014/04/01/byd-china-electric -car_n_4964233.html.

6. Contract between BYD Motor, Inc., and the Office of the City Clerk, Council/Public Services Division, signed by Micheal Austin (Director, BYD Motor, Inc.), March 7, 2011.

7. Vincent Fernando, "Here Is Exactly How Warren Buffett's Chinese Auto Company BYD Copied Competitor Designs Piece by Piece," *Business Insider*, February 11, 2010, www .businessinsider.com/here-is-exactly-how-warren-buffetts-chinese-auto-company-byd -copied-competitor-designs-piece-by-piece-2010-2.

8. Alex Crippen, "Warren Buffett Invests in Chinese Company Developing 'Green' Cars," *CNBC*, September 27, 2008, www.cnbc.com/id/26916857.

9. Sheehan, "How China's Electric Car Dreams Became a PR Nightmare in America."

10. Echo Huang and Tripti Lahiri, "Nine Years Ago Warren Buffett Bet on an Unknown Chinese Battery Maker, and It's Sort of Paying Off," *Quartz*, September 25, 2017, qz.com/1083571 /nine-years-ago-warren-buffett-put-a-bet-on-byd-then-an-unknown-chinese-cellphone -battery-maker/.

11. "Google Public Data: Unemployment Rate - Seasonally Adjusted, Lancaster, CA," Google, www.google.com/publicdata/explore?ds=z1ebjpgk2654c1_&met_y=unemployment_rate &hl=en&dl=en.

12. "Google Public Data: Unemployment Rate - Seasonally Adjusted, Lancaster, CA."

13. "Crime and Arrest Statistics Publications - 1996-Present," Los Angeles County Sheriff's Department, shq.lasdnews.net/CrimeStats/LASDCrimeInfo.html.

14. Felicity Barringer, "With Help from Nature, a Small Town Aims to be a Solar Capital," *New York Times*, April 8, 2013, www.nytimes.com/2013/04/09/us/lancaster-calif-focuses-on -becoming-solar-capital-of-universe.html.

15. "China Investment Monitor."

16. Sheehan, "How China's Electric Car Dreams Became a PR Nightmare in America."

17. Huang and Lahiri, "Nine Years Ago Warren Buffett Bet on an Unknown Chinese Battery Maker."

18. Mark Landler, "U.S. and China Reach Climate Accord after Months of Negotiations," *New York Times*, November 11, 2014, www.nytimes.com/2014/11/12/world/asia/china-us -xi-obama-apec.html.

19. Jennifer Medina, "Chinese Company Falling Short of Goals for California Jobs," *New York Times*, October 25, 2013, www.nytimes.com/2013/10/26/us/chinese-company-falling -short-of-goal-for-california-jobs.html.

20. "Election Results: April 12, 2016," City of Lancaster, www.cityoflancasterca.org/about-us /departments-services/city-clerk/2016-election-results.

21. Bill Emmott, *Japanophobia: The Myth of the Invincible Japanese* (New York: Crown, 1993).

22. Thomas J. Prusa, PhD, "The Contribution of the Japanese-Brand Automotive Industry to the United States Economy: 2015 Update," econweb.rutgers.edu/prusa/Contributions/prusa %20contributions%20-%20update%20with%202015%20data.pdf. Note: This study was prepared for the Japan Automobile Manufacturers Association.

23. Mark Kane, "BYD Wins 10 of 12 Vehicle Categories in Bus RFP in Washington & Oregon," *InsideEVs*, September 12, 2015, insideevs.com/byd-wins-10-of-12-vehicle-categories -in-bus-rfp-in-washington-oregon.

24. Mark Madler, "BYD Opens Expansion Warehouse in Lancaster," *San Fernando Valley Business Journal*, September 27, 2018, www.sfvbj.com/news/2018/sep/27/byd-builds-5m -warehouse-lancaster.

25. "The China Footprint: FDI," *MacroPolo*, macropolo.org/china-footprint/fdi/.

26. Robert King, "Is BYD Co. Fairly Valued?," *Seeking Alpha*, November 15, 2010, seekingalpha .com/article/236824-is-byd-co-fairly-valued.

CHAPTER 6: A PHOENIX RISING FROM THE TOXINS

1. Blanca Torres, "Will the Bayview Benefit from Lennar's Massive Shipyard Project?," *San*

Francisco Business Times, July 8, 2014, www.bizjournals.com/sanfrancisco/blog/real-estate/2014/07/lennar-shipyard-bayview-community-benefits-s-f.html.

2. Phillip Matier and Andrew Ross, "S.F.-China Development Deal Falls Apart," *San Francisco Chronicle*, April 11, 2013, www.sfgate.com/bayarea/matier-ross/article/S-F-China-development-deal-falls-apart-4427448.php.

3. Author interview with executives of Golden Gate Global, the company charged with raising money from EB-5 investors and lending it to the project's developer.

4. Lindsey Dillon, "Redevelopment and the Politics of Place in Bayview-Hunters Point," UC Berkeley, *ISSC Working Paper Series* (2011), 12, escholarship.org/uc/item/9s15b9r2.

5. "2017 Profile of International Activity in U.S. Residential Real Estate," National Association of Realtors: Research Department, July 2017.

6. Ana Swanson, "How China Used More Cement in 3 Years Than the U.S. Did in the Entire 20th Century," *Washington Post*, March 24, 2015, www.washingtonpost.com/news/wonk/wp/2015/03/24/how-china-used-more-cement-in-3-years-than-the-u-s-did-in-the-entire-20th-century.

7. "Palo Alto Market and Overview," Zillow, www.zillow.com/palo-alto-ca/home-values.

8. Carol Blitzer, "Chinese Homebuyers Hone In on Palo Alto," *Palo Alto Weekly*, September 4, 2013, www.paloaltoonline.com/news/2013/09/04/chinese-homebuyers-hone-in-on-palo-alto.

9. Christine Johnson, "Episode 3: Career Ending Podcast," *Infill Podcast*, October 1, 2016, www.sfyimby.org/uncategorized/2016101episode-3-career-ending-podcast.

10. Matier and Ross, "S.F.-China Development Deal Falls Apart."

11. "The China Footprint: EB-5," *MacroPolo*, macropolo.org/china-footprint/eb-5.

12. Author interviews with executives at both Lennar Corporation and Golden Gate Global, the EB-5 regional center that raised money for the project.

13. "Breaking Ground: Chinese Real Estate Investment in the United States," Asia Society and the Rosen Consulting Group, May 16, 2016, asiasociety.org/northern-california/breaking-ground-chinese-investment-us-real-estate.

14. "Breaking Ground."

15. Michael Cole, "China Buys More US Real Estate with $200 Million LA Deal," *Mingtiandi*, January 6, 2014, www.mingtiandi.com/real-estate/outbound-investment/china-buys-more-us-real-estate-with-200-million-la-deal/.

16. Roxana Popescu, "Rising Above the Tangled Traffic of Los Angeles in a Luxury Condo," *Washington Post*, October 18, 2018, www.washingtonpost.com/realestate/rising-above-the-tangled-traffic-of-los-angeles-in-a-luxury-condo/2018/10/17/6ef1daf6-b79a-11e8-a7b5-adaaa5b2a57f_story.html.

17. Emily Fancher, "7 Major Chinese Investment and Development Deals in the Bay Area," *San Francisco Business Times*, January 15, 2015, www.bizjournals.com/sanfrancisco/blog/real-estate/2015/01/chinese-investment-bay-area-sf-oceanwide-zarsion.html.

18. Fancher, "7 Major Chinese Investment and Development Deals in the Bay Area."

19. "2017 Profile of International Activity in U.S. Residential Real Estate."

20. Xin Jiang, "A Perspective on Chinese Home Buyers," *Palo Alto Weekly*, October 27, 2016, paloaltoonline.com/news/2016/10/27/a-perspective-on-chinese-buyers.

21. Author interviews with executives at Lennar Corporation and Golden Gate Global.

22. Shawn Boburg, "How Jared Kushner Built a Luxury Skyscraper Using Loans Meant for Job-Starved Areas," *Washington Post*, May 31, 2017, www.washingtonpost.com/investigations/jared-kushner-and-his-partners-used-a-program-meant-for-job-starved-areas-to-build-a-luxury-skyscraper/2017/05/31/9c81b52c-4225-11e7-9869-bac8b446820a_story.html.

23. Bianca Barragan, "Less Than a Year-Old, Downtown LA's Hotel Indigo is For Sale, Seeking $280M," *Curbed: Los Angeles*, February 1, 2018, la.curbed.com/2018/2/1/16960290/metropolis-hotel-indigo-for-sale-greenland-usa.

CHAPTER 7: "CHINESE AMERICANS FOR TRUMP"

1. "Chinese Laborers Excluded from U.S.," History, last updated December 13, 2018, www.history.com/this-day-in-history/chinese-laborers-excluded-from-u-s.

2. "1990 Census Page: Selected Historical Decennial Census Population and Housing Counts," U.S. Census Bureau, www.census.gov/population/www/censusdata/hiscendata.html.

3. Judy Yung, Gordon H. Chang, Him Mark Lai, eds., *Chinese American Voices: From the Gold Rush to the Present* (Berkeley and Los Angeles: University of California Press, 2006), 222.

4. "1990 Census Page."

5. Ellen D. Wu, *The Color of Success: Asian Americans and the Origins of the Model Minority* (Oxford: Oxford University Press, 2013).

6. "1990 Census Page."

7. Scott D. Seligman, *The First Chinese American: The Remarkable Life of Wong Chin Foo* (Hong Kong: Hong Kong University Press, 2013), xxii.

8. Mark Arax, "Lily Lee Chen: Her Roots—and Perhaps Her Political Goals—Lie Beyond Monterey Park," *Los Angeles Times*, November 14, 1985, articles.latimes.com/1985-11-14/news/ga-2678_1_monterey-park/3.

9. 萧东，"王湉访谈：华人维权不能总是抗议," *China Press*, March 22, 2017, www.uschinapress.com/2017/0322/1099437.shtml.

10. Timothy Fong, *The First Suburban Chinatown: The Remaking of Monterey Park, California* (Philadelphia: Temple University Press, 1994), 111.

11. Mike Ward, "Libel Suit Over Chen's Reaction to Sign Rejected," *Los Angeles Times*, December 12, 1985, articles.latimes.com/1985-12-12/news/ga-16393_1_libel-suit.

12. Orla O'Sullivan, "Peter Liang Cop Conviction Makes Asian American Tiger Roar," *Asia Times*, February 20, 2016, www.atimes.com/article/peter-liang-cop-conviction-makes-asian-american-tiger-roar.

13. Kaiser Kuo, "Why Are So Many First-Generation Chinese Immigrants Supporting Donald Trump?," *SupChina*, November 3, 2016, supchina.com/2016/11/03/many-first-generation-chinese-immigrants-supporting-donald-trump.

MATT SHEEHAN served as a foreign correspondent in China and is currently a nonresident fellow at the Paulson Institute's think tank, MacroPolo. There he researches and writes on the Sino–U.S. technology relationship and ties between California and China. In 2018, he was short-listed for the Young China Watcher of the Year Award. Sheehan grew up in the San Francisco Bay Area and spent over five years living in mainland China. His writing has been published in *Vice News*, *The WorldPost*, *Foreign Policy*, and *The Atlantic*. He is based in Oakland, California. To explore photos, videos, and interactive graphics related to this book, visit transpacificexperiment.com.

Printed in the United States
by Baker & Taylor Publisher Services